GREAT RELIGIONS OF MODERN MAN

Judaism

GREAT RELIGIONS OF MODERN MAN
Richard A. Gard, *General Editor*

BUDDHISM
Edited by Richard A. Gard

CHRISTIANITY: CATHOLICISM
Edited by George Brantl

CHRISTIANITY: PROTESTANTISM
Edited by J. Leslie Dunstan

HINDUISM
Edited by Louis Renou

ISLAM
Edited by John Alden Williams

JUDAISM
Edited by Arthur Hertzberg

Judaism

EDITED BY

Arthur Hertzberg

GEORGE BRAZILLER

NEW YORK   1962

ACKNOWLEDGMENTS

The editor wishes to thank the following for permission to reprint the material included in this volume:

ATHENEUM PUBLISHERS—for selection from André Schwarz-Bart, *The Last of the Just*, copyright © 1960 by Atheneum House, Inc.

DOUBLEDAY & COMPANY, INC.—for selections from Arthur Hertzberg, *The Zionist Idea*, copyright 1959 by Arthur Hertzberg, reprinted by permission of Doubleday & Company, Inc.

FARRAR, STRAUS & CUDAHY, INC.—for selection from *At the Turning*, by Martin Buber, copyright 1952 by Martin Buber, used by permission of the publishers;—and for selection from *The Sabbath*, by A. J. Heschel, copyright 1951 by Abraham Joshua Heschel, used by permission of the publishers.

PHILIPP FELDHEIM, INC.—for selections from S. R. Hirsch, *The Nineteen Letters of Ben Uziel*, published by Philipp Feldheim, Inc.

HARPER & BROTHERS—for selection from Louis Finkelstein, *The Jews: Their History, Culture and Religion*, reprinted by permission of the publisher.

JEWISH PUBLICATION SOCIETY OF AMERICA—for selection from Nina Salaman, *Selected Poems of Judah Halevi*.

DR. FRANZ KOBLER and the "ARARAT" PUBLISHING SOCIETY LTD.—for selections from F. Kobler, *Treasury of Jewish Letters*.

THE MACMILLAN COMPANY—for selections from Mordecai M. Kaplan, *The Future of the American Jews*, copyright 1948 by The Macmillan Company.

THE RABBINICAL ASSEMBLY OF AMERICA—for selections from *The Weekday Prayer Book*, copyright by The Rabbinical Assembly of America.

SCHOCKEN BOOKS, INC.—for selections from *Franz Rosenzweig: His Life and Thought*, by Nahum N. Glatzer, copyright 1953 by Schocken Books, Inc.;—for selections from *Language of Faith*, edited by Nahum N. Glatzer, copyright 1947 by Schocken Books Inc.;—for selections from *Yamim Noraim*, by S. Y. Agnon, copyright 1946 by Schocken Books, Inc.;—for selections from *Time and Eternity*, ed. by Nahum N. Glatzer, copyright 1946 by Schocken Books, Inc. The preceding selections are reprinted by permission of Schocken Books, Inc.

MARTIN SECKER & WARBURG LTD.—for selection from André Schwarz-Bart, *The Last of the Just*.

SONCINO PRESS LTD.—for selection from Sperling & Simon (trans.), *The Zohar*.

YALE UNIVERSITY PRESS—for selections from Saadia Gaon, *The Book of Beliefs and Opinions*, trans. Samuel Rosenblatt.

לְהוֹרַי
א״מ הרב צבי אלימלך
בן הרב אברהם זצ״ל
א״מ נחמה שפרה
בת הקדוש משולם שו״ב מלמברג הי״ד

FOR MY PARENTS

RABBI AND MRS. ZVI ELIMELECH HERTZBERG

WHOSE LIFE IS A LESSON
IN THE WAY OF JEWISH
FAITH

I want to express my warm thanks to my good friend, Rabbi Jules Harlow, who labored with me in the selection of source material for this volume and in the work of translation, where necessary.

Contents

Preface

The very notion of attempting this volume is an impertinence. It is not possible to represent a spiritual literature that spans three millennia in the compass of a short book. The informed reader will miss much that he would have preferred to see included. Unfortunately, the task of the editor is to choose those passages which, in his judgment, are the most representative. An anthologist is therefore really writing his own book through the words of others.

The specific premise on the basis of which this work was constructed is my belief that there is an essential unity which underlies Jewish faith through all its changing expressions. Judaism is here treated conceptually. Its basic values and affirmations serve as divisions, while selections from the Jewish literary tradition are organized to show the integrity of the Jewish spirit through the ages.

Because the Jewish religion is so heavily involved in the historical experience of the Jewish people, it would be helpful if this book were read in conjunction with a history of the Jews. There are many such volumes in all the major languages of the world.

I cannot lay down this task without expressing my gratitude to my wife for her participation in the work attendant upon preparing this book. It is my prayer, in the words of a classic Jewish utterance, that "as I leave this house of study, the Almighty may find this work not displeasing to Him and that He may help me to enter other houses of study, for His Name's sake."

A. H.

Englewood, New Jersey
June 9, 1961

Introduction

God made covenant with a particular people that it should be His priesthood. To this people, the seed of Abraham, the slaves He had just redeemed from Egypt, He revealed the Torah, the Law which they were to obey, as the particular burden of the Jews and as the sign of their unique destiny in the world. He chose the land of Canaan as His inheritance and that of His people, the Holy Land which would forever remain the place in which He would most clearly be manifest.

God exists in the world and cares for all men, for are not the children of Israel, as Amos said, no more to Him than the Ethiopians? It was out of His love for mankind as a whole that He taught all men His way of redemption, the Torah, in His revelation in the desert of Sinai, to show that, like the desert, the Law belongs to anyone who dares to claim it. God does not speak to man only in the Holy Land, for He addressed Noah in the land between the rivers, Abraham in Ur, Moses in Midian, and He spoke even to Balaam, who came to curse the Jews in the desert of Sinai. The Talmud contains a vision of the end of days, in which the holiness that is particular to the land of Israel will "spread out" to encompass all the lands.

Either of the two sets of assertions just above is true as description of Judaism, but neither is true without the other. It would be easy to say that these two versions of Judaism, the so-called "universal" and "particular" aspects, are in uneasy tension; this has indeed been said by non-Jewish commentators and polemicists for many centuries. From the perspective of one who stands inside the Jewish tradition, in the faith and experience of the Jewish believer, such a distinction does not exist. Jewish faith addresses itself not only to the Jews; it prescribes the Law and the way of salvation for all mankind.

The Jewish ideas of God, Torah, and the people of Israel, as well as the lesser but quite important doctrine of the Holy Land, do not represent a catechism or a theology, for there is none such in Judaism. They are the lasting values, areas of concern, foci, or problems (call them what you will) around which the mass of Jewish spiritual devotion and thought through the ages has organized itself. Men of simple faith, scholars, mystics, and philosophers have differed from one another in their understanding and interpretation of these values. Nonetheless Judaism has remained recognizably one faith through all these permutations because, at least until the last century or so, the contemporary age of doubt, the normative tradition has been believed, and obeyed, by all Jews who intended to remain within the fold. Jews have regarded it as self-evident that the God of all the world had made them His priest-people, His "suffering servant," to live by the Law and to bear the burden of the woes that might come to them. Their task is to achieve redemption for themselves and to lead mankind to the day when, in the words of the liturgy, "the Lord will be One and His name One."

The truest key to understanding Judaism in its own terms is to be found in its concept of the "chosen people." This doctrine of "chosenness" is a mystery—and a scandal. It was already a mystery to the Bible itself, which ascribed the Divine choice, not to any inborn merits of the Jews, but to the unknowable will of God. It soon became, and has remained, a scandal to the Gentiles—and even to some Jews. There have been many attempts through the ages to defend and explain this doctrine.

Several such explanations, culled from the writings of medieval and modern Jewish thinkers, appear in this book, as well as a modern attack on this doctrine by a radical American Jewish theologian, whose version of Judaism is naturalist and religio-cultural. Certainly the secularist versions of Jewish experience, like some forms of Zionism, have tended to abandon this doctrine. It is nonetheless my view that Judaism is inconceivable without it. This does not mean that any man, certainly not one of our own troubled generation, can dare assert that he knows the meaning of this mystery. Perhaps it is enough for this moment to know that the mystery exists; perhaps that is all that any other generation really knew. Nevertheless, a few words about what the idea of the "chosen people" implies need to be added.

Obviously there can be no "chosen people" unless there is a God who does the choosing. History, especially modern history, knows too many examples of self-chosen peoples. No matter how high and humanitarian a "civilizing mission" such a people may assign to itself, self-chosenness has invariably degenerated into some form of the notion of a master race. Nor can we attempt to rationalize the classical Jewish concept of the chosen people, as some nineteenth-century Jewish theologians did, by arguing that various peoples have particular talents innate within them, e.g. the Greeks for art and philosophy, the Germans for order, the English and Americans for liberty, and the Jews for religion. Quite apart from the massive evidence from sociology and allied disciplines that such thinking is untrue, it has about it an air of arrogance which is morally repugnant. A "chosen people" has a right to exist and so think of itself only if there is a God in the world who is more than a First Cause or the order of the cosmos. He has to be conceived as the Creator who has not

washed His hands of creation, who cares for and speaks
to man, to whom what man does is not a matter of indif-
ference. Such a God can be imagined as choosing a particular people for the task of strictest obedience to His
will, as an instrument in His hand for the redemption of
mankind and as a teacher whom God Himself keeps from
pride by applying to His chosen people the severest of
judgments.

Classical Judaism is, therefore, a *revealed* religion. The
very notion of revelation is in itself of the utmost difficulty, not only to the unbeliever but especially to the believer. What need does God have of man at all? Why
should He have wished to speak to man? Even if one's
faith in His revelation is of the most orthodox kind, there
still remains the question: What does the Divine command require of me, of my individual life in the context
of my immediate situation?

Stripped bare of all argument, there are only two possible approaches to religion: either man invented God for
man's own purposes, or God created man to achieve His
purposes. The first alternative is the favorite one of the
last several centuries. Some have approved of man's in-
ventiveness and others have denounced it as an unneces-
sary and even harmful illusion. Especially since Voltaire,
the idea of God has been explained as the antidote that
man has devised of the menace of the world and to death.
It is a crutch that man can, indeed ought to, discard—so
this argument goes. There is no real comfort for the tradi-
tionalist in the classical philosophical and theological attempts to prove that God exists. Each of the well-known
"proofs"—that creation implies a Creator, that the design
of the world implies a Designer, etc.—has been refuted in
the realm of philosophical argument, and a verdict of "not
proved" has been returned by the jury of reason.

I say *not proved*, and not *disproved*. Philosophical argument can indeed produce no undeniable proof of God's
existence, but neither can it make it certain beyond argument that there is no God. The choice can only be made
by faith. Man surveys the world, and it can appear to him
as an uncaring universe, indifferent and perhaps chaotic,
to which he gives some passing meaning, or he can view
it as purposeful, though like Job, he may not comprehend
its purposes. Here we are confronted by an ultimate
choice, and we cannot argue ourselves into one or the
other position.

Judaism, the religion of the Bible, is the classical para-
digm of a God-made religion. It is the assertion—not the
philosophical proof—that God exists and that He has
spoken and speaks to man, giving him clues to the road
that he must follow. A God who cares about man is likely
to have revealed Himself to His favorite creation, though
this is not an absolute necessity, for He could have so created the world that man's destiny would work itself out
without immediate contact with the Divine; but a God
who has chosen a people for a role of transcendent importance in the scheme of redemption must have informed
it of His choice, though here, too, it is just possible that
the choice can exist without its knowledge. Classical Judaism believes that this people is conscious of its ap-
pointment, for God has spoken to it. The Jewish faith has,
therefore, from the earliest time, even in the Bible itself,
confronted the question of what is true and what is false
revelation.

To be sure, every man can experience the Divine revelation, but he can also imagine that he is experiencing it
while really engaged in self-delusion. Revelation must
therefore be personal but not personalist. For the Jew,
the form into which the revelation is cast is the Law, and

Judaism throughout all the ages is therefore a tension between true and false prophets, between religious enthusiasts who come to recharge the experience of the obedient believer with refreshed devotion to the Law and those enthusiasts who come to break it in the name of some "higher" experience.

If a prophet should arise among you or a dreamer of dreams, even one who gives you a sign or a miracle. And these signs and miracles of which he speaks to you come to pass, as he says, Let us follow after other gods which you have not known and let us serve them. Do not listen to the words of that prophet or that dreamer of dreams; for the Lord your God is testing you to know whether you love the Lord your God with all your heart and with all your soul. You shall follow after the Lord your God with all your heart and with all your soul. You shall follow after the Lord your God and fear Him, keeping His commandments and obeying His voice; you shall serve Him and cleave unto Him (Deut. 13:2–5).

In every age Jewish religious expression is rich in mystical fervor. Such fervor is regarded as valid so long as it remains the handmaiden of obedience to the original revelation, so long as it is judged by it and does not presume to become its judge.

What the Divine revelation contains has of course been at issue between Judaism and both Christianity and Islam for many centuries. In the realm of history, in the actual living experience of an all too often persecuted minority, this debate has had large and tragic consequences, but it has had relatively little effect on the Jewish faith. Occasionally a philosophical theologian within Jewry, e.g. Maimonides, has posited a missionary role among the Gentiles for the daughter religions which have sprung from the Bible, but throughout the ages all Israel has stood fast in the faith that the Torah is the inheritance of the congregation of Jacob. It is only in the modern age that the meaning of revelation, which means, most crucially, the binding character of the Torah, has become the most serious and severe problem for Jewish religious thought.

Biblical criticism of the modern kind has tended to undermine the Talmudic notions that every word in the Torah was dictated by the Lawgiver to Moses on Sinai and that the further tradition of interpretation in the Talmud and the later writings has been guided by Divine inspiration. Religious anthropology has called into question the idea that the ritual prescriptions of the Bible are unique and God-given, for many parallels to them have been found, especially in ancient near-Eastern religions. Above all, the political and intellectual emancipation of modern Jewry, the entry of large segments of this community into the general life of Western man, has been regarded by most Jews as a primary practical objective. The life of obedience to the inherited Law requires of the Jew a considerable conscious apartness. Inevitably, it has therefore been regarded as a bar on the road to complete social integration.

The first two attacks, from Biblical criticism and the anthropology of religion, were not directed against Judaism alone. They were part of a major current which has dominated Western thought in the last several centuries, the criticism of revealed religion in the name of reason and science. The story of the defense of Judaism against such attack is not essentially different from the history of Western religious thought as a whole. It is by now commonly agreed that scholarly investigation into the composition of the text of the Bible, no matter what the results of such study may be, cannot by its very nature pass final judgment on the faith in revelation. As for the argument from anthropology, man is obviously more than the chemical elements that make up his body. By the same token, a religious system is quite another thing than the sum of its individual practices.

For Judaism, however, the theological problem in modern times has been made more acute by the historic implications of the changing political and social history of the Jews. From the beginning of the Exile in the year 70 until the eighteenth century all Jews lived as a separate enclave both in Christian Europe and in Moslem North Africa and the Near East. With the beginning of the social and political emancipation of Jewry, the overarching theme of Jewish experience in the nineteenth century became the finding of ways to cease being outside society. Jewish thought devoted itself to definitions of Jewish faith and identity which would make it possible for the Jews to think about themselves as very much like everybody else, as a religion among religions, a group among groups, or as a nation among nations. Hence Jewish religious thought was more radically "Westernized" than it had ever been before, even by the most philosophical of medieval Jewish theologians. It was defined, especially by liberal theologians, as a religious denomination among the several which dominated West European culture. The Law therefore became a problem not only because it was socially inconvenient. It was even more fundamentally in question because, of all the key values of Judaism, it was the most foreign, the hardest to explain, within an outlook that proceeded in the form and mode of Western philosophical theology.

Authentic Judaism is inconceivable without the Law. To be sure, there is a difference between moral principle and ceremonial observance. The Talmudic tradition rules that on the Day of Atonement man can find forgiveness from God for his sins in the realm of ritual, but no ceremony can absolve him of his sins against other men, for he can atone only by redressing the wrong. Many other proofs of this distinction could be added. It is nonetheless an essential of the faith that the regimen that has been ordained for the religious practice of the Jew is God-given. This people was chosen to be a corporate priesthood, to live within the world and yet apart from it. Its way of life is the appointed sign of its difference. At the end of time, in a completely redeemed world, this unique way will perhaps disappear, but the world is not yet redeemed and the Messiah has not yet come.

It remains to be added that, in terms of a famous distinction, Judaism is a religion not of nature but of history. There are many passages in the Bible which sing the praises of God in nature, but the characteristic Jewish experience of God is the awareness of His presence in human events. Every aspect of the Jewish tradition is pervaded by the memory of His redemptive act in the exodus from Egypt. Almost the whole of the religious calendar is an act of recalling the past experience of the Jewish people as the record of God's relationship to it. The emphasis of Jewish faith is therefore neither on metaphysical speculation nor on dogma but on human action. Life is the arena of moral choice, and man can choose the good. He can make himself worse than the beast or he can ascend to but little lower than the angels. Every man plays his role, for good or ill, in the redemptive history of mankind, for man is God's partner in the work of creation.

Judaism constructs its present out of a memory reaching back to Abraham and looking forward to the Messianic age for humanity as a whole. It is the way which began with the breaking of the idols and with risking all for the sake of God. To lead is often to suffer, and throughout all the centuries Judaism has found in the tragedy which is so much of Jewish history, in its role as the "suffering servant" of God, the surest sign of its ordained task.

The Jews have often been restless under the burden. Even before the modern age, some have longed for peace and ease, for the quest for a "normal" identity and destiny is human, all too human. It is, at very least, untrue to history. Jewish experience has not been like that of all the nations, and the generation which has witnessed both Hitler and the third return to Zion engages in great self-delusion if it imagines that the place of the Jew in the world is as yet "normalized." Like Jonah, some Jews may attempt to cease prophesying against Nineveh, but Nineveh is always there. Jonah's knowledge that God wants something special from him is the inescapable and continuing groove of Jewish experience.

CHAPTER ONE

People

THE FACT OF THE COVENANT

God's initial covenant, with Abraham, was with the head of a family, and the Jewish people was conceived as the ever-increasing number of his descendants. Hence to this day the convert to Judaism is not only accepted into the faith; the ritual prescribes that he be adopted into the family as a child of Abraham. The covenant with Moses is a new and wider one, with a people as a whole. This is symbolized by the "new name" by which God makes Himself known.

And when Abram was ninety nine years old, the Lord appeared to Abram and said to him, "I am God Almighty; walk before Me, and be perfect. And I will make My covenant between Me and you and I will multiply you exceedingly." Abram fell on his face and God spoke with him, saying "As for Me, behold, My covenant is with you, and you shall be the father of a multitude of nations. Neither shall your name be called any more Abram, but your name shall be Abraham, because I have made you the father of a multitude of nations. And I will make you exceedingly fruitful, and I will make nations of you, and kings shall come out of you. And I will establish My covenant between Me and you and your seed after you throughout their generations for an everlasting covenant, to be God to you and to your seed after you. And I will give to you, and to your seed after you, the land of your sojournings, all the land of Canaan, for an everlasting possession, and I will be their God."[1]

And God spoke to Moses saying, "I am the Lord. I appeared to Abraham, to Isaac and to Jacob as God Almighty but by My name of Lord I did not make Myself known to them. And I established My covenant with them, to give them the land of Canaan, the land of their sojournings, wherein they dwelled. Moreover I have heard the groaning of the children of Israel whom the Egyptians keep in bondage and I have remembered My covenant. Therefore say to the children of Israel, 'I am the Lord, who will bring you out from under the burdens of the Egyptians, and will deliver you from their bondage, and will deliver you with an outstretched arm and with great judgments. And I will take you to Myself for a people and I will be your God; and you shall know that I am the Lord your God who brought you out from under the burdens of the Egyptians. And I will bring you into the land concerning which I lifted up My hand to give it to Abraham, Isaac and Jacob. I will give it to you for a heritage; I am the Lord.' "[2]

THE NATURE OF THE COVENANT

The covenant with God binds the Jewish people to the task of being a corporate priesthood. God redeemed them from slavery in Egypt, let them hear His voice, led them to the promised land and vowed to keep faith with all future generations of this people. They in turn must keep His statutes as ordained in the Bible. The covenant is, however, unbreakable. They will be punished for their sins and judged by stricter standards than those God applies to other men, but He will never put them utterly aside and find a new love.

Now, therefore, if you will obey My voice and keep My covenant, you shall be My own possession among all the peoples, for all the earth is mine, and you shall be to Me a kingdom of priests and a holy nation.[3]

You shall therefore keep all My statutes and all My ordinances, and do them, lest the land, into which I bring you to dwell, vomit you out. And you shall not walk in the customs of the nations which I am casting out before you; they have done all these things and therefore I abhorred them. But to you I say: Possess their land which I will give you for an inheritance, a land flowing with milk and honey. I am the Lord your God, who have set you apart from other people. You shall therefore separate the clean beast from the unclean, and the clean fowl from the unclean; you shall not defile your souls by beast or by fowl or by anything with which the ground teems, which I have set apart for you to hold unclean. You shall be holy to Me, because I the Lord am holy, and I have separated you from other people, that you should be Mine.[4]

You shall not defile the land in which you live, in the midst of which I dwell, for I the Lord dwell in the midst of the people of Israel.[5]

Ask of the days of old, that have been before your time from the day that God created man upon the earth, from one end of heaven to the other, whether a great thing like this has ever happened or was ever heard of. Did ever a people hear the voice of God speaking out of the midst of fire, as you have heard, and live? Has God attempted to go and take to Himself a nation from the midst of another nation, by trials, signs and wonders, by war, a mighty hand and an outstretched arm, and by great terrors, according to all that the Lord your God did for you in Egypt before your eyes? To you it was shown, that you might know that the Lord, He is God, and there is no other besides Him. From heaven He made you hear His voice, that He might teach you. And on earth He showed you His great fire, and you heard His words out of the midst of the fire. And because He loved your fathers, and chose their seed after them, and brought you out of Egypt with His Presence, with His great power, to drive out nations greater and mightier than you from before you, to bring you in, to give you their land for an inheritance, as it is this day; know therefore this day and lay it to your heart, that the

Lord, He is God in heaven above and in the earth beneath, and there is no other.[6]

Moses summoned all Israel and said to them: Hear, O Israel, the statutes and the ordinances which I speak in your hearing this day, and you shall learn them and be careful to do them. The Lord our God made a covenant with us in Horeb. Not with our fathers did the Lord make this covenant, but with us, who are all of us here alive this day.[7]

You all stand this day before the Lord your God, your princes, your tribes, your elders and your officers, all the people of Israel, your children and your wives, and the stranger that is in the midst of your camp, from those that hew wood to those that draw water; that you enter into the covenant of the Lord your God, and into His oath, which this day the Lord your God makes with you, that He may establish you this day as a people to Himself, and that He may be your God, as He has spoken to you, and as He swore to your fathers, Abraham, Isaac and Jacob. Not with you only do I make this covenant and this oath, but with him that stands here with us this day before the Lord our God and also with him that is not here with us this day.[8]

I will betroth you to Me forever. I will betroth you to Me in righteousness and in justice, in love and in mercy. I will betroth you to Me in faithfulness, and you shall love the Lord.[9]

The Holy One, praised be He, said to Hosea "Your children have sinned." Hosea should have said "They are Your children, children of Your dear ones, children of Abraham, Isaac and Jacob; show them Your mercy." However, not only did he not say this, but he said "Lord of the universe! The entire world belongs to You. Displace them with another people." The Holy One, praised be He, thought: What shall I do with this old man? I shall tell him to marry a harlot and to beget children of harlotry and then I shall tell him to send her away. If he will be able to send her away, I will send Israel away. And it is written "The Lord said to Hosea: Go, take to yourself a wife of harlotry and have children of harlotry. . . . So he went and took Gomer the daughter of Dibla'im . . . " [Hosea 1:2–3]. When two sons and a daughter had been born to him, the Holy One, praised be He, said to Hosea "Could you not have learned from Moses, your teacher? Whenever I spoke with him he separated from his wife. You must do likewise." Hosea answered "Lord of the universe! I have children from her. I cannot put her away or divorce her." The Holy One said to him "Your wife is a harlot and your children are children of harlotry; you do not even know if they are really yours. Yet you refuse to divorce her. How, then, should I act toward Israel? They are the children of those whom I have tested, the children of Abraham, Isaac and Jacob, and one of the four possessions which I have acquired in My world: The Torah, heaven and earth, the Temple and Israel. And yet you tell Me to supersede them with another people!"

When he realized that he had sinned, Hosea rose to ask mercy for himself. The Holy One, praised be He, said to him "Before you ask mercy for yourself, ask mercy for Israel."[10]

In the rabbinic commentary on the Song of Songs the Biblical image is changed. This great paean to love is interpreted as referring to the love between God and His people, Israel. The beloved is beautiful because she decks herself as a bride in her proper jewelry, i.e. deeds which represent the obedient and sacrificial love borne by Israel to God. Israel is adorned by daily prayer (the Shema, i.e. "Hear, O Israel, the Lord our God, the Lord is One"); the receptacle on the right front doorpost of every Jewish home which contains the Shema (the mezuzah); the phylacteries (tephillin, or tefillin), the black receptacles to be worn on head and arm, near the heart, by every adult male in weekday morning prayer; and the citron (ethrog, or etrog) and palm tree (lulab, or lulav) used in the ritual of the Sukkoth holiday (see below, Chapter IV).

"You are beautiful, my love" (Song of Songs 1:15). You are beautiful through the commandments, both positive and negative, beautiful through loving deeds, beautiful in your house with the heave-offering and the tithes . . . beautiful in the law of circumcision, beautiful in prayer, in reciting the *Shema*, in observing the laws of *Mezuzah* and *Tefillin, etrog* and *lulav*, beautiful too in repentance and in good works, beautiful in this world and beautiful in the world to come.[11]

The author of the following epistle is Maimonides (1135–1206), Moses ben Maimon, the towering figure of medieval Jewish learning in both philosophy and rabbinic law. He is here (in 1172) strengthening the resolve of Yemenite Jewry to withstand persecution.

. . . And now let me deal with the rest of the contents of your epistle. I reply to it in the Arabic language, in order that all may easily understand, for all are concerned in what I shall communicate. The news that the government under which you live ordered all Jews in South Arabia to apostacize, in the same manner as the ruling powers in Western countries have acted towards us, made us turn pale with terror. The whole community shares your grief. . . . Our minds are bewildered; we feel unable to think calmly, so terrible is the alternative in which Israel has been placed on all sides, from the East and from the West. . . .

Know for certain that what we believe in is the Law of God given through the father of the prophets. That by its teaching the heavenly legislator intended to constitute us an entirely distinct people. The selection was not due to our inherent worth. Indeed we have been distinctly told so in the Scriptures. But because our progenitors acted righteously through their knowledge of the Supreme Being, therefore we, their descendants, reap the benefit of their meritorious deeds. . . .

My brethren, it behooves us to keep ever present before our minds the great day of Sinai, for the Lord has forbidden

us ever to forget it. Rear your offspring in a thorough understanding of that all-important event. Explain before large as-
semblies the principles it involves, show that it is a lucid
mirror reflecting the truth: aye, the very pivot upon which our
religion turns. . . . Know, moreover, you who are born in
this covenant and raised in this belief, that the stupendous
occurrence, the truth of which is testified by the most trusty
of witnesses, stands in very deed alone in the annals of mankind. For a whole people heard the word of God and saw the
glory of the Divinity. From this lasting memory we must draw
our power to strengthen our faith even in a period of persecution and affliction such as the present one.

My brethren! Hold fast to the covenant, be immovable in
your convictions, fulfill the statutes of your religion. . . . Rejoice that you suffer trials, confiscation, contumely, all for the
love of God, to magnify His glorious name. It is the sweetest
offering you can make. . . . Should ever the necessity of flee-
ing for your lives to a wilderness and inhospitable regions
arise, painful as it may be to sever oneself from dear associations or to relinquish one's property, you should still endure
all, and be supported by the consoling thought that the Omni-
present Lord, who reigns supreme, can recompense you com-
mensurately to your deserts, in this world and in the World to
come. . . . It often happens that a man will part from his
kindred and friends and travel abroad, because he finds his
earnings inadequate to his wants. How much more readily
ought we to follow the same course, when we stand in danger
of being denied the means to supply our *spiritual* necessities.[12]

THE NATURE OF THE COVENANT PEOPLE

By obeying the divine commandments the people that
God has chosen will experience His nearness to a degree
greater than that of all other peoples. Obedience to the
Law is therefore not slavery to a divine despot; it is the
way of regular encounter with God. Law in Judaism is
not the enemy of mystical experience; it *is* that experi-

ence, generalized and regularized for all kinds and conditions of men.

But why did God choose this people? There are several partial answers: the merits of their ancestors, chiefly Abraham, who accepted the One God and broke with idolatry; their comparative virtue; their humility and their faithfulness. The first reason, the argument based on the merit of Abraham, recurs everywhere in Jewish literature, and especially in the liturgy. The others (and more can be added) indicate that the question remained a question—and a source and guarantor of humility.

I have taught you statutes and ordinances, as the Lord my God has commanded me; so shall you do in the land which you shall possess. And you shall observe and fulfill them, for this is your wisdom and your understanding in the sight of the peoples that, hearing all these statutes, they may say: Behold a wise and understanding people, a great nation. For what great nation is there that has God so near to them, as the Lord our God is whenever we call upon Him? And what great nation is there that has statutes and ordinances so righteous as all this law which I set before you this day?[13]

For you are a holy people to the Lord your God; the Lord your God has chosen you to be His own treasure, out of all the peoples that are upon the earth. Not because you surpass all nations in number did the Lord set His love upon you and choose you, for you are the fewest of any people, but because the Lord has loved you, and because He would keep His oath which He swore to your fathers has He brought you out with a mighty hand and redeemed you from the house of bondage, out of the hand of Pharaoh, king of Egypt. Know therefore that the Lord your God is God, the faithful God, keeping His covenant and mercy with those that love Him and keeping His commandments to a thousand generations, and repaying those that hate Him, to destroy them, immediately rendering to them what they deserve. Keep therefore the commandment and the statutes and the ordinances which I command you this day to do.[14]

Not because of your righteousness or the uprightness of your heart are you going in to possess their land, but because of the wickedness of these nations the Lord your God is driving them out from before you, and that He may confirm the word which the Lord swore to your fathers, to Abraham to Isaac and to Jacob.[15]

The people of Israel are dear to God, for they are called His children. They are especially dear in that they were made aware of this, as it is written, "You are the children of the Lord your God . . ." [Deut. 14:1]. The people of Israel are dear to God, for to them was given the beloved instrument [the Torah]. They are especially dear in that they were made aware that to them was given the precious instrument by which the world was created, as it is written, "For I have given you good doctrine; do not forsake My Torah" [Prov. 4:2].[16]

"You have declared this day concerning the Lord that He is your God and that you will walk in His ways . . . and the Lord has declared this day that you are a people for His own possession . . ." [Deut. 26:17–18]. The Holy One, praised be He, said to Israel: You have made Me unique in the world and I shall make you unique in the world. You have made Me unique, as it is written "Hear, O Israel, the Lord is our God, the Lord is *One*" [Deut. 6:4], and I will make you unique, as it is written "Who is like Your people Israel, a nation that is *one* in the earth . . ." [I Chron. 17:21].[17]

"It was not because you were more in number than any other people that the Lord set His love upon you and chose you, for you were the fewest of all peoples" [Deut. 7:7]. The Holy One praised be He said to Israel: I set My love upon you because even when I grant you greatness you make yourselves small [i.e. humble] before Me. I gave greatness to Abraham, and he said "Behold, I am dust and ashes" [Gen. 18:27]; to Moses and Aaron, and they said "But what are

we?" [Ex. 16:7]; to David, and he said "I am a worm, not a
man" [Ps. 22:7]. But the other nations of the world are not
like you. I gave greatness to Nimrod, and he said "Let us
build for ourselves a city, and a tower with its top in the
heavens . . ." [Gen. 11:4]; to Pharaoh and he said "Who is
the Lord?" [Ex. 5:2] . . . to Nebuchadnezzar and he said "I
will ascend above the heights of the clouds; I will make myself like the Most High" [Isa. 14:14].[18]

This people has been compared to the dust [". . . your descendants shall be like the dust of the earth . . ." Gen. 28:14]
and it has been compared to the stars [". . . I will multiply
your descendants as the stars of the heavens . . ." Gen. 22:17].
When they go down, they go down to the dust of the earth;
but when they rise, they rise to the stars.[19]

Rabbi Abba bar Aha said: One cannot determine the nature of this people. When asked to contribute for making the
golden calf, they give; and when asked to contribute for con-
structing the Tabernacle, they give.[20]

"And you shall take on the first day [of Sukkot] the fruit
of goodly trees, branches of palm trees and boughs of leafy
trees, and willows of the brook; and you shall rejoice before
the Lord your God seven days" [Lev. 23:40]. ". . . the fruit
of goodly trees . . ." refers to Israel. Just as the *etrog* [citron]
has both taste and fragrance, so Israel has men who have both
learning and good deeds. ". . . branches of palm trees . . ."
refer to Israel. Just as the fig has a taste but has no fragrance,
so Israel has men who have learning but have no good deeds.
". . . boughs of leafy trees . . ." refer to Israel. Just as the
myrtle has fragrance but has no taste, so Israel has men who
have goods deeds but have no learning. ". . . willows of the
brook . . ." refer to Israel. Just as the willow has neither taste
nor fragrance, so Israel has men who have neither learning
nor good deeds. What does the Holy One, praised be He, do
with them? . . . He stated, "Let them be interrelated, united
in one group, and they will be able to atone for one another.
When Israel does so, I will be exalted. . . ."[21]

Judah Halevi, the author of the following passage, was born in Spain toward the end of the eleventh century, and died either on the way to or in the Holy Land in 1140. He was the greatest of medieval Hebrew poets and philosophers. Tradition and revelation, rather than reason, are the sources of faith—so he argues in his book called the *Kuzari*. The form of this volume, from which the statement here about Israel is excerpted, is based on a historic fact. The Khazars, a people of large though temporary power in southern Russia (740–1250), were converted to Judaism, in preference to Christianity or Islam. The *Kuzari* was written as a series of imaginary religious disputations before the king of the Khazars by representations of all three faiths, culminating in his accepting Judaism.

Israel amidst the nations is like the heart amidst the organs of the body; it is at one and the same time the most sick and the most healthy of them. . . .

Our relation to the Divine Influence is the same as that of the soul to the heart. For this reason it is said: "You only have I known of all the families of the earth, therefore I will punish you for all your iniquities" [Amos 3:2]. These are the illnesses. As regards its health. . . . He does not allow our sins to become overwhelming, or they would destroy us completely by their multitude. . . . Just as the heart is pure in substance and matter, and of even temperament, in order to be accessible to the intellectual soul, so also is Israel in its component parts. In the same way as the heart may be affected by disease of the other organs . . . caused through contact with malignant elements, thus also is Israel exposed to ills originating in its inclinations towards the Gentiles, as it is said: "They were mingled among the heathens and learned their works" [Ps. 106:35]. . . . The trials which meet us are meant to prove our faith, to cleanse us completely, and to remove all taint from us.[22]

THE BURDEN OF THE COVENANT

To be God's chosen people is a merit and a distinction. It is also the explanation for Jewry's tragedies. The Babylonian captivity after the destruction of the First Temple in 589 B.C.E. and the Exile of the Jews from the Holy Land after the razing of the Second Temple by the Romans in the year 70 were both great crises of faith. Had God put the Jews aside? No. They had sinned, perhaps no more than other peoples, but it was their duty to be more obedient.

Hear this word that the Lord has spoken against you, O children of Israel, against the whole family which I brought up out of the land of Egypt, saying: You only have I known of all the families of the earth; therefore will I punish you for all your iniquities.[23]

Are you not as the children of the Ethiopians to Me, O children of Israel? says the Lord. Did I not bring up Israel out of the land of Egypt, and the Philistines out of Caphtor, and the Syrians out of Kir? Behold, the eyes of the Lord God are upon the sinful kingdom, and I will destroy it from the face of the earth, but I will not utterly destroy the house of Jacob, says the Lord. For behold, I will command, and I will sift the house of Israel among all nations, as corn is sifted in a sieve, yet not the least grain shall fall to the ground. All the sinners of My people shall fall by the sword, who say, "The evil shall not approach, and shall not come upon us."[24]

The image here is essentially that of the comment above on the Song of Songs. Israel is God's faithful mate. It is ornamented by obedience to every one of His laws, not to just a few; it is faithful to the home, the Temple, which was its meeting place with its beloved divine mate; it is faithful to God even unto death.

"Your eyes are doves" [Song of Songs 1:15]. The dove is faithful; Israel was likewise faithful to the Holy One, praised be He, at Sinai. For they did not say that ten commandments, or twenty or thirty, were enough for them, but they said, "All that the Lord has spoken we will do and we will obey" [Ex. 24:7]. The dove is distinguishable among all other birds; Israel is likewise distinguished, by deeds. The dove is modest; Israel is likewise modest. . . . The dove does not leave its nest even if someone has taken its brood; Israel likewise continues to visit the Temple site even though the Temple has been destroyed. The dove journeys, and returns to its nest; Israel likewise "shall come eagerly like birds from Egypt and like doves from Assyria" [Hos. 11:11]. Others are attracted to the dove; likewise, converts are attracted to Israel. The dove, unlike other birds, offers its neck for slaughter without struggling; children of Israel likewise give their lives for the Holy One praised be He. The dove does not leave its mate; Israel likewise does not leave the Holy One, praised be He. The dove atones for sins; Israel likewise atones for the nations of the world.[25]

THE COVENANT WITH ALL MEN

Noah is the ancestor of all mankind, and to him God made the promise that no matter what its sins, humanity would never be utterly destroyed, as it had been at the Flood. But covenant here too involves commandment. Noah's descendants must obey the moral law and forsake idolatry. Salvation is not only for the "chosen people," or those who join it by conversion. It is open to all, if they but obey the law of righteousness.

God spoke to Noah and to his sons, saying: Behold, I will establish My covenant with you and with your seed after you, and with every living creature that is with you, the fowl, the cattle, and every beast of the earth with you, that come forth out of the ark, all the beasts of the earth. I will establish My covenant with you; all flesh shall no more be destroyed with the waters of a flood, neither shall there be a flood to waste the earth. And God said: This is the sign of the covenant which I make between Me and you and every living creature that is with you, for perpetual generations. I will set My bow in the clouds, and it shall be the sign of a covenant between Me and the earth. And whenever I cover the sky with clouds, My bow shall appear in the clouds, and I will remember My covenant with you and with every living creature of all flesh, and there shall no more be waters of a flood to destroy all flesh.[26]

The sons of Noah were given seven commandments, forbidding idolatry, adultery, bloodshed, profaning God's name, injustice, robbery, and cutting the flesh or a limb from a living animal.[27]

I call heaven and earth as witnesses: The spirit of holiness rests upon each person according to the deed that each does, whether that person be non-Jew or Jew, man or woman, manservant or maidservant.[28]

The Holy One, praised be He, does not disqualify any creature; He accepts everyone. The gates are always open, and whoever wants to enter may enter.[29]

Rabbi Jeremiah used to say: How do we know that even a non-Jew who fulfills the Torah is to be considered as the High Priest? Scripture states, "You shall therefore keep My statutes and My ordinances which, if *a man* do, he shall live by them" [Lev. 18:5]. . . . And he said: Scripture does not state "This is the Law of the Priests, Levites and Israelites" but "This is the Law of man, O Lord God" [II Sam. 7:19]. And he said: Scripture does not state "Open the gates, that the Priests, Levites and Israelites may enter" but "Open the gates, that the righteous nation that keeps faithfulness may enter" [Isa. 26:2]. And he said: Scripture does not state

"This is the gate of the Lord; the Priests, Levites and Israelites shall enter therein" but "This is the gate of the Lord; the righteous shall enter therein" [Ps. 118:20].[30]

. . . As to your question about the nations, know that the Lord desires the heart, and that the intention of the heart is the measure of all things. That is why our sages say, "The pious men among the Gentiles have a share in the world to come," namely, if they have acquired what can be acquired of the knowledge of God, and if they ennoble their souls with worthy qualities. There is no doubt that every man who ennobles his soul with excellent morals and wisdom based on the faith in God, certainly belongs to the men of the world to come. That is why our sages say, "Even a non-Jew who studies the Torah of our master Moses may be compared to a High Priest."[31]

Judaism does accept converts. They are indeed especially precious to God. Their virtue is not so much that they have accepted the Jewish faith, for good men can attain salvation in their own religions. It is that they have taken upon themselves the special burden of Jewish destiny and obligation of becoming part of a priest-people, by choice and adoption "children of Abraham."

"You shall have one ordinance both for the stranger and for the native" [Num. 9:14]. [For the rabbis, "stranger" means proselyte.] Thus, this verse teaches that Scripture makes the proselyte equal to the native-born Jew as regards all the commandments of the Torah.[32]

A proselyte who has come of his own accord is dearer to God than all the Israelites who stood before Him at Mount Sinai. Had the Israelites not witnessed the thunders, lightnings, quaking mountains and sound of trumpets, they would not have accepted the Torah. The proselyte, who saw not one of these things, came and surrendered himself to the Holy One, praised be He, and took the yoke of Heaven upon himself. Can anyone be dearer to God than such a person?³³

If anyone desires to be a convert during these times [*probably a period of persecution*], they should say to him, "Why do you want to convert? Do you not know that Israelites today are harried, and oppressed, persecuted and harassed, and that they suffer?" If he says, "I know and I am not worthy," he is accepted at once, and they explain some of the lighter and some of the more stringent commandments to him. . . . And as they tell him of the punishments for transgressing commandments, so they tell him of the rewards for observing them. . . . However, they do not speak with him at great length nor do they go into great detail. If he agrees to accept everything, he is circumcised at once. . . . After he is healed, he must undergo ritual immersion and two scholars stand by, telling him some of the lighter and some of the more stringent commandments. After the ritual immersion he is an Israelite in every respect.³⁴

Why was Abraham circumcised at the age of ninety-nine? To teach that if a man wants to convert he should not say, "I am too old; how can I convert?" This is the reason why Abraham was not circumcised until the age of ninety-nine.³⁵

What follows here is a legal decision by Maimonides in answer to a question posed by a convert.

. . . You ask me if you, too, are allowed to say in the blessings and prayers you offer alone or in the congregation: *"Our* God and God of *our* fathers," "You who have sanctified *us* through Your commandments," "You who have separated *us,*" "You who have chosen *us,*" . . . "You who have brought *us* out of the land of Egypt," . . . and more of this kind.

Yes, you may say all this in the prescribed order and not change it in the least. In the same way as every Jew by birth says his blessings and prayers, you, too, shall bless and pray alike, whether you are alone or pray in the congregation. The reason for this is that Abraham, our father, taught the people, opened their minds, and revealed to them the true faith and the unity of God; he rejected the idols and abolished their adoration; he brought many children under the wings of the Divine Presence; he gave them counsel and advice, and ordered his sons and the members of his household after him to keep the ways of the Lord forever, as it is written, "For I have known him to the end that he may command his children and his household after him, that they may keep the way of the Lord, to do righteousness and justice" [Gen. 18:19]. Ever since then whoever adopts Judaism and confesses the unity of the Divine Name, as it is prescribed in the Torah, is counted among the disciples of Abraham, our father, peace be with him. These men are Abraham's household, and he it is who converted them to righteousness.

In the same way as he converted his contemporaries through his words and teaching, he converts future generations through the testament he left to his children and household after him. Thus Abraham, our father, peace be with him, is the father of his pious posterity who keep his ways, and the father of his disciples and of all proselytes who adopt Judaism.[36]

MODERN THINKING ABOUT THE COVENANT

The concepts of revelation, the Law, and the "chosen people" all became problematic for modern Jewish theologians, as stressed above in the essay which introduces this volume. The thinkers represented here are each interpreting it anew, several in the conscious desire to formulate it so that it is consonant with the general thought of their own generations.

Kaufmann Kohler (1843–1926), a leading figure of American Reform Judaism, identified religion with moral progress and chosenness with a corporate mission to effect it. Judaism in Biblical days had been the most progressive faith of its time; it would continue to be so, he asserted, by constantly reforming and purifying itself, by abandoning outworn ideas and practices in the name of ever higher ideals. To Kohler, revelation is thus progressive and not bound even by the event on Sinai.

. . . The election of Israel cannot be regarded as a single divine act, concluded at one moment of revelation, or even during the Biblical period. It must instead be considered a divine call persisting through all ages and encompassing all lands, a continuous activity of the spirit which has ever summoned for itself new heralds and heroes to testify to truth, justice and sublime faith, with an unparalleled scorn for death, and to work for their dissemination by words and deeds and by their whole life. Judaism differs from all other religions in that it is neither the creation of one great moral teacher and preacher of truth, nor seeks to typify the moral and spiritual sublimity which it aims to develop in a single person, who is then lifted up into the realm of the superhuman. Judaism counts its prophets, its sages and its martyrs by generations; it is still demonstrating its power to reshape and regenerate religion as a vital force. Moreover, Judaism does not separate religion from life, so as to regard only a segment of the common life and the national existence as holy. The entire people, the entire life, must bear the stamp of holiness and be filled with priestly consecration. Whether this lofty aim can ever be completely attained is a question not to be decided by short sighted humanity, but only by God, the Ruler of history. It is sufficient that the life of the individual as well as that of the people should aspire toward this ideal.

Of course, the election of Israel presupposes an inner calling, a special capacity of soul and tendency of intellect which fit it for the divine task. The people which has given mankind its greatest prophets and psalmists, its boldest thinkers and its noblest martyrs, which has brought to fruition the three great world-religions, the Church, the Mosque and— mother of them both—the Synagogue, must be the religious people *par excellence*. It must have within itself enough of the heavenly spark of truth and of the impetus of the religious genius as to be able and eager, whenever and wherever the opportunity is favorable, to direct the spiritual flight of humanity toward the highest and holiest.[37]

Mordecai Kaplan (born in 1881) is the leader of American Jewish religious naturalism, i.e. of a version of religion without revelation. "God" is the term man uses for the sum of his highest ideals. Obviously there can be no "chosen people," in such a system. Even here, in the boldest anticlassicist among modern Jewish theologians, one can perceive a re-echo of one part—but only one part —of the teaching of Amos, that the Jews are no better than the Ethiopians. But Amos also believed that they were in covenant with the living God who had chosen them to do and to suffer more than others.

The apologists for the doctrine of Israel's election do not take the trouble to think through to a conclusion the role of religion in human civilization. Formerly the adherents of all the traditional religions of the Western world maintained that religion was supernaturally revealed truth. That such truth was transmitted only by one's own people was sufficient evidence that only one's own people had been chosen. Since it was assumed that salvation could be achieved only through revealed truth, the possession of that truth imposed the obligation to convey it to others and to induct them into one's own "chosen" community by way of conversion.

But when one abandons the idea of supernatural revelation, what becomes of religion? If religious truth is independent of any historic self-revelation of God to a particular people, then it is no different from scientific truth in being accessible to and attainable by all mankind. Indeed, one of the main criteria of truth is its universal applicability to and conformity with universal reason. . . .

A religion is the organized quest of a people for salvation, for helping those who live by the civilization of that people to achieve their destiny as human beings. In the course of that quest, the people discovers religious truth and abiding values. These truths and values, like all others, are universal. They are not the monopoly of the group that discovers them. They may be discovered by other groups as well. Religions are distinct from one another not so much ideationally as existentially. Each religion represents a particular area of collective life marked out by the *sancta* of the group. These are a definite product of the group's unique historic experience. Such *sancta* are its saints and heroes, its sacred literature, its holy places, its common symbols, its customs and folkways, and all objects and associations which have been hallowed, because of their relation to that people's quest for salvation. There is no more reason for having all the world adopt the *sancta* of one people or church than for all people to wear an identical type of garment. What is important is that the *sancta* of each people or church help to humanize all who belong to it, by implementing those universal values which it should share with all other peoples and churches. *A religion is universal, if its conception of God is one that imposes on its adherents loyalty to a universally valid code of ethics. It is only in that sense that the Jewish religion is universal.*[38]

Martin Buber, the leading Jewish existentialist theologian, profoundly believes in the fact of the encounter between God and the Jewish people. For him it is an event which recurs in the personal experience of each Jew, so long as he chooses to be a Jew and to hear the voice of God addressing him. Buber thus affirms the classical notions of both God and Israel, but the traditional idea of the Law is absent. In the encounter with God, as the individual hears Him speaking to the deepest recesses of his being, each man hears what he can hear—and obeys that which he has personally heard.

What does it mean to become a "people of God?" A common belief in God and service to His name do not constitute a people of God. Becoming a people of God means rather that the attributes of God revealed to it, justice and love, are to be made effective in its own life, in the lives of its members with one another; justice materialized in the indirect mutual relationships of these individuals; love in their direct mutual relationships, rooted in their personal existence. Of the two, however, love is the higher, the transcending principle. This becomes unequivocally clear from the fact that man cannot be just to God; he can, however, and should, love God. And it is the love of God which transfers itself to man; "God loves the stranger," we are told, "so you too shall love him." The man who loves God loves also him whom God loves.[39]

Edmond Fleg (born in 1876), the Franco-Jewish man of letters, is a historical mystic. The ancient tradition could find only one reason for God's choice on which all agreed, the merit of Abraham and the virtue of those of his progeny who followed in his courageous and faithful ways. This affirmation is here used as the central value, blended with intellectual liberalism and passionate love for the Jewish past.

People ask me why I am a Jew. It is to you that I want to answer, little unborn grandson. . . .

I am a Jew because, born of Israel and having lost her, I have felt her live again in me, more living than myself.

I am a Jew because, born of Israel and having regained her, I wish her to live after me, more living than in myself.

I am a Jew because the faith of Israel demands of me no abdication of the mind.

I am a Jew because the faith of Israel requires of me all the devotion of my heart.

I am a Jew because in every place where suffering weeps, the Jew weeps.

I am a Jew because at every time when despair cries out, the Jew hopes.

I am a Jew because the word of Israel is the oldest and the newest.

I am a Jew because the promise of Israel is the universal promise.

I am a Jew because, for Israel, the world is not yet completed; men are completing it.

I am a Jew because, above the nations and Israel, Israel places Man and his Unity.

I am a Jew because, above Man, image of the divine Unity, Israel places the divine Unity, and its divinity. . . .

And I say to myself: From this remote father [Abraham] right up to my own father, all these fathers have handed on to me a truth which flowed in their blood, which flows in mine; and shall I not hand it on, with my blood, to those of my blood?

Will you take it from me, my child? Will you hand it on? Perhaps you will wish to abandon it. If so, let it be for a greater truth, if there is one. I shall not blame you. It will be my fault; I shall have failed to hand it on as I received it.[40]

Samson Raphael Hirsch (1808–1888) was a rabbi in Germany and the founder of neo-orthodox Judaism. These words of his are not different, except in rhetoric, from what we have found in earlier centuries.

Because men had eliminated God from life, nay, even from nature, and found the basis of life in possessions and its aim in enjoyment, deeming life the product of the multitude of human desires, just as they looked upon nature as the product of a multitude of gods, therefore, it became necessary that a people be introduced into the ranks of the nations which, through its history and life, should declare God the only creative cause of existence, fulfillment of His will the only aim of life; and which should bear the revelation of His will, rejuvenated and renewed for its sake, unto all parts of the world as the motive and incentive of its coherence. This mission required for its carrying out a nation poor in everything upon

which the rest of mankind reared the edifice of its greatness
and its power; externally subordinate to the nations armed
with proud reliance on self, but fortified by direct reliance on
God; so that by suppression of every opposing force God
might reveal Himself directly as the only Creator, Judge and
Master of nature and history. . . .

"One God, Creator, Lawgiver, Judge, Guide, Preserver,
and Father of all beings; all beings His servants, His children,
man also His child and servant, from His hand all, and this
all to be used only for the fulfillment of His will, since this
alone is sufficient for a proper attainment of the purposes of
life, while all other human occupations and pursuits are but
paths which lead to the goal of the fulfillment of the mission
of humanity."

The proclaiming of these great truths was to be the chief,
if not the sole, life-task of this people.[41]

Has Israel any other task than to teach all the races of
man to recognize and worship the Only-One as their God?
Is it not Israel's unceasing duty to proclaim through the example of its life and history Him as the universal Lord and
Sovereign? The Bible terms Israel *segulah*, "a peculiar treasure," but this designation does not imply, as some have falsely
interpreted, that Israel has a monopoly of the Divine love and
favor, but, on the contrary, that God has the sole and exclusive claim to Israel's devotions and service; that Israel may not
render Divine homage to any other being. [*Segulah* means a
property belonging exclusively to one owner, to which no
other has any right or claim.] Israel's most cherished ideal is
that of the universal brotherhood of mankind.[42]

The greatest spiritual representative of classical Judaism in the twentieth century was Abraham Isaac Kook
(1865–1935), who became in 1921 the chief rabbi of
Palestine. Kook's mysticism was a reaffirmation of the
holiness of the Jewish faith, practices, land, and people
and of the divine meaning of their interaction and unity.
The selection from his writings should be read, though he

did not write it as such, as a homily on the paragraph
from the prescribed daily morning prayers, which concludes this chapter.

The world and all that it contains is waiting for the Light
of Israel, for the Exalted Light radiating from Him Whose
Name is to be praised. This people was fashioned by God to
speak of His glory; it was granted the heritage of the blessing
of Abraham so that it might disseminate the knowledge of
God and it was commanded to live its life apart from the
nations of the world. God chose it to cleanse the whole world
of all impurity and darkness; this people is endowed with a
hidden treasure, with the Torah, the means by which the
Heaven and the Earth were created.

The Light of Israel is not a utopian dream, or some abstract morality, or merely a pious wish and a noble vision.
It does not wash its hands of the material world and all its
values, abandoning the flesh, and society and government to
wallow in their impurity, and forsaking the forces of nature,
which fell in the Fall of Man, to remain in their low estate.
It is, rather, a raising of all of life. . . .

Redemption is continuous. The Redemption from Egypt
and the Final Redemption are part of the same process, "of
the mighty hand and outstretched arm," which began in Egypt
and is evident in all of history. Moses and Elijah belong to
the same redemptive act; one represents its beginning and the
other its culmination, so that together they fulfill its purpose.
The spirit of Israel is attuned to the hum of the redemptive
process, to the sound of the waves of its labors which will end
only with the coming of the days of the Messiah.

It is a grave error to be insensitive to the distinctive unity
of the Jewish spirit, to imagine that the Divine stuff which
uniquely characterizes Israel is comparable to the spiritual
content of all the other national civilizations. This error is
the source of the attempt to sever the national from the religious element of Judaism. Such a division would falsify both
our nationalism and our religion, for every element of thought,
emotion, and idealism that is present in the Jewish people be-

longs to an indivisible entity, and all together make up its specific character.[43]

From the Prayer Book

Deep is Your love for us, O Lord our God;
Bounteous is Your compassion and tenderness.
You taught our fathers the laws of life,
And they trusted in You, Father and King.

For their sake be gracious to us, and teach us,
That we may learn Your laws, and trust in You.
Father, merciful Father, have compassion upon us;
Endow us with discernment and understanding.

Grant us the will to study Your Torah,
To heed its words and to teach its precepts.
May we observe and practice its instruction,
Lovingly fulfilling all its teachings.

Enlighten our eyes in Your Torah,
Open our hearts to Your commandments.
Unify our hearts with singleness of purpose
To hold You in reverence and in love.

Unify our hearts to revere and to love You;
Then shall we never be brought to shame.
We will delight and exult in Your help;
In Your holiness do we trust.

Bring us safely from the corners of the earth,
And lead us in dignity to our holy land.
You, O God, are the Source of salvation;
You have chosen us from all peoples and tongues.

You have drawn us close to You;
We praise You and thank You in truth.
With love do we thankfully proclaim Your unity,
And praise You who chose Your people Israel in love.[44]

CHAPTER TWO

God

GOD IS

The Bible does not regard God's existence as something to be proved. It does not ever entertain the thought that the universe was self-created or is eternal; and if the universe had a beginning in time, who but God could have created it? Surely God has not abandoned creation. He cares for all men, indeed for everything that is.

In the beginning God created the heavens and the earth.[1]

Who has measured the waters in the hollow of his hand, and weighed the heavens with his palm? Who has measured the dust of the earth in a measure and weighed the mountains in scales, and the hills in a balance? Who has meted out the spirit of the Lord? Who has been His counsellor; who has taught Him? With whom has He consulted and who has instructed Him, and taught Him the path of justice, and taught Him knowledge and showed Him the way of understanding? Behold, the nations are as a drop of a bucket, and are counted as the smallest grain of a balance; behold the islands are as a little dust. And Lebanon is not enough to burn, nor the beasts thereof sufficient for a burnt offering. All nations are before Him as if they had no being at all, and are counted to Him as nothing, and vanity. To whom then will you liken God? What likeness will you compare to Him? The image which the craftsman has melted and the goldsmith spread over with gold, the silversmith casting silver chains? He has chosen strong wood, that will not rot; he seeks a skillful workman to set up an idol that shall not be moved.

Do you not know? Have you not heard? Has it not been told you from the beginning? Have you not understood the foundations of the earth? It is He that sits above the globe of the earth, and the inhabitants thereof are as grasshoppers, He that stretches out the heavens as a curtain, and spreads them out as a tent to dwell in; that brings princes to nothing; He makes the judges of the earth as a thing of nought. Scarce are they planted, scarce are they sown, scarce has their stock taken root in the earth when He blows upon them, and they are withered, and a whirlwind takes them away as stubble. To whom, then, would you liken Me, that I should be equal? says the Holy One.[2]

Praised are You, O Lord our God, King of the universe.
You fix the cycles of light and darkness;
You ordain the order of all creation.
You cause light to shine over the earth;
Your radiant mercy is upon its inhabitants.

In Your goodness the work of creation
Is continually renewed day by day.
How manifold are Your works, O Lord.
With wisdom You fashioned them all.
The earth abounds with Your creations.[3]

The Lord is my shepherd; I shall not want.
He makes me lie down in green pastures,
He leads me beside still waters.
He restores my soul;
He guides me on paths of justice, for His name's sake.

Though I walk through the valley of the shadow of death,
I shall fear no evil, for You are with me.
Your rod and Your staff do comfort me.

You prepare a table before me in the presence of my
    enemies.
You anoint my head with oil, my cup overflows.
Surely goodness and mercy shall follow me
All the days of my life;
And I shall live in the house of the Lord forever.[4]

Man's proper response to such a God is gratitude and reverence. The psalm and prayer of thanksgiving that follow here are prescribed in the prayer book for the festivals of Passover, Shabuoth, and Sukkoth; for the first day of the lunar month, which is a half holiday; and for Hanukkah, the holiday which commemorates the victory of the Jews over their Syrian Greek persecutors of the second century B.C.E.

Sing praises, O you servants of the Lord;
Praise the glory of the Lord. Halleluyah!

Praised is the glory of the Lord, now and always;
From sunrise to sunset, praised is the Lord.

Supreme over all nations is the Lord;
His glory is high over all the heavens.

Who is like the Lord our God, enthroned on high,
Yet bending low to survey all heaven and earth?

He raises the poor from the dust;
He lifts the needy from the ash heap.

He places them in the seats of the noble;
He seats them with the princes of His people.

He transforms the childless mistress of a home
Into a joyous mother of children. Halleluyah![5]

All creation praises You, O Lord our God.
The pious and the just who do Your will,
And all Your people of the house of Israel
Join in thanking You with joyous song.

They praise, exalt, sanctify and revere
Your sovereign glory, O our King.

To You it is good to give thanks;
To Your glory it is fitting to sing.

You are God from beginning of time to its end.
Praised are You, O Lord, acclaimed with praises.[6]

The world is not God. i.e. Judaism is not pantheistic, but God is in the world. Man's sins may make Him more remote, but that is man's fault, for God is always present for "those who call upon Him in truth."

Am I not a God near at hand, says the Lord, and not a God far off? Can any hide himself in secret places that I shall not see him? Do I not fill heaven and earth?[7]

There is nothing on earth which is apart from the *Shekhinah* [God's Presence].[8]

God fills the universe just as the soul fills the body of man.[9]

An emperor said to Rabbi Joshua ben Hananya: "I want to see your God." He replied, "You cannot see Him." "Nevertheless," the emperor said, "I want to see Him!" Rabbi Joshua stood him in the summer sun, and said "Look at the sun." "I cannot," answered the emperor. Rabbi Joshua said, "The sun is but one of the servants who stand in the presence of the Holy One, praised be He, and you cannot look at the sun. Is it not truer still that you cannot see God's Presence?"[10]

Originally, the *Shekhinah* [Presence of God] was on earth. When Adam sinned, it rose to the nearest firmament. When Cain sinned, it rose to the second. When the generation of Enosh sinned [in idolatry], it rose to the third. When the generation of the Flood sinned, it rose to the fourth. When the generation of the dispersal of nations [who tried to erect the Tower of Babel] sinned, it rose to the fifth firmament. When the men of Sodom sinned, it rose to the sixth. The wickedness of the Egyptians in the time of Abraham caused the *Shekhinah* to retreat to the seventh and most remote firmament.
The righteous counteracted the above effect. Abraham brought the *Shekhinah* down to the sixth firmament, Isaac brought it to the fifth, Jacob brought it to the fourth, Levi to the third, Kehat to the second and Amram to the first firmament. Moses brought it back from the heavens to earth.[11]

The passage immediately below is from the *Zohar*
(Book of Splendor), the basic text of the *kabbalah* (cabala). In its present form this book dates from the thirteenth century, when it was "edited" by the Spanish mystic
Moses de León, who announced it as an ancient text of
the second century. This is almost certainly not true, but
the book does reflect a well-developed older tradition of
mystical speculation. The dominant Jewish tradition has
always regarded *kabbalah* gingerly and with some suspicion. Mystic speculation can enrich the faith, but it must
be curbed lest it substitute mystical transports and even
magic for the life of obedience to divine commandment.

"And Sarah was listening at the tent door, behind him"
[Gen. 18:10]. Rabbi Judah began a discourse with the verse:
"Her husband is known in the gates, when he sits among the
elders of the land" [Prov. 31:23].

The Holy One, praised be He, is transcendent in His glory,
he is hidden and removed far beyond all ken; there is no one
in the world, nor has there ever been one whom His wisdom
and essence do not elude, since He is recondite and hidden
and beyond all ken, so that neither the supernal nor the lower
beings are able to commune with Him until they utter the
words: "Blessed is the glory of the Lord from His place"
[Ezek. 3:12].

The creatures of the earth think of Him as being on high,
declaring "His glory is above the heavens" [Ps. 113:4], while
the heavenly beings think of Him as being below, declaring
"His glory is over all the earth" [Ps. 57:12], until they both,
in heaven and on earth, concur in declaring "Blessed be the
glory of the Lord from His place" [Ezek. 3:12], because He
is unknowable and no one can truly understand Him. . . .

For there is door within door, grade behind grade, through
which the glory of the Holy One is made known. Hence here
the "tent door" is the door of righteousness, referred to in the
words, "Open to me the gates of righteousness" [Ps. 118:19],
and this is the first entrance door: through this door a view

is opened to all the other supernal doors. He who succeeds in entering this door is privileged to know both it and all the other doors, since they all repose on this one.

At the present time this door remains unknown because Israel is in exile; and therefore all the other doors are removed from them, so that they cannot know or commune; but when Israel will return from exile, all the supernal grades are destined to rest harmoniously upon this one. Then men will obtain a knowledge of the precious supernal wisdom of which hitherto they knew not, as it is written, "And the spirit of the Lord shall rest upon him, the spirit of wisdom and understanding, the spirit of counsel and might, the spirit of knowledge and of the fear of the Lord" [Isa. 11:2].[12]

Under the challenge of Aristotelian philosophy, as understood by the Arabs after the ninth century, Jewish thinkers felt constrained to develop their own philosophical apologetics. Here are two famous examples of such explanations of the doctrine of God. The first is by Saadia (882–942), who is second only to Maimonides among medieval Jewish scholars. Saadia was a native of Egypt and head (*gaon*) of the academy in Sura, Babylonia. His *Book of Beliefs and Opinions*, from which this passage is taken, is the first major work of medieval Jewish philosophical theology.

With respect to the category of *relation*, I say that it would be improper to connect anything with the Creator in an anthropomorphic manner or to relate it to Him, because He has existed since eternity, that is a time when none of the things created were connected with Him or related to Him. . . . When, therefore, we note that the Scriptures call God *king* and present human beings as His slaves and the angels as ministering to Him . . . all that is merely a means of expressing reverence and esteem. For the human beings most highly esteemed by us are the kings. God is also called "king" in the sense that He can do whatever He wishes and that His command is always carried out. . . .

Apropos of the category of *place*, I say that it is inconceivable for several reasons that the Creator should have any need for occupying any place whatsoever. First of all He is Himself the Creator of all space. Also He originally existed alone, when there was as yet no such thing as place. It is unthinkable, therefore, that as a result of His act of creation He should have been transported into space. Furthermore, space is required only by a material object. . . .

As for the assertion of the prophets that God dwells in heaven, that was merely a way of indicating God's greatness and His elevation, since heaven is for us the highest thing we know of. . . . The same applies to statements to the effect that God dwells in the Temple, such as "And I will dwell among the children of Israel" [Ex. 29:45] and "The Lord dwells in Zion" [Joel 4:21]. The purpose of all this was to confer honor upon the place and the people in question. . . .

As regards the category of *time*, it is inconceivable that the concept of time could be applied to the Creator because of the fact that He Himself is the Creator of all time. Furthermore, He existed originally alone when there was as yet no such thing as time. It is, therefore, unthinkable that time should have effected any locomotion or change in Him. Moreover, time is nothing else than the measurement of the duration of corporeal beings. He, however, who has no body, is far removed from such concepts as time and duration. If, nevertheless, we do describe God as being enduring and permanent, that is done only by way of approximation. . . .

As regards the matter of *possession*, inasmuch as all creatures are God's creation and handiwork, it is not seemly for us to say that He possesses one thing to the exclusion of another, nor that He possesses the one to a greater and the other to a lesser degree. If we, nevertheless, see Scriptures assert that a certain people is His peculiar property and His possession and His portion, as they do in the statement, "For the portion of the Lord is His people, Jacob the lot of His inheritance" [Deut. 32:9], that is done merely as a means of conferring honor and distinction. For, as it appears to us, every man's portion and lot are precious to him. Nay the

Scriptures even go so far as to declare God, too, figuratively to be the lot of the pious and their portion, as they do in their statement, "O Lord, the portion of mine inheritance and of my cup" [Ps. 16:5]. This is, therefore, also an expression of special devotion and esteem. . . .

As for the category of *position*, inasmuch as the Creator is not a physical being, it is unseemly to speak of Him as having any such position as sitting or standing or the like. Nay, it is impossible because He is not a physical being, and because originally there existed nothing outside of Himself.[18]

Maimonides here expounds the doctrine of God's "negative attributes," which means that anything that man may ascribe to God is a limitation of His absolute being. This passage is a crucial point in the argument of the greatest Jewish philosophical classic, *The Guide of the Perplexed.*

It would be extremely difficult for us to find, in any language whatsoever, words adequate to this subject, and we can only employ inadequate language. In our endeavour to show that God does not include a plurality, we can only say "He is one," although "one" and "many" are both terms which serve to distinguish quantity. We therefore make the subject clearer, and show to the understanding the way of truth by saying that He is one but does not possess the attribute of unity.

The same is the case when we say God is the First (*kadmon*), to express that He has not been created; the term *kadmon*, "First," is decidedly inaccurate, for it can in its true sense only be applied to a being that is subject to the relation of time; the latter, however, is an accident to motion which again is connected with a body. Besides, the attribute *kadmon* ("first" or "eternal") is a relative term, being in regard to time the same as the terms "long" and "short" are in regard to a line. Both expressions, "created" and "eternal" (or "first"), are equally inadmissible in reference to any being to which the attribute of time is not applicable, just as we do not say "crooked" or "straight" in reference to taste, "salted" or "insipid" in reference to the voice. These subjects are not un-known to those who have accustomed themselves to seek a true understanding of the things, and to establish their prop-erties in accordance with the abstract notions which the mind has formed of them, and who are not misled by the inaccuracy of the words employed. All attributes, such as "the First," "the Last," occurring in the Scriptures in reference to God, are as metaphorical as the expressions "ear" and "eye." They simply signify that God is not subject to any change or in-novation whatever; they do not imply that God can be de-scribed by time, or that there is any comparison between Him and any other being as regards time, and that He is called on that account "the first" and "the last." In short, all similar expressions are borrowed from the language commonly used among the people. In the same way we use "One" (*ehad*) in reference to God, to express that there is nothing similar to Him, but we do not mean to say that an attribute of unity is added to His essence.

Know that the negative attributes of God are the true attributes. . . . God's existence is absolute. . . . It includes no composition. . . . We comprehend only the fact that He exists, not His essence (i.e. we comprehend only that He is, but not what He is). Consequently it is a false assumption to hold that He has any positive attribute; for He does not possess existence in addition to His essence; it therefore cannot be said that the one (either existence or essence) may be de-scribed as an attribute of the other; much less has He in addition to His existence a compound essence, consisting of two constituent elements to which the attribute could refer; still less has He accidents, which could be described by an attribute. Hence it is clear that He has no positive attribute whatever. The negative attributes, however, are those which are necessary to direct the mind to the truths which we must believe concerning God; for, on the one hand, they do not imply any plurality, and, on the other, they convey to man the highest possible knowledge of God; e.g. it has been estab-lished by proof that some being must exist besides those things which can be perceived by the senses, or apprehended by the mind; when we say of this being, that it exists, we mean that its non-existence is impossible. We thus perceive that such a being is not, for instance, like the four elements, which are animate, and we therefore say it is living, expressing thereby that it is not dead. We call such a being incorporeal, because we notice that it is unlike the heavens, which are living, but material.

Seeing that it is also different from the intellect, which, though incorporeal and living, owes its existence to some cause, we say it is the first (*kadmon*), expressing thereby that its existence is not due to any cause. We further notice that the existence, that is the essence, of this being is not limited to its own existence; many existences emanate from it, and its influence is not like that of the fire in producing heat or that of the sun in sending forth light, but consists in constantly giving them stability and order by well-established rule, as we shall show (heat comes from fire, light from the sun, as natural consequences of the properties of fire and of the sun. There is no intention or will in either of them; but that which comes from God emanates from His will). We say, on that account, it has power, wisdom and will, i.e. it is not feeble or ignorant, or hasty, and does not abandon its creatures; when we say that it is not feeble, we mean that its existence is capable of producing the existence of many other things; by saying it is not ignorant, we mean "it perceives" or "it lives,"—for everything that perceives is alive—by saying "it is not hasty, and does not abandon its creatures," we mean that all these creatures preserve a certain order and arrangement; they are not left to themselves, or produced aimlessly, but whatever condition they receive from that being is given them with design and intention. We thus learn that there is no other being like unto God, and we say that He is One, i.e. there are not more Gods than one.[14]

The rabbinic tradition was largely antispeculative.

Why was the world created with the letter *Beth*? [*Beth* is the first letter of the first word in the Torah, *Bereshith*, "In the beginning."] Just as the shape of the letter *Beth* is closed

on three sides and open toward the front, so you do not have
permission to be concerned with that which is below or above
the earth, nor with what happened before this world came to
be. Rather, you should be concerned with what happened
since the Creation of the world, with what lies before you on
earth.[15]

There were four who entered the Pardes [*Rashi*: they
ascended to the highest firmament, that of *God*]: Ben Azai,
Ben Zoma, Elisha ben Abuyah, and Rabbi Akiva. Ben Azai
looked in the direction of the *Shekhinah* and died. . . . Ben
Zoma looked and went mad. . . . Elisha ben Abuyah became
irreligious. Rabbi Akiva came out unharmed.[16]

Maimonides as guide to Jewish law was accepted as
the paramount authority. As philosophical theologian his
work occasioned embittered controversy. Pietists were less
impressed by his brilliant answers to doubters than they
were upset by the clarity with which he posed the arguments of the unbelievers. They preferred not to enter this
field at all. Here Hayyim ibn Musa (1390–1460), a
Spanish rabbi and writer, expresses this view.

In my youth I heard a preacher preach about God's being
one and one only, in a speculating manner—in the manner of
philosophers. And he said many times over that if He were
not one only God, then this and that would necessarily follow.
Thereupon a man rose, one of those who "tremble at the
word of the Lord" [Isa. 66:5], and said: "Misfortune came
upon me and mine at the great disaster in Sevilla (Pogrom of
1391). I was beaten and wounded, until my persecutors
desisted because they thought I was dead. All this have I
suffered for my faith in 'Hear, O Israel, the Lord our God,
the Lord is One.' And here you are, dealing with the traditions of our fathers in the manner of a speculating philosopher, and saying: 'If He were not one only God, then this
and that would necessarily follow.' I have greater faith in the

tradition of our fathers, and I do not want to go on listening
to this sermon." And he left the house of prayer and most of
the congregation went with him.[17]

Here are three nonphilosophical views of God, which
are quite characteristic of rabbinic piety and its sense of
at-homeness with Him.

How do we know that the Holy One, praised be He, prays?
It is written, "I will bring them to My holy mountain and
make them rejoice in My house of prayer" [Isa. 56:7]. This
verse states not *their* house of prayer" but *"My* house of
prayer," from which we infer that the Holy One, praised be
He, prays. What is His prayer? Rav Tuviah bar Zutra, quoting
Rav, said, "May it be My will that My compassion overcomes
My wrath, and that it prevail over My attribute of strict justice. May I deal with My children according to the attribute
of compassion; may I not deal with them according to the
strict line of justice."[18]

Rabbi Judah said, quoting Rav: The day consists of twelve
hours. During the first three hours, the Holy One, praised be
He, is engaged in the study of Torah. During the second three
He sits in judgment over His entire world. When He realizes
that the world is deserving of destruction, He rises from the
Throne of Justice, to sit in the Throne of Mercy. During the
third group of three hours, He provides sustenance for the entire world, from huge beasts to lice. During the fourth, He
sports with the Leviathan, as it is written, "Leviathan, which
You did form to sport with" [Ps. 104:26]. . . . During the
fourth group of three hours (according to others) He teaches
schoolchildren.[19]

Rabbi Nehemiah said: When the Israelites did that wicked
deed [i.e. when they constructed and worshiped the golden
calf] Moses sought to appease God, who was angry with them.
He said, "Lord of the universe! They have made an assistant

for You. Why should You be angry with them? This calf will assist You: You will cause the sun to shine and the calf will cause the moon to shine; You will take care of the stars and the calf will take care of the planets; You will cause the dew to fall and the calf will make the winds to blow; You will cause the rain to fall and the calf will cause vegetation to sprout." The Holy One, praised be He, said to Moses, "You are making the same mistake that the people are making! This calf is not real!" Moses then replied, "If that is so, why should You be angry with Your children?"[20]

Rabbi Israel Baal-Shem Tov (1698–1760), the founder of Hasidism, sums up what, with varying emphases, has been the mainstream of Jewish thought about God's existence. We know that God is by reason, by faith and by tradition. We require all these sources of knowledge. Incidentally, exactly this view had already been stated by Saadia more than eight centuries before in his *Book of Beliefs and Opinions. (See below,* Chapter III).

Why do we say "Our God and the God of our fathers"? [Introductory phrase in many prayers.] There are two sorts of persons who believe in God. The one believes because his faith has been handed down to him by his fathers; and his faith is strong. The other has arrived at faith by dint of searching thought. And this is the difference between the two: the first has the advantage that his faith cannot be shaken, no matter how many objections are raised to it, for his faith is firm because he has taken it over from his fathers. But there is a flaw in it: it is a commandment given by man, and it has been learned without thought or reasoning. The advantage of the second man is that he has reached faith through his own power, through much searching and thinking. But his faith too has a flaw: it is easy to shake it by offering contrary evidence. But he who combines both kinds of faith is invulnerable. That is why we say "Our God," because of our searching, and "the God of our fathers," because of our tradition.

And a like interpretation holds when we say "The God of Abraham, the God of Isaac, and the God of Jacob" [Introductory phrase of the *Amidah* prayer], for this means: Isaac and Jacob did not merely take over the tradition of Abraham, but sought out the divine for themselves.[21]

GOD IS ONE

On this subject all Jewish teachings throughout the ages speak with one voice. For this faith countless martyrs have died in all the centuries.

Hear O Israel, the Lord our God, the Lord is one.[22]

You shall have no gods before Me. You shall not make to yourself a graven image, or the likeness of anything that is in heaven above or in the earth beneath or in the waters under the earth. You shall not bow down to them or serve them, for I, the Lord your God, am a jealous God, visiting the iniquity of the fathers upon the children to the third and fourth generation of those that hate Me, and showing mercy to the thousandth generation of those that love Me and keep My commandments.[23]

Not to us, O Lord, not to us belongs the glory,
But to You, for Your faithful mercy.

Let not nations say: "Where is their God?"
When our God is in the heavens above;
Whatever is pleasing to Him He does.

Pagan idols are of silver and gold;
They are fashioned by human hands.
They have mouths, but cannot speak;
Eyes have they, but cannot see.

They have hands, but cannot feel;
Feet have they but cannot walk;
Their throats cannot utter a sound.
As they are, so be their makers,
All who put their trust in them.

Let Israel trust in the Lord;
He is your help and your shield.
House of Aaron, trust the Lord;
He is your help and your shield.

You who revere the Lord, trust the Lord;
He is your help and your shield.

The Lord is mindful of us and will bless us.
He will bless the house of Israel;
He will bless the house of Aaron;

He will bless all those that revere Him,
Blessing alike the lowly and the great.
The Lord will multiply blessings upon you,
Blessings upon you and your children.

Blessed are you of the Lord,
Maker of heaven and earth.

The heavens are the heavens of the Lord;
The earth He has given to mankind.

The dead cannot praise the Lord,
Nor those who go down into silence,
But we praise the Lord now and forevermore. Halleluyah![24]

The law against idolatry is basic to all the commandments
in the Torah. . . . Whoever transgresses all of the commandments breaks off the yoke of the Torah, annuls the covenant
between God and Israel and misrepresents the Torah. The
same is true of whoever transgresses the one commandment
against idolatry.[25]

Rabbi Hanina said: The seal of the Holy One, praised be
He, is truth. [In Hebrew, the word for *truth* is spelled with
three letters, אמת, the first, middle, and last letters of the
alphabet.] Resh Lakish said: Truth (*emet*) is spelled with the
first, middle and last letters of the alphabet to teach that "I
am first, I am last, and beside Me there is no God" [Isa.
44:6]. "I am first" for I received nothing from another; "and
beside Me there is no God," for I have no partner; "and with
the last, I am He" [Isa. 41:4]—I shall never transmit My
sovereignty to another.[26]

Let us praise Him, Lord over all the world;
Let us acclaim Him, Author of all creation.

He made our lot unlike that of other peoples;
He assigned to us a unique destiny.

We bend the knee, worship, and give thanks
To the King of kings, the Holy One, praised is He.

He unrolled the heavens and established the earth;
His throne of glory is in the heavens above;
His majestic Presence is in the loftiest heights.

He and no other is God and faithful King,
Even as we are told in His Torah:
Remember now and always that the Lord is God;
Remember no other is Lord of heaven and earth.

We therefore hope in You, O Lord our God,
That we shall soon see the triumph of Your might,
That idolatry shall be removed from the earth,
And false gods shall be utterly destroyed.

Then will the world be a true Kingdom of God,
When all mankind will invoke Your name,
And all the earth's wicked will return to You.

Then all the inhabitants of the world will surely know
That to You every knee must bend,
Every tongue must pledge loyalty.

Before You, O Lord, let them bow in worship;
Let them give honor to Your glory.
May they all accept the rule of Your kingdom.
May You reign over them soon through all time.

Sovereignty is Yours in glory, now and forever.
So is it written in Your Torah:
The Lord shall reign for ever and ever.

Such is the assurance uttered by the prophet:
The Lord shall be King over all the earth;
That day the Lord shall be One and His name one.[27]

GOD IS MORAL

He is the Lord of all the world, creating evil as well as good, but He desires the good. The classic ages of Judaism, in Bible and Talmud, did not really imagine or regard as real the question whether the good is whatever God wills, or whether God is bound to will only the good. It was certain that He is especially identified with the good and responsive to finding it in man's conduct. As we have already seen, Judaism does not insist that the faithful can or even should know all the attributes of God, or even very much about God's action in the world. One thing, however, is undoubted, that He demands righteous conduct from man and will punish him for his transgressions.

The Lord, the Lord, a God merciful and gracious, slow to anger, and abounding in steadfast love and faithfulness, keeping steadfast love for thousands, forgiving iniquity and transgression and sin, but who will by no means clear the guilty, visiting the iniquity of the fathers upon the children and the children's children, to the third and the fourth generation.[28]

Know in your heart that as a man disciplines his son the Lord your God disciplines you.[29]

When you come to appear before Me, who required these things at your hands, that you should walk in My courts? Offer sacrifices no more in vain; it is an offering of abomination to Me. New Moon and Sabbath, the holding of convocations—I cannot endure iniquity along with solemn assembly. My soul hates your new moons and your appointed seasons; they have become troublesome to Me, I am weary of bearing them. When you stretch forth your hands, I will turn away My eyes from you; when you multiply prayer, I will not hear, for your hands are full of blood. Wash yourselves, be clean, put away the evil of your devices from before My eyes; cease

to do perversely. Learn to do well; seek justice, relieve the
oppressed, judge the fatherless, defend the widow.

Come now and let us reason together, says the Lord.
Though your sins be as scarlet, they shall be white as snow;
though they be red as crimson, they shall be white as wool.
If you are willing, and hearken to Me, you shall eat the good
things of the land; but if you refuse, and provoke Me, the
sword shall devour you, for the mouth of the Lord has
spoken.[30]

"The Rock, His work is perfect, for all His ways are just.
A God of faithfulness without iniquity, just and right is He"
[Deut. 32:4]. His work is perfect as regards all who come
into the world, and one should not criticize His ways. A man
should not ponder, saying "If I had three hands or three feet,
if I could walk on my head, if I had eyes in the back of my
head, how nice it would be." He is a God of justice. He
judges each person justly and gives him what he deserves.
He is a God of faithfulness. He had faith in the world and
so He created it. He did not create men that they should be
wicked, but that they should be righteous, as it is written "God
made man upright, but they have sought out many devices"
[Eccles. 7:29].[31]

Rabbi Joshua said "Wherever you find a description of the
greatness of the Holy One, praised be He, you find a description of His consideration for the lowly. This is written in the
Torah, repeated in the Prophets, and stated for the third time
in the Writings. In the Torah it is written: "For the Lord
your God is God of gods and Lord of lords . . . " [Deut.
10:17], and in the verse following it is written, "He executes
justice for the fatherless and the widow" [Deut. 10:18]. It is
repeated in the Prophets: "For thus says the high and lofty
One who inhabits eternity, whose name is holy; 'I dwell in
the high and holy place' " [Isa. 57:15]. And the verse continues "and also with him who is of a contrite and humble
spirit" (*ibid.*). It is stated for the third time in the Writings:
"Extol Him who rides upon the skies, whose name is the
Lord" [Ps. 68:5], and in the verse following it is written
"Father of the fatherless and protector of widows" [Ps.
68:6].[32]

"Then Moses said to God 'If I come to the people of Israel and say to them "The God of your fathers has sent me to you" and they ask "What is His name?" what shall I say to them?' " [Ex. 3:13]. Moses asked the Holy One, praised be He, to tell him His great name. "And God said to Moses 'I am what I am' " [Ex. 3:14]. Rabbi Abba bar Mamal said: The Holy One, praised be He, said to Moses "You want to know My name. I am called according to My deeds. At various times I am called Almighty, Lord of hosts, God, and Lord. When I judge My creatures, I am called God. When I wage war against the wicked, I am called Lord of hosts. When I suspend the punishment of man's sins, I am called Almighty. And when I have compassion upon My world, I am called Lord. Thus Scripture states 'I am what I am'; I am called according to My deeds."[33]

"You, O Lord, are ever on high" [Ps. 92:8]. You are always right. When a mortal king sits in judgment, all the people praise him when he grants a pardon. But no one praises him when he orders punishment, for they know that passion has played a part in his judgment. However, this is not so of the Holy One, praised be He. Whether He pardons or punishes, "You, O Lord, are ever on high." . . . Rav Huna, in the name of Rav Aha, said: It is written, "I will sing of mercy and justice; to You, O Lord, will I sing" [Ps. 101:1]. In this Psalm, David was saying: Be it one way or the other [whether God pardons me or punishes me] to You, O Lord, will I sing. . . . Rabbi Judah bar Ilai said: It is written, "The Lord gave, the Lord has taken away; praised be the name of the Lord" [Job 1:21]. When He gives, He gives in mercy; when He takes away, He takes away in mercy.[34]

"Then the Lord said to Cain [after the latter killed Abel] 'Where is Abel, your brother?' He answered, 'I do not know. Am I my brother's keeper?' " [Gen. 4:9]. Cain said: "You, O Lord, are the Keeper, the one who should watch over all creatures, and yet You ask me concerning Abel." This situation may be compared to that of a thief who stole at night and was not caught. The following morning, the watchman caught him and asked, "Why did you steal?" The thief an-

swered, "I am a thief and I did not abandon my profession.
But your profession demands that you watch at the gate. Why
did you abandon your profession? And now you ask me why
I stole!" Thus, too, did Cain speak to God: "I killed Abel;
but You have created in me the impulse to evil. You are the
Keeper of all and yet You permitted me to kill him. *You* have
killed him! If You had accepted my offering as You accepted
his, I would not have been jealous of him."[35]

Thus spoke the Holy One, praised be He: If I create the
world solely on the basis of My attribute of Mercy, its sins
will become too many. If I create it by My attribute of strict
Justice, how will the world be able to exist? Therefore, I will
create it with both attributes, both Justice and Mercy, and
would that it stand.[36]

Franz Rosenzweig (1887–1929), the last great theologian of German Jewry, here speaks for the whole of
Jewish thought about God and His moral nature.

To His people, God the Lord is simultaneously the God of
retribution and the God of love. In the same breath, they call
on Him as "our God" and as "King of the universe," or—to
indicate the same contrast in a more intimate sphere—as "our
Father" and "our King." He wants to be served with trembling and yet rejoices when His children overcome their fear
at His wondrous signs. Whenever the Scriptures mention His
majesty, the next verses are sure to speak of His meekness. He
demands the visible signs of offering and prayer brought to
His name, and of the "affliction of our soul" in His sight. And
almost in the same breath He scorns both and wants to be
honored only with the secret fervor of the heart, in the love
of one's neighbor, and in anonymous works of justice which
no one may recognize as having been done for the sake of
His name. He has elected His people, but elected it to visit
upon them all their iniquities. He wants every knee to bend
to Him and yet He is enthroned above Israel's songs of praise.

[Ps. 22:4] Israel intercedes with Him in behalf of the sinning peoples of the world and He afflicts Israel with disease so that those other people may be healed [Isa. 53]. Both stand before God: Israel His servant, and the kings of the peoples; and the strands of suffering and guilt, of love and judgment, of sin and atonement, are so inextricably twined that human hands cannot untangle them.[37]

MAN MUST LOVE AND SERVE GOD

How does man serve God? By imitating His ways—"as He is just and merciful so must you be just and merciful" —and by absolute devotion, even to death.

You shall love the Lord your God with all your heart, with all your might, and with all your soul.[38]

And now, Israel, what does the Lord your God require of you but that you fear the Lord your God, and walk in His ways, and love Him, and serve the Lord your God with all your heart and with all your soul, to keep the commandments of the Lord, and His statutes, which I command you this day? Behold, heaven, and the heaven of heaven, the earth and all things therein, belong to the Lord your God. And the Lord had a delight in your fathers, and He loved them, and chose their seed after them, that is to say, you, out of all peoples, as it is this day. Circumcise therefore the foreskin of your heart, and stiffen your neck no more, because the Lord your God is the God of gods, and the Lord of lords, the great God, the mighty and the awful, who regards not persons, nor takes bribes. He executes justice for the fatherless and the widow, loves the stranger, and gives him food and raiment. Do you therefore love strangers, for you were strangers in the land of Egypt. You shall fear the Lord your God, and serve Him only; to Him shall you cleave and by His name shall you swear. He is your glory and your God, that has done for you these great things, which your eyes have seen. With seventy souls your fathers went down into Egypt; and behold now the Lord your God has multiplied you as the stars of heaven.³⁹

Praise the Lord, all nations. Laud Him, all peoples. Great is His love for us; everlasting His faithfulness. Halleluyah!⁴⁰

"You shall love the Lord your God with all your heart, with all your soul, and with all your might" [Deut. 6:5] . . . Rabbi Eliezer said, "Since this verse states 'with all your soul' [i.e. life] why does it state 'with all your might' [i.e. substance]? And since it states 'with all your might' why does it state 'with all your soul'? The reason is that for a man who holds his life as more precious than his wealth, it is written 'with all your soul.' And for a man who holds his wealth as more precious than his life it is written 'with all your might.' " Rabbi Akiva said, " 'With all your soul' means that you should love Him even if He takes your soul."⁴¹

Rabbi Shabtai Hurwitz (1590–1660) an East European scholar, is the author of a will in which this passage occurs.

My master, my father, of blessed memory, wrote in his book that when the time of death draws near, Satan stands near the dying man and tempts him saying, "Deny the God of Israel." The mind of a man in that state is weakened—may the Merciful one save us. Therefore I proclaim from this time forth before God praised be He and His *Shekhinah*, before the heavenly court and the earthly court, that if, God forbid, I should make any unseemly statement near the time of my death, the words shall be null and void, without any binding power. But what I say now does have validity: I accept and bear witness that the Holy One, praised be He, is the First Cause, Creator of all things, eternal, existing before the first and enduring after the last. "Hear, O Israel, the Lord our God, the Lord is One." "Praised be His glorious kingdom for ever and ever." These are the principles which I accept now and to eternity.⁴²

Moses Luzatto (1707–1747) was an Italian poet and
mystic. He is the author of a famous ethical tract, the
Mesillat Yesharim ("Way of the Upright"), which is the
source of the next three passages.

There are many ways of profaning the Name, and one must
be constantly mindful of the glory of his Creator. In whatever
one does, he must be alert and careful that it does not produce anything which could be a profanation of the glory of
Heaven. We have learned, "Whoever profanes the name of
Heaven in secret will be punished openly. It makes no difference whether the Name was profaned unwittingly or inten-
tionally" [Mishnah *Avot* 4:4]. When the sages asked for an
example of profaning the Name, Rav said, "If a man of my
reputation should buy meat without paying for it immediately" [*Yoma* 86a]. Rabbi Johanan said, "If a man of my
reputation should walk a distance of four *amot* without medi-
tating on the Torah or without *tefillin*." Every man, according
to his status and how he is looked upon by his contemporaries, must be careful not to do anything which is improper
for a man of his standing. The more one is honored and
learned, the more must he be careful in his religious observance. If he does not act in this way, the Name of Heaven is
profaned through him. For it honors the Torah when one who
devotes a great amount of time to studying it also devotes a
great amount of time to virtue and to self-improvement. But
whoever lacks such virtue, though he studies a great deal,
disgraces the study of Torah. This is a profanation of the
name of God, praised be He, who gave us His holy Torah
and commanded us to be occupied in studying it as a means
to attaining our perfection.[43]

A major principle in the service of God is joy. David declares, "Serve the Lord with gladness; come into His Presence
with singing" [Ps. 100:2]. "Let the righteous be joyful; let
them exult before God; let them be jubilant with joy" [Ps.
68:4]. Our sages said, "The *Shekhinah* rests only upon one
who performs a commandment in a joyous spirit" (*Shabbat*
30b).[44]

There are three elements in the love of God: joy, devotion and zeal. To love God is to passionately desire His nearness, praised be He, and to pursue His holiness, as one pursues something he strongly desires, until mentioning His name, praised be He, or speaking His praise, or studying His Torah or His divine nature becomes a source of pleasure and delight as real as that of one who strongly loves the wife of his youth, or his only son. In the latter case, even speaking of them is a delight. And Scripture states, "As often as I speak of him, I remember him still; therefore my heart yearns for him . . . " [Jer. 31:19]. Surely whoever truly loves his Creator will not neglect serving Him for any reason in the world, unless he is physically prevented from doing so. He will not need to be coaxed or enticed into serving Him. On the contrary, unless prevented by some great obstacle, his heart itself will lift him. This is the desirous quality which the early saints, the holy ones of the Highest, were privileged to attain. . . .

Surely there must be no ulterior motive in such love. One should love the Creator, praised be He, not because He is good to him, or grants him wealth or success, but one should love Him as naturally and as obligingly as a son loves his father. Indeed, Scripture states, "Is He not your father, who created you?" [Deut. 32:6]. The test of this love is during a time of hardship and trouble. . . . "Whatever Heaven does is for the best" (*Berakhot* 60b). This means that even hardship and trouble are apparent evils which in reality are good. . . . Thus one should realize that whatever the Holy One praised be He does to him, whether it affect his body or his property, is for his own good, even though he does not understand how it could be for his own good. Thus neither hardship nor suffering would lessen his love for God.[45]

Here, too, Rabbi Israel Baal-Shem Tov's words, from his "testament," can stand as a summary of the view of Judaism.

. . . A man who makes efforts to cleave to God has no time to think of unimportant matters; when he constantly serves the Creator, he has no time to be vain. . . . If a man should suddenly be faced by a beautiful woman, or by any other of the fair and lovely objects of this world, he should immediately think to himself: "Where does this beauty come from, if not from the divine power which permeates the world? It follows that the source of this beauty is on high. Why, then, should I be drawn after a part? It would be better for me to be drawn after the All, the Source and Root of all partial beauty." When a man tastes something good and sweet, he should realize that the sweetness on high is the power which sustains it. Perception of any good quality is an experience of the Eternal, praised be He. . . . Thus when a man hears something amusing which brings him some joy, he should realize that it is but a portion from the world of love. Every man must serve God, praised be He, with all his might, for all of this is a divine need. God desires that man serve Him in all ways. At times a man walks and speaks with other men, and then he is unable to study the Torah. Even then he must cleave to God and be conscious of His unique- ness. When a man travels and can neither pray nor study in his usual manner, he must serve Him in other ways. Let him not be troubled over this, for God, praised be He, desires that man serve Him in all ways, sometimes one way, sometimes another. . . . A major principle in serving the Creator is to be rid of sadness as much as possible. Weeping is very bad, for man must serve God in joy. However, if the weeping is caused by joy, then it is very good. One should not thoroughly investigate each one of his acts, for through such a state of mind the impulse to evil intends to make one fearful that he is not fulfilling his duties, and thus bring him to sadness. And sadness is a great obstacle to the service of the Creator, praised be He. Even if a man has committed a sin he should not be overly sad, lest he neglect the service of God. He should, of course, be sad because of the sin, but he should then return to rejoice in the Creator, praised be He.[46]

CHAPTER THREE

Torah: Teaching and Commandment

RATIONALE FOR COMMANDMENT

"The Torah was given only as a means of purifying men" —so runs a famous rabbinic dictum. It is no impossible set of demands, meant for angels or a very few men of superior piety. Its wisdom and ordinances are the way of holiness for all men, even the most ordinary among them. Through obedience we resist the temptations that come to us on each and every day—so Rashi, Rabbi Solomon ben Isaac (1040–1105), the classic commentator on the Bible and Talmud, explains the third of the passages immediately below.

And when your son shall ask you in time to come, saying, "What mean the testimonies, the statutes and the ordinances which the Lord our God has commanded us?" then you shall say to your son, "We were bondmen of Pharaoh in Egypt, and the Lord brought us out of Egypt with a mighty hand. And the Lord wrought signs and wonders, great and very grievous, in Egypt against Pharaoh and all his house, before our eyes. And He brought us out from there, that He might bring us in and give us the land which He swore to our fathers. And the Lord commanded that we should do all these statutes, and that we should fear the Lord our God, that it might be well with us all the days of our life, as it is at this day. And He will be merciful to us if we keep and do all this commandment before the Lord our God, as He has commanded us."[1]

This commandment which I command you this day is not too hard for you, nor is it far away from you. It is not in heaven, that you should say, "Who shall go up to heaven, to bring it to us, and make us hear it, that we may fulfill it?" Nor is it beyond the sea, that you should say, "Who shall go over the sea for us, to bring it to us, and make us hear it, that we may fulfill it?" But the word is very near to you, in your mouth and in your heart, that you may do it.[2]

Rabbi Simlai expounded: Six hundred and thirteen commandments were transmitted to Moses on Mount Sinai. Three hundred sixty five of them are negative commandments [i.e. prohibitions], corresponding to the number of days in the solar year. The remaining two hundred forty eight are positive commandments [i.e. injunctions], corresponding to the number of limbs in the human body.[3]

After Moses, David came and reduced the six hundred thirteen commandments to eleven, as it is written: "Lord, who shall sojourn in Your tabernacle? Who shall dwell on Your holy mountain? He who walks blamelessly, and does what is right, and speaks truth in his heart, who does not slander with his tongue, and does no evil to his friend, nor takes up a reproach against his neighbor, in whose eyes a reprobate is despised, but honors those who fear the Lord, who swears to his own hurt and does not change, who does not put out his money at interest, and does not take a bribe against the innocent" [Ps. 15:1–5]. . . .

Then Isaiah came and reduced the commandments to six, as it is written "He who walks righteously and speaks uprightly, he who despises the gain of oppressions, who shakes his hands lest they hold a bribe, who stops his ears from hearing of bloodshed, and shuts his eyes from looking upon evil" [Isa. 33:15]. . . . Then Micah came and reduced them to three, as it is written, "It has been told you, O man, what is good, and what the Lord requires of you: To do justice, to love mercy, and to walk humbly with your God" [Mic. 6:8]. . . . Then Isaiah came again and reduced them to two. "Thus says the Lord: Keep justice and do righteousness" [Isa. 56:1]. Amos came and reduced them to one, as it is

written, "Thus says the Lord to the house of Israel: Seek
Me and live" [Amos 5:4]. . . . Habakkuk came and also
reduced them to one, as it is written, "The righteous shall
live by his faith" [Hab. 2:4].[4]

Rabbi Huna and Rabbi Jeremiah said in the name of Rabbi
Hiyya bar Abba: It is written, "They have forsaken Me and
have not kept My law" [Jer. 16:11]. This is to say: "If only
they *had* forsaken Me but kept My law! Since they then would
have been occupied with it, the light which is in it would have
restored them to the right path."[5]

". . . remember all the commandments of the Lord, to do
them, not to follow after your heart and your eyes, which
you are inclined to go after wantonly" [Num. 15:40]. The
heart and the eyes are the panders of the body; they excite
the senses. "So you shall remember and do all My commandments, and be holy to your God" [Num. 15:41]. The human
situation may be compared to that of a man who fell into the
sea. The helmsman threw him a rope and said "Hold on to
the rope. Do not let go, for should you let go of it, you will
lose your life." Thus spoke the Holy One, praised be He, to
Israel: "So long as you hold fast to the commandments, 'you
who hold fast to the Lord your God are all alive this day' "
[Num. 4:4]. And it is written, 'Hold on to instruction, do not
let go; guard it, for it is your life' [Prov. 4:13].[6]

The accepted Jewish view of Torah as the way of "normal holiness" is expounded by a modern exponent, Rabbi
Louis Finkelstein (born in 1895), the head of Conservative Judaism in America.

Judaism is a way of life that endeavors to transform virtu-
ally every human action into a means of communion with
God. Through this communion with God, the Jew is enabled
to make his contribution to the establishment of the Kingdom
of God and the brotherhood of man on earth. So far as its
adherents are concerned, Judaism seeks to extend the concept

of right and wrong to every aspect of their behavior. Jewish rules of conduct apply not merely to worship, ceremonial and justice between man and man, but also to such matters as philanthropy, personal friendships and kindnesses, intellectual pursuits, artistic creation, courtesy, the preservation of health and the care of diet.

So rigorous is this discipline, as ideally conceived in Jewish writing, that it may be compared to those specified for members of religious orders in other faiths. A casual conversation or a thoughtless remark may, for instance, be considered a grave violation of Jewish Law. It is forbidden as a matter not merely of good form but of religious law, to use obscene language, to rouse a person to anger or to display unusual ability in the presence of the handicapped. The ceremonial observances are equally detailed. The ceremonial law expects each Jew to pray thrice every day, if possible at the synagogue; to recite a blessing before and after each meal; to thank God for any special pleasure, such as a curious sight, the perfume of a flower, or the receipt of good news; to wear a fringed garment about his body; to recite certain passages from Scriptures each day and to don *tephillin* [cubical receptacles containing certain Biblical passages] during the morning prayers. . . .

Like every other authentic experience, piety cannot stop short of the home. If religion were to be merely ecclesiastical, it would soon cease to be that too. The Psalmist who was told "Let us go up to the house of the Lord" rejoiced because in his own house the reality of God was never forgotten. Throughout Jewish history the attempt to reproduce in the home the order and mood of the place of worship has never been relaxed.

The interrelationship of sanctity and home has been responsible for at least two significant results. On the one hand, the Jew did not remain a stranger to the ceremonial and purpose of his sacred institutions. On the other hand, his home and home life were transfigured. His residence became a habitation of God.

This sanctification of the home was achieved by a religious discipline whose purpose was constantly to prompt a remembrance of God. The Jew who visited the ancient Temple, for example, readily understood that the elaborate rites, precautions, exactitudes and purifications were the appropriate expression of the beauty of holiness. "If you were to serve a king of flesh and blood," the saintly Hillel once reminded a guest, "would you not have to learn how to make your entrances and exits and obeisances? How much more so in the service of the King of kings!"

That such fastidiousness was therefore required in God's House the Jew accepted unquestionably. The forms reminded him of God. And because they did, and because Israel's teachers tried to prevent the Jew from forgetting God even when he was away from the Sanctuary, corresponding rituals were introduced into the Jewish home. Thus the Jewish home became a sanctuary in miniature, its table an altar, its furnishings instruments for sanctity.[7]

THE TORAH AS WISDOM

The Torah is commandment, but it is much more than that. At its widest, the concept means more than even the teaching contained in the Bible. It is the whole of the sacred tradition, especially as expressed in all the writings of the faith, from the Bible to the present. Study of Torah is a commandment several times enjoined in the Bible itself. To know that such study is as important an act of Jewish piety as prayer, in some senses indeed more important, is crucial to understanding the genius of Judaism and of Jewry. Hence, in all the past ages, when few men could read, illiteracy was little known among Jews and learning was always the most highly prized of all attainments.

The words of the Torah are compared to a life-giving medicine. A king who inflicted a severe wound upon his son put a plaster upon the wound. He said, "My son, so long as this plaster is on your wound, eat and drink what you like, wash with either hot or cold water, and you will suffer no harm. But if you should remove this plaster, you will suffer." Thus the Holy One, praised be He, said to the Israelites, "I created within you the impulse to evil, but I created the Torah as a medicine. So long as you occupy yourselves with the Torah, the impulse to evil will not dominate you. But if you do not occupy yourselves with the Torah, you will be delivered into the power of the impulse to evil.[8]

Resh Lakish said: "The commandment of the Lord is pure" [Ps. 19:9]. If one's intent is pure, the Torah for him becomes a life-giving medicine, purifying him to life. But if one's intent is not pure, it becomes a death-giving drug, purifying him to death.[9]

Rabbi Meir said: Whoever occupies himself with the study of the Torah with no ulterior motive merits many things. Furthermore, the entire world is indebted to him. He is called beloved friend [of God]. He loves God and mankind, and he causes God and mankind to rejoice. The Torah clothes him with humility and fear of the Lord, and it prepares him to be just, pious, upright and faithful. It keeps him far from sin and it brings him near to virtue. Through him men enjoy counsel and sound wisdom, insight and strength, as it is written, "I have counsel and sound wisdom, I have insight, I have strength" [Prov. 8:14]. [In that chapter of Proverbs, wisdom, or Torah, is speaking.] It gives him sovereignty and dominion and discerning judgment. The secrets of the Torah are revealed to him; he becomes like a neverfailing spring and like a river which never halts. He becomes modest, patient and forgiving of insult; it magnifies him and exalts him above all the works of creation.

Rabbi Joshua ben Levi said: Every day a heavenly voice echoes forth from Mount Horeb [Sinai, where the Torah was given], proclaiming "Woe to mankind for contempt of the Torah." . . .

This is the way to acquire knowledge of the Torah: Eat bread with salt, drink water by measure [Ezek. 4:11], sleep on the ground, live a life of constraint, and toil in the Torah.

If you do this, "You shall be blessed and it shall be well with you" [Ps. 128:2]. You shall be blessed in this world, and it shall be well with you in the world to come. Seek not greatness for yourself, and do not covet honor. Practice more than you learn. Crave not after the table of kings, for your table is greater than theirs and your crown is greater than theirs, and your master is faithful; He will pay you the reward of your labor. . . .

Rabbi Jose ben Kisma said: I once was walking on a road when a man met me and greeted me, "Shalom." I returned his greeting "Shalom." He said, "Rabbi, where are you from?" I said, "From a great city of sages and scribes." He said, "Rabbi, should you wish to live with us in our place, I would give you a million gold dinars, and precious stones and pearls." I said, "Were you to give me all the silver, gold, precious stones and pearls in the world, I would live only in a place of Torah. Thus is it written in the book of Psalms by David the king of Israel, 'The law [Torah] of Your mouth is better to me than thousands of gold and silver pieces' " [Ps. 119:72]. Furthermore, when a man dies, neither silver, gold, precious stones nor pearls accompany him; only Torah and good deeds alone, as it is written, "When you walk it shall lead you, when you lie down it shall watch over you, and when you awake it shall be with you" [Prov. 6:22]. "When you walk it shall lead you" in this world. "When you lie down it shall watch over you" in the grave. "And when you awake it shall be with you" in the world to come. . . .

Rabbi Hananiah ben Akashya said: The Holy One, praised be He, desired to favor Israel. Therefore He increased for them the Torah and commandments, as it is written, "The Lord was pleased, for His righteousness' sake, to magnify His law [Torah] and to make it glorious" [Isa. 42:21].[10]

"On the third new moon after the people of Israel had gone forth out of the land of Egypt, on this day they came into the wilderness of Sinai" [Exodus 19:1]. Ben Zoma said: This verse does not state "on that day" but "on this day," as if to say that on *this* day they have come to the wilderness of Sinai [the site of Revelation]. Whenever you are engaged in the study of Torah, you can say, "It is as though I have received the Torah at Sinai on *this* day." Furthermore, it is written, "*This* day the Lord your God commands you to do these statutes and ordinances. . . ." [Deut. 26:16].[11]

Rabbi Judah would send Rabbi Assi and Rabbi Ammi to organize religious education in the towns of the Land of Israel. When they came to a town they would say to the people, "Bring to us the guardians of the town." They would bring to them the captain of the guard and the magistrate. The Rabbis would say, "These are not the guardians of the town. These are its destroyers!" When the people asked, "Who are the guardians of the town?" the rabbis would answer, "The scribes and the teachers, who meditate upon, teach and preserve the Torah day and night." This is in accordance with what is written, "You shall meditate therein day and night" [Joshua 1:8]. And it is written, "Unless the Lord builds the house, those who build it labor in vain" [Ps. 127:1]. . . . Rabbi Huna said: Study Torah, even if not for its own sake. Though it be studied at first not for its own sake, this will lead one to study it for its own sake.[12]

Lest you say "I will study Torah that I might be called wise, or sit in the Academy, or be rewarded with length of days in the world to come," it is written "You shall love the Lord your God" [Deut. 6:5]. [The action must be motivated only by love of God.][13]

Rabbi Eliezer said: When the evil power comes to seduce man, let him drag it to the Torah and thus depart from the evil power. Come and see that thus have we learned: When the evil power stands before the Holy One, praised be He, to accuse the world for evil deeds, the Holy One, praised be He, shows compassion for the world and gives mankind counsel by which it can escape the evil power, so that it will dominate neither them nor their deeds. What is this counsel?—To be occupied with the Torah. How do we know this? It is written, "The commandment is a lamp and the Torah is a light, and the reproofs of discipline are the ways of life [Prov. 6:23]. What words follow that verse? "To preserve you from the evil woman, from the smooth tongue of the adventuress" [Prov. 6:24]. The latter verse refers to the impurity in the world, the "other force" continually standing before the Holy One, praised be He, to accuse mankind for its sins.[14]

The Torah declares, "I was the instrument of the Holy One, praised be He." It is the way of the world that when a mortal king builds a palace he builds it not from his own plans but with the advice of an architect. And the architect in turn has blueprints and charts to guide him how to construct the rooms and chambers. So, too, the Holy One, praised be He, was guided by the Torah in creating the world.[15]

The Torah was given publicly and openly, in a place to which no one had any claim. Had it been given in the land of Israel, the nations of the world could have said "We have no portion in it." Therefore it was given in the wilderness, publicly and openly, in a place to which no one had any claim. Everyone who desires to accept, let him come and accept it.[16]

The next passage is from the Daily Prayer Book. That He gave Israel the Torah is the surest sign of God's love.

You have loved the house of Israel with everlasting love; You taught Your people the Torah and commandments; You instructed them in its statutes and its judgments.

O our God, when we lie down as when we are awake, we shall always think and speak of Your ordinances, and rejoice in the Torah and its commandments.

It is Your Torah that sustains us throughout life; on its teachings will we meditate day and night. May You never take away Your love from us.

Praised are You, O Lord, who loves Your people Israel.[17]

CHALLENGES TO FAITH IN TORAH

Persecution makes living the life ordained by the Torah difficult and dangerous. In the face of Roman tyranny after the destruction of the Second Temple in the year 70 the rabbis had to distinguish between those laws for which man should accept martyrdom and those which he could disobey rather than risk his life.

"You shall therefore keep My statutes and My ordinances, by doing which a man shall live" [Lev. 18:5]. Rabbi Ishmael said: If in a time of persecution an Israelite should be told in private "Worship this idol and you shall not be killed," he should worship the idol. How do we know this to be so? Because it is written, "by doing which a man shall live," not "by doing which a man shall die." However, if he is told to do this in public, is he to obey? No. For it is written, "You shall not profane My holy name, but I will be hallowed among the children of Israel" [Lev. 22:32].[18]

It was resolved in the upper chambers of the house of Nithya in Lydda [in southern Palestine] by a majority vote that should a man be offered the alternative of transgressing one of the Torah's commandments or be killed, he may transgress, except for the commandments against idolatry, incest (including adultery) and murder.[19]

Doubt is the other danger to the life of Torah. Saadia attempts to deal with this problem in the three paragraphs quoted next.

There may be some men who would give up their adherence to the Bible because many of the commandments are not clearly explained in it. My answer to them is that the Bible is not the sole basis of our religion, for in addition to it we have two other bases. One of these is anterior to it; namely, the fountain of reason. The second is posterior to it; namely, the source of tradition. Whatever, therefore, we may not find in the Bible, we can find in the two other sources. Thus are the commandments rounded out quantitatively as well as qualitatively.[20]

"Could not God have bestowed upon His creatures complete bliss and permanent happiness without giving them commandments and prohibitions? Nay it would seem that His kindness would in that case have contributed even more to their well-being, because they would be relieved of all exertion for the attainment of their bliss."

Let me, then, say in explanation of this matter that, on the contrary, God's making His creatures' diligent compliance with His commandments the means of attaining permanent bliss is the better course. For according to the judgment of reason the person who achieves some good by means of the effort that he has expended for its attainment obtains double the advantage gained by him who achieves this good without any effort but merely as a result of the kindness shown him by God. In fact, reason recognizes no equality between these two. This being the case, then, the Creator preferred to assign to us the ampler portion in order that our reward might yield us a double benefit, not merely a compensation exactly equivalent to the effort, as Scripture also says: "Behold, the Lord God will come as a Mighty One, and His arm will rule for Him; behold, His reward is with Him, and His recompense before Him" [Isa. 40:10].[21]

This rationalization of the Law is by Samson Raphael Hirsch.

And as for the Law, is it really a preventative of all the joys of life, a hindrance and an obstacle to the gratification of the natural human craving for pleasure? Examine once the precepts and ordinances of the Law from beginning to end and tell me what legitimate desire it forbids to gratify, what natural impulse it would destroy or extirpate.

On the contrary, it purifies and sanctifies even our lower impulses and desires by applying them with wise limitation to the purposes designated by the Creator.

Righteousness is the Law's typical end and aim, the gratification of physical lust and passion is never its object. Therefore are the lower cravings subordinated to higher law and limited by the Creator's wisdom for His infinitely wise purposes; but as means of attaining proper and necessary ends, the Law recognizes these desires as perfectly moral, pure and human, and their carrying out as just and as legitimate as the fulfillment of any other human task or mission.

What the Law, however, firmly and unyieldingly opposes is the deification of wealth and lust as the sole aim and controlling impulse of our lives; but it not only permits their pursuit within the limits set by Divine wisdom, but declares the effort to gain them a duty as sacred and binding as any other human obligation, and condemns the purposeless and unreasonable abstinence from permitted indulgences as sin. ...

Does not this law erect a wall of separation between its adherents and the rest of mankind? It does, I admit, but had it not done so Israel would long since have lost all consciousness of its mission, would long since have ceased to be itself.[22]

Solomon Schechter (1847–1915), the greatest figure of Conservative Judaism, was perhaps the most eloquent "defender of the faith" ever to write in English.

It is an illusion to speak of the burden which a scrupulous care to observe six hundred and thirteen commandments must have laid upon the Jew. Even a superficial analysis will discover that in the time of Christ many of these commandments were already obsolete (as for instance those relating to the tabernacle and to the conquest of Palestine), while others concerned only certain classes, as the priests, the judges, the soldiers, the Nazirites, or the representatives of the community, or even only one or two individuals among the whole population, as the King and the High Priest. Others, again, provided for contingencies which could occur only to a few, as for instance the laws concerning divorce or levirate marriages, whilst many—such as those concerning idolatry, and incest, and the sacrifice of children to Moloch—could scarcely have been considered as a practical prohibition by the pre-Christian Jew, just as little as we can speak of Englishmen as lying under the burden of a law preventing them from burning widows or marrying their grandmothers, though such acts would certainly be considered as crimes. Thus it will be found by a careful enumeration that barely a hundred laws remain which really concerned the life of the bulk of the people. If we remember that even these include such laws as belief in the unity of God, the necessity of loving and fearing Him, and of sanctifying His name, of loving one's neighbour and the stranger, of providing for the poor, exhorting the sinner, honouring one's parents and many more of a similar character, it will hardly be said that the ceremonial side of the people's religion was not well balanced by a fair amount of spiritual and social elements. Besides, it would seem that the line between the ceremonial and the spiritual is too often only arbitrarily drawn. With many commandments it is rather a matter of opinion whether they should be relegated to the one category or the other.

Thus the wearing of the Tephillin or phylacteries has, on the one hand, been continually condemned as a meaningless superstition, and a pretext for formalism and hypocrisy. But, on the other hand, Maimonides, who can in no way be suspected of superstition or mysticism, described their importance in the following words: "Great is the holiness of the Tephillin; for as long as they are on the arm and head of man he is humble and God-fearing, and feels no attraction for frivolity or idle things, nor has he any evil thoughts, but will turn his heart to the words of truth and righteousness." The view which Rabbi Johanan, a Palestinian preacher of the third century, took of the fulfillment of the Law, will probably be found more rational than that of many a rationalist of today. Upon the basis of the last verse in Hosea, "The ways of the Lord are right, and the just shall walk in them, but the transgressors shall fall therein," he explains that while one man, for instance, eats his paschal lamb with the purpose of doing the will of God who commanded it, and thereby does an act of righteousness, another thinks only of satisfying his appetite by the lamb, so that his eating it (by the very fact that he professes at the same time to perform a religious rite) becomes a stumbling block for him. Thus all the laws by virtue of their divine authority—and in this there was in the first century no difference of opinion between Jews and Christians—have their spiritual side, and to neglect them implies, at least from the individual's own point of view, a moral offense.

The legalistic attitude may be summarily described as an attempt to live in accordance with the will of God, caring less for what God is than for what He wants us to be. But, nevertheless, on the whole this life never degenerated into religious formalism. Apart from the fact that during the Second Temple there grew up laws, and even beliefs, which show a decided tendency towards progress and development, there were also ceremonies which were popular with the masses, and others which were neglected. Men were not, therefore, the mere soulless slaves of the Law; personal sympathies and dislikes also played a part in their religion. Nor were all the laws actually put upon the same level. With a happy inconsistency men always spoke of heavier and slighter sins, and by the latter—excepting, perhaps, the profanation of the Sabbath—they mostly understood ceremonial transgressions.[23]

Kohler here states the Reform doctrine of the Law—or rather its rationale for abandoning it. He is obviously impaled on the dilemmas of wanting Israel separate as a "priest-people" and yet wanting it to be part of society as a whole; of desiring the life of obedience and wanting to loose the ancient bonds.

Undoubtedly the Law, as it embraced the whole of life in its power, sharpened the Jewish sense of duty, and served the Jew as an iron wall of defense against temptations, aberrations, and enticements of the centuries. As soon as the modern Jew, however, undertook to free himself from the tutelage of blind acceptance of authority and inquired after the purpose of all the restrictions of the Law laid upon him, his ancient loyalty to the same collapsed and the pillars of Judaism seemed to be shaken. Then the leaders of Reform, imbued with the prophetic spirit, felt it to be their imperative duty to search out the fundamental ideas of the priestly law of holiness and, accordingly, they learned how to separate the kernel from the shell. In opposition to the orthodox tendency to worship the letter, they insisted on the fact that Israel's separation from the world—which it is ultimately to win for the divine truth—cannot itself be its end and aim, and that blind obedience to the law does not constitute true piety. Only the fundamental idea, that Israel as the "first-born" among the nations has been elected as a priest-people, must remain our imperishable truth, a truth to which the centuries of history bear witness by showing that it has given its life-blood as a ransom for humanity, and is ever bringing new sacrifices for its cause. Only because it has kept itself distinct as a priest-people among the nations could it carry out its great task in history; and only if it remains conscious of its priestly calling and therefore maintains itself as the people of God, can it fulfill its mission. Not until the end of time, when all of God's children will have entered the kingdom of God, may Israel, the high-priest among the nations, renounce his priesthood.[24]

The greatest of modern Hebrew poets, Hayyim Nah-man Bialik (1873–1934), speaks here in exalted sum-mary of the meaning of Torah within the Jewish heritage.

The concept of "Torah" attained in the esteem of the [Jew-ish] people an infinite exaltation. For them the Torah was almost another existence, a more spiritual and loftier state, added to or even taking the place of secular existence. The Torah became the center of the nation's secret and avowed aspirations and desires in its exile. The dictum "Israel and the Torah are one" was no mere phrase; the non-Jew cannot appreciate it, because the concept of "Torah," in its full national significance, cannot be rendered adequately in any other tongue. Its content and connotations embrace more than "religion" or "creed" alone, or "ethics" or "commandments" or "learning" alone, and it is not even just a combination of all these, but something far transcending all of them. It is a mystic, almost cosmic, conception. The Torah is the tool of the Creator; with it and for it He created the universe. The Torah is older than creation. It is the highest idea and the living soul of the world. Without it the world could not exist and would have no right to exist. "The study of the Torah is more important than the building of the Temple." "Knowledge of the Torah ranks higher than priesthood or kingship." "Only he is free who engages in the study of the Torah." "It is the Torah that magnifies and exalts man over all creatures." "Even a heathen who engages in the study of the Torah is as good as a High Priest." "A bastard learned in the Torah takes precedence over an ignorant High Priest." [Quotations are from rabbinic literature.]

Such is the world outlook to which almost seventy generations of Jews have been educated. In accordance therewith their spiritual life was provisionally organized for the interim of the exile. For it they suffered martyrdom and by virtue of it they lived. The Jewish elementary school was established shortly before the destruction of Jerusalem and has survived to this day. As a result of such prolonged training, the nation has acquired a sort of sixth sense for everything connected with the needs of the spirit, a most delicate sense and always the first to be affected, and one possessed by almost every individual. There is not a Jew but would be filled with horror by a cruel decree "that Jews shall not engage in the Torah." Even the poorest and meanest man in Israel sacrificed for the teaching of his children, on which he spent sometimes as much as half of his income or more. Before asking for the satisfaction of his material needs, the Jew first prays daily: "And graciously bestow upon us knowledge, understanding, and comprehension." And what was the first request of our pious mothers over the Sabbath candles? "May it be Your will that the eyes of my children may shine with Torah." Nor do I doubt that if God had appeared to one of these mothers in a dream, as He did once to Solomon, and said, "Ask, what shall I give unto you?" she would have replied even as Solomon did, "I ask not for myself either riches or honor, but O Lord of the universe, may it please You to give unto my sons a heart to understand Torah and wisdom to distinguish good from evil" [Based on I Kings 3:9-11].[25]

CIRCUMCISION

The rest of this section is devoted to some characteristic practices and institutions which are ordained by the Jewish faith. Circumcision is the most ancient of Jewish rituals, and it has not changed to the present day.

And God said to Abraham: You therefore shall keep My covenant, and your seed after you, throughout their generation. This is My covenant, which you shall keep, between Me and you and your seed after you, every male among you shall be circumcised. You shall be circumcised in the flesh of your foreskin, that it may be a sign of the covenant between Me and you. An infant of eight days old shall be circumcised among you, every male throughout your generations, he that is born in your house, as well as he that is bought with money of any foreigner, that is not of your seed. He that is born in your house and he that is bought with your money must be circumcised, and My covenant shall be in your flesh for an everlasting covenant. The male who is uncircumcised in the flesh of his foreskin, that soul shall be destroyed out of his people, because he has broken My covenant.[26]

If a child is sick he is not circumcised until he becomes well.[27]

Rabbi Ishmael says: Great is circumcision, whereby the covenant was made thirteen times [the word "covenant" is repeated thirteen times in the seventeenth chapter of Genesis, where the commandment is given]. Rabbi Jose says: Great is circumcision, for it overrides even the stringency of the Sabbath [circumcision may be performed on the Sabbath if it is the eighth day after birth]. Rabbi Joshua ben Korha says: Great is circumcision, for it was not suspended so much as an hour even for the sake of Moses [*See* Ex. 4:24*f*]. . . . Rabbi says: Great is circumcision, for despite all the religious duties which Abraham fulfilled, he was not called "perfect" until he was circumcised, as it is written, "Walk before Me and be perfect, and I will make My covenant [i.e. circumcision] between Me and you" [Genesis 17:1–2]. Great is circumcision, for the Holy One, praised be He, had not created the world but for it, as it is written "Thus says the Lord: But for My covenant [i.e. circumcision] day and night, I had not set forth the ordinances of heaven and earth" [Jer. 33:25].[28]

A man who brings his son to be circumcised is to be compared to a High Priest bringing meal offering and libation to the Temple altar. From this they say that a man is obliged to prepare a joyous feast on the day on which he is privileged to circumcise his son.[29]

The Israelites who came out of Egypt faithfully observed one commandment: they circumcised their infant sons. The Egyptians told them: Why must you circumcise your sons? Let them grow up like the Egyptians and you will eventually take the heavy load of slavery off your shoulders. The Israelites answered: Did Abraham, Isaac and Jacob forget their Father in heaven? Should their children forget Him?[30]

MARRIAGE

The family is the basic unit of society. Its integrity and purity must be guarded as a sacred obligation. Within the family husbands and wives have set and specified obligations to one another.

It is not good that man should be alone. I will make a helper fit for him.[31]

Therefore a man leaves his father and his mother and cleaves to his wife, and they become one flesh.[32]

When a man is newly married, he shall not go out with the army or be charged with any business. He shall be free at home one year, to be happy with his wife, whom he has taken.[33]

A woman of valour, who can find?
Her worth is far above rubies.
The heart of her husband trusts in her,
And he shall have no need of spoils.
She will render him good and not evil
All the days of her life. . . .
She opens her mouth with wisdom,
And the law of kindness is on her tongue.
She looks well to the ways of her household,
And eats not the bread of idleness.
Her children rise up, and call her blessed,
Her husband also, and he praises her:
"Many daughters have done valiantly,
But you surpass them all."
Charm is deceitful and beauty is vain,
But a God-fearing woman is much to be praised.
Give her of the fruit of her hands,
And let her works praise her in the gates.[34]

A wife must do the following for her husband: grind flour,
bake bread, wash clothes, cook food, give suck to her child,
make ready his bed and work in wool. If she brought him
one maidservant [from her father's house], she need not grind
or bake or wash. If she brought two maidservants, she need
not cook or give her child suck. If she brought three maidservants, she need not make ready his bed or work in wool.
If four, she may sit all day and do nothing. Rabbi Eliezer
says: Even if she brought one hundred maidservants he should
force her to work in wool, for idleness leads to unchastity.[35]

If a man has vowed to have no intercourse with his wife,
the School of Shamai say that she may consent for two weeks;
the School of Hillel say, for one week. Disciples of the sages,
for purposes of study of the Torah, may stay away from their
wives for thirty days without their consent. Laborers [whose
work takes them to another city] may stay away for one week
without their wives' consent. The marital duty enjoined upon
husbands by the Torah [. . . he shall not diminish her marital
rights . . . Ex. 21:10] is as follows: every day for those that
are unemployed, twice a week for laborers, once a week for

donkey-drivers [who lead caravans for short distances], once
every thirty days for camel drivers, [who lead caravans for
longer distances], and once every six months for sailors. So
Rabbi Eliezer.[36]

No man may abstain from fulfilling the commandment "Be
fruitful and multiply" [Gen. 1:28], unless he already has
children. According to the School of Shamai, "children" here
means two sons, while the School of Hillel states that it means
a son and a daughter, for it is written, "Male and female
created He them" [Gen. 5:2]. If he married a woman and
lived with her for ten years and she bore no child, he is not
permitted to abstain from fulfilling the commandment. If he
divorced her she may marry another, and the second husband
may live with her for ten years. If she had a miscarriage, the
period of ten years is reckoned from the time of the miscarriage. The duty to be fruitful and multiply is incumbent upon
the man but not upon the woman. Rabbi Johanan ben Baroka
says: Concerning them both it is written: "God blessed them
and God said to them: Be fruitful and multiply" [Gen.
1.28]."[37]

Rabbi Eliezer said: Whoever does not fulfill the duty of
procreation is compared to a murderer, as it is said: "Whoever sheds the blood of man, by a man shall his blood be
shed" [Gen. 9:6], and immediately following it is written "Be
fruitful and multiply" [Gen. 9:7]. Rabbi Akiva said: Such a
man is compared to one who diminishes the divine image, as
it is said "for God made man in His image" [Gen. 9:6] and
immediately following it is written "Be fruitful and multiply"
[Gen. 9:7]. Ben Azzai said: It is as though he did both.[38]

"I will establish My covenant between Me and you and
your descendants after you . . . to be God to you and to your
descendants after you" [Gen. 17:7]. If you have no descendants, upon whom will the *Shekhinah* rest? Upon trees
and stones?![39]

Rabbi Hanilai said: A man who has no wife lives without
joy, without blessing, without good. Without joy, for it is

written "you and your household shall rejoice" [Deut. 14:26]. Without blessing, for it is written "that a blessing may rest on your house" [Ezekiel 44:30]. Without good, as it is written "It is not good for man to be alone" [Gen. 2:18]. . . . Rabbi bar Ulla said: He lives without peace. . . . Rabbi Joshua ben Levi said: A man who knows that his wife fears heaven and does not fulfill his marital duty of cohabitation is to be called a sinner. . . . Rabbi Eleazar said: A man who has no wife is not even a man, as it is stated: "Male and female He created them and He named *them* 'man' " [Gen. 5:2]. . . . "I will make man a helper to set over against him" [Gen. 2:18]. If he proves deserving, she will be a helper; if not, she will be against him.[40]

In Palestine, when a man marries, they ask him: "Finds or Found?" "Finds," as it is said "He who finds a wife finds something good" [Prov. 18:22]. "Found," as it is said "I have found the woman whose heart is snares and nets and whose hands are fetters more bitter than death" [Eccles. 7:26].[41]

If a man and wife prove deserving, the *Shekhinah* dwells among them; if not, a fire consumes them.[42]

There is no greater adultery than when a woman thinks of another man while her husband is alone with her.[43]

It is already clear that Judaism does not regard sexual union as a concession to the flesh but as a proper and sacred act. The flesh need not be the enemy of the spiritual life; true spirituality raises the flesh to make it, too, a servant of God. Rabbi Nahman of Bratslav (1772–1811), the great-grandson of the Baal-Shem Tov and himself a great figure of the Hasidic movement, is the author of the passage that follows.

The whole world depends on the holiness of the union between man and woman, for the world was created for the sake of God's glory and the essential revelation of His glory comes through the increase of mankind. Man must therefore sanctify himself in order to bring to the world holy people through whom God's glory will be increased. . . .

In truth all experiences of the Divine Unity and Holiness depend on the union between man and woman, for the ultimate meaning of this act is very lofty. Alas, darkness and falsehood tend to grow stronger and to spread so much blackness that we no longer see the truth at all. Union between man and woman becomes so tainted with imperfection that one can almost begin to believe the lie that there is no true holiness in this act.

Union represents the state in which breathing is suspended. It is therefore the opposite of the state of longevity, for, as is well known, many die of this passion. It is also the opposite of wisdom, for many people are driven mad by it. But through the act of union in holiness and purity life is increased and years are added. Through it "man sees life with his wife" and attains wisdom and elevation of the spirit.[44]

A characteristic form of rabbinic legal writing, from its origins two millennia ago, is the responsum, i.e. a question of Jewish law asked of an authority and answered by him in writing, giving his reasons for his decision. The two tragic questions that follow were asked in Kovno, Lithuania, in the Nazi era, of a young rabbi, Ephraim Oshry. That they were asked speaks eloquently of the persistence of Jewish piety under the most extreme of circumstances; that they had to be asked at all shouts out deafeningly the tale of man's inhumanity and of Jewry's suffering.

QUESTION: On the twentieth day of Iyar, 5712 (1942), the wicked ones [i.e. the Germans] published a decree that should they discover a Jewish woman pregnant they would put her to death. I was asked whether it was permissible for Jewish women imprisoned in the ghetto to use contraceptives to prevent pregnancy and thus to avoid endangering their lives.

RESPONSE: In *Yebamot* 12b we read that three categories of women may use contraceptives—a minor [under twelve years of age], a pregnant woman, and a nursing mother. A minor may, lest she become pregnant and, as a result, die. A pregnant woman may, lest she be aborted. And a nursing mother may, lest her child be prematurely weaned and die. . . . In the *Tosafot* it is written that women who are not in any of these categories are forbidden to use contraceptives and willfully destroy seed, even though the obligation "to be fruitful and multiply" is incumbent upon men, not women. . . .

In the case before us, there certainly would be danger to life, for if it would become known to the impure murderers, may they be cursed, that a woman is pregnant, they would put her to death. [As earlier authorities have stated], why should we forbid them the use of contraceptives since in this instance there is not what could be called willful destruction of seed? The latter term applies only when it is fitting to sow this seed. Since this is not a place in which it is fitting to do so, this is not to be termed "destruction of seed." Under these circumstances, a woman is obligated to use contraceptives when a pregnancy would endanger life. There is then no ban of destruction of seed in this case. . . . Furthermore [the discovery by the Germans of pregnant Jewish women, implying disobedience to their decree] can have bad consequences for the entire community. Thus everyone must agree that in this case it is permissible to use contraceptives during intercourse.[45]

QUESTION: Immediately after we were liberated from the ghetto I was asked an important and dreadful question which concerned not only the person who came to me but also many other Jewish women who survived the atrocities committed against them when they were seized by the oppressors and their bodies ravished by German officers, may their name be cursed.

This is the question: A young woman of good family, one of the respected families of Kovno, came to me weeping. She was very unhappy and without comfort, for she, like many of our poor sisters, had been seized and humiliated by the accursed Germans. In addition to abusing her body they had tattooed on her arm the legend: "Whore for Hitler's Troops."

After liberation she had succeeded in finding her husband and the two of them intended to renew their marriage and on the pillars of purity and sanctity to build a proper Jewish home. They wanted to build a family again, since they had lost all their children at the hands of the Germans. However, when her husband saw the dreadful words tattooed on her arm he was taken aback, declaring that they had to clarify whether she was permitted to him or not, since, when the enemy had seized her and had done with her as they pleased, perhaps there had been an element of consent in her submission. Thus she came to me to ask what to do, her eyes asking mercy.

RESPONSE: Maimonides [*Hilkhot Na-arah B'tulah, halakhah* 2], in differentiating between one who seduces and one who rapes, states that the former does so with the woman's consent while the latter acts against her will. If it occurred in the field we assume that she was forced unless witnesses testify that she consented. If it occurred in the city we assume that she was seduced since she did not call out, unless witnesses testify that she had been forced [e.g. he threatened her with a sword, saying he would kill her if she called out]. . . .

The case before us occurred in the city and since she did not cry out you might assume that she consented. However everyone knows that the sword of the oppressors was constantly held over each and every one of these women. Calling out would have been of no avail, for who would have interrupted them? Since there was no escape for these unfortunate women, this case is surely stronger than that cited by Maimonides [when he states that even in the city the girl is considered to have been forced if witnesses testify that she was threatened with the sword], for in the case before us we are all witnesses that the sword was constantly over their heads and that whoever refused was put to death. Thus surely this poor woman is permitted to her husband and there is absolutely no suspicion that she was at all co-operative, for she also saw what they did to Jewish men, women and children, that they slaughtered them without mercy. Surely these oppressors were abominable in her eyes and she could not have willingly consented in any way to lie with them. . . .

This leads to the conclusion that in our case she definitely is believed when she states that she was forced. For in addition [to what has been cited above] many authorities are of the opinion that also in the city and in the absence of witnesses a girl is believed when she claims "I was forced."

Far be it from anyone to cast aspersion on these honorable Jewish women. On the contrary, it is our duty to proclaim the reward they will be granted by "the One who hears the plea of the destitute." . . . He will heal their sorrow and bestow upon them the blessings of womanhood. . . . We must avoid causing them sorrow and anguish. There are instances in which women in similar circumstances were divorced by their husbands. Alas for us that such a thing has happened in our time.

In my opinion there is no need to make any effort to remove the contemning legend from the bodies of such women. On the contrary, it should be preserved. It should be considered not a sign of disgrace and shame but as a symbol of honor and courage . . . and an enduring reminder that we shall yet see the defeat of the transgressors from whose face is blotted any human semblance. They are like beasts of the forest and voracious wolves, hastening to spill innocent blood and to put to death the pious and the upright. This legend upon the arms of innocent and pure souls will always remind us of that which is written in the Torah of Moses, the man of God, "Sing aloud, O you nations, of His people; for He avenges the blood of His servants, and renders vengeance to His adversaries" [Deut. 32:43].[46]

Here is the text of the wedding ceremony. In Jewish law anyone may perform a wedding, for Jews are essentially married by consent. The passing of a ring, or any object of value, from groom to bride represents a contract which is valid if it is witnessed by two other adult male Jews. The prayers which surround this act represent the ancient engagement rituals, before it, and seven blessings said on behalf of the congregation afterward, if a *minyan* (a minimum quorum of ten male adults) is present. It must be added that nowadays the wedding ritual is conventionally read by a rabbi.

You that come in the name of the Lord are blessed.

May He who is supreme in might, blessing and glory bless this bridegroom and bride.

A cup of wine is filled and held by the officiant as he recites:

Praised are You, O Lord our God, King of the universe, Creator of the fruit of the vine.

Praised are You, O Lord our God, King of the universe, who sanctified us with Your commandments, and commanded us concerning forbidden marriages, who forbade us those to whom we are not married, and permitted us those married to us by means of the wedding ceremony and the bridal canopy. Praised are You, O Lord, who sanctifies Your people Israel through the wedding ceremony beneath the bridal canopy.

The cup of wine is presented first to the bridegroom and then to the bride.

The bridegroom then places the ring on the finger of his bride, and says:

By this ring you are consecrated to me as my wife in accordance with the law of Moses and the people of Israel.

The cup of wine is refilled, and held by the officiant as he recites:

Praised are You, O Lord our God, King of the universe, Creator of the fruit of the vine.

Praised are You, O Lord our God, King of the universe, who created all things for Your glory.

Praised are You, O Lord our God, King of the universe, Creator of man.

Praised are You, O Lord our God, King of the universe, who created man and woman in Your image, fashioning woman in the likeness of man, preparing for man a mate, that together they might perpetuate life. Praised are You, O Lord, Creator of man.

May Zion rejoice as her children in joy are restored to her.

Praised are You, O Lord, who causes Zion to rejoice at her children's return.

Grant great joy to these beloved companions, as You did to the first man and woman in the Garden of Eden. Praised are You, O Lord, who grants joy to bride and groom.

Praised are You, O Lord our God, King of the universe, who created joy and gladness, bride and groom, mirth, song, delight and rejoicing, love and harmony, peace and companionship. O Lord our God, may there be heard in the cities of Judah and in the streets of Jerusalem voices of joy and gladness, voices of bride and groom, the jubilant voices of those joined in marriage under the bridal canopy, the voices of young people feasting and singing. Praised are You, O Lord, who causes the groom to rejoice with his bride.[47]

PARENTS AND CHILDREN

That children must love and honor their parents is undoubted. However, the sources emphasize that, patriarchal though ancient Jewish society was, the duty to honor parents applied in equal measure to the father and the mother. The parent-child relationship was not one way, for parents have specified duties toward their children.

Honor your father and your mother, that your days may be long in the land which the Lord your God gives you.[48]

Cursed be he who dishonors his father or his mother.[49]

There are three partners in a man: The Holy One, praised be He, his father and his mother. When a man honors his parents, the Holy One says: It is as though I were dwelling among them and they were honoring Me. Rabbi says: He-who-spoke-and-the-world-was-created knows that a child honors his mother more than his father. Therefore [Ex. 20:12], the Holy One, praised be He, preceded honoring one's father to honoring one's mother. He-who-spoke-and-the-world-was-created knows that a child fears his father more than his mother. Therefore [Lev. 19:3] the Holy One, praised be He, preceded the fear of one's mother to fear of one's father. When a man pains his father and his mother, the Holy One, praised be He, says: I did well in not dwelling among them for had I done so, they would have caused Me pain.[50]

They asked Rav Ulla: To what point must one honor his parents? He told them: Go and see how a non-Jew named Dama ben Netinah treated his father in Ashkelon. The sages once sought to conclude a business transaction with him, through which he would gain 600,000 gold *denarii*. But the key to his vault was under the pillow of his sleeping father, and he refused to disturb him.[51]

The disciples of Rabbi Eliezer the great asked him to give an example of honoring one's parents. He said: Go and see what Dama ben Netinah did in Ashkelon. His mother was feeble minded and she used to strike him with a shoe in the presence of the council over which he presided, but he never said more than "It is enough, mother." When the shoe fell from her hand he would pick it up for her, so that she would not be troubled.[52]

Rabbi Simeon ben Johai said: Great is the duty of honoring one's parents, for the Holy One, praised be He, gave it status greater than the duty of honoring Him. Concerning the Holy One it is written "Honor the Lord with your substance" [Prov. 3:9]. How is this done? By leaving grain in the field, giving priestly and poor tithes, observing the commandments of *Sukkah* and *Lulav, Shofar, Tefillin* and *Tzitzit*, feeding the hungry, giving drink to the thirsty, and clothing the naked. If you have the means to do these, then you are obligated to do them, but if you do not have the means you are not obligated. However, when it comes to honoring your parents, whether you are a man of substance or not, you are obligated to "honor your father and your mother" [Ex. 20:12]—even if you have to beg from door to door.[53]

It is written "Honor your father and your mother" [Ex. 20:12] and it is written "Honor the Lord with your substance"

[Prov. 3:9]. Scripture compares honoring one's parents with honoring God.[54]

"Every one shall revere his parents and you shall observe My Sabbaths; I am the Lord" [Lev. 19:3]. One might think that honoring parents could have precedence over Sabbath observance. Therefore this verse is written in this way, to state that "all of you are obligated to honor Me."[55]

Scripture everywhere speaks of the father before the mother. Does the honor due the father exceed the honor due the mother? Therefore Scripture states: "Every one shall fear his mother and his father" [Lev. 19:3], to teach that both are equal. However, the sages have said: Scripture everywhere speaks of the father before the mother because both a man and his mother are bound to honor the father. So too in the study of Torah. If the son has gained much wisdom while he sat before his teacher, his teacher comes before his father, since both he and his father are bound to honor the teacher.[56]

A father is obligated to see that his son is circumcised, to redeem him [if he is the first-born], to teach him Torah and a craft and to find a wife for him. Some say that he must teach his son to swim. Rabbi Judah said: Whoever does not teach his son a craft is considered as having taught him thievery.[57]

Rav said: A father should never favor one son more than the others, for because of a little extra silk which Jacob gave to Joseph, his brothers became jealous, sold him into slavery and it came about that our ancestors went down to Egypt.[58]

Whoever hears a section of the Torah from his grandson is considered as hearing it at Mount Sinai on the day of Revelation, as it is written ". . . make them known to your children and your children's children . . . on the day that you stood before the Lord your God at Horeb" [Deut. 4:9–10].[59]

Rabbi Hiyya bar Abba did not eat breakfast before he reviewed the previous day's verse with the child and taught him a new verse. Rabba bar Rav Huna did not eat breakfast before he took the child to school.[60]

". . . and teach them to your children, to speak of them" [Deut. 11:19]. From this it is said: When a child begins to speak, his father should speak with him in the holy tongue and teach him Torah. If he does not do so, it is as though he buries him.[61]

KASHRUTH (DIETARY LAWS)

The most pervasive of Jewish rituals, for they are observed by the faithful in the very act of eating to sustain life, are the laws of kashruth, the regulations about forbidden and permitted foods. There have been many attempts through the ages to "explain" these rules. There are several such remarks to be found in the section below, culminating in the concluding three paragraphs, written by Maimonides. Essentially the traditional writings have produced two basic reasons for kashruth: that these laws represent a curbing of man's animal appetites and that they were ordained as a way of setting the Jews apart in their day to day life, so that they might be conscious of their responsibility as members of a priest-people. Contemporary Reform Judaism has rejected these laws, though at least one of its leaders, Kaufmann Kohler, knew that this left it with the problem of finding "other methods to inculcate the spirit of holiness in the modern Jew, to render him conscious of his priestly mission." Ultimately, the laws of kashruth cannot be rationalized. The believer accepts them as part of a total system, the Jewish way to holiness, ordained by God. The nonbeliever may cling to kashruth out of sentiment or attachment to a cultural past, but this clinging has demonstrably seldom outlasted one generation of disbelief.

Therefore to this day the Israelites do not eat the sinew of the hip which is upon the hollow of the thigh, because he touched the hollow of Jacob's thigh on the sinew of the hip.[62]

You shall be consecrated to Me. Therefore you shall not eat any flesh that is torn by beasts in the field; you shall cast it to the dogs.[63]

You shall not boil a kid in its mother's milk.[64]

These are the animals which you may eat of all the beasts of the earth. Whatsoever divides the hoof and is wholly cloven-footed, and chews the cud, among the beasts, you may eat. But whatsoever chews the cud and has a hoof but divides it not, such as the camel, you shall not eat, but shall reckon it among the unclean. The rock-badger, which chews the cud but does not divide the hoof, is unclean. The hare too, for it chews the cud but does not divide the hoof. And the swine, because, though it divides the hoof, it does not chew the cud. The flesh of these you shall not eat, nor shall you touch their carcasses, because they are unclean to you.[65]

These you may eat, of all that are in the waters: Everything in the waters that has fins and scales, whether in the seas or in the rivers, you may eat. But anything that is in the sea or the rivers that has no fins and scales . . . is an abomination to you. . . . Of their flesh you shall not eat.[66]

If any man of the house of Israel or of the strangers that dwell among them, should eat blood, I will set My face against his soul, and will cut him off from among his people. For the life of the flesh is in the blood, and I have given it to you, that you may make atonement with it upon the altar for your souls; for it is blood that makes atonement by reason of the life. Therefore I have said to the children of Israel: No soul of you, nor of the strangers that dwell among you, shall eat blood. Any man of the children of Israel or of the strangers that dwell among them, who by hunting takes any beast or fowl which is lawful to eat, shall pour out its blood and cover it with earth. For the life of all flesh is in the blood; therefore I have said to the children of Israel: You shall not eat the blood of any flesh, because the life of the flesh is in the blood, and whoever eats it shall be cut off.[67]

You shall not eat anything that dies of itself. You may give it to the alien that is in your towns, that he may eat it, or you may sell it to a foreigner. For you are a people holy to the Lord your God.[68]

The following signs disqualify cattle [making it *trefah* and so unfit for consumption]: if the gullet is pierced or the windpipe torn; if the membrane of the brain is pierced; if the heart is pierced through to the cells; if the spine is broken and the spinal cord severed; if the liver is completely missing; if the lung is pierced or defective (Rabbi Simeon says it is not *trefah* unless its bronchial tubes are pierced); if the maw is pierced, or the gall-bladder or the intestines; if the inner stomach is pierced or if the greater part of its outer coating is torn (Rabbi Judah says a handbreadth in larger cattle, or the greater part in smaller cattle); if the third stomach or the second stomach is pierced on its outermost side; if the beast has fallen from a roof or has most of its ribs broken; if it has been mauled by a wolf (Rabbi Judah says: if small cattle have been mauled by a wolf, large cattle by a lion, small birds by a hawk and larger birds by a vulture). This is the general rule: If the animal could not have remained alive for twelve months in like state, it is *trefah*.[69]

No flesh may be cooked in milk [to avoid the possibility of transgressing the law against boiling a kid in its mother's milk: Ex. 23:19; 34:26; Deut. 14:21], excepting the flesh of fish and locusts. No flesh may be served on the table together with cheese, excepting the flesh of fish and locusts. . . . A man may tie up meat and cheese in the same cloth provided that they do not touch one another. . . . If a drop of milk fell upon a piece of meat that was cooking in a pot and there was enough to give its flavor to that piece, that piece cannot be eaten. If a man stirred the pot and there was enough to give the flavor of the milk to everything in it, none of it can be eaten.[70]

"These are the living things which you may eat" [Lev. 11:2]. . . . "The way of God is perfect, the promise of the Lord proves true. He is a shield for all who take refuge in

Him" [II Sam. 22:31; Ps. 18:31]. The ways of the Holy One praised be He are perfect. What can it matter to Him whether an animal is slaughtered according to prescribed ritual or whether it is simply stabbed with no regard to ritual, before it is eaten? Does it benefit Him or does it harm Him in any way? What can it matter to Him if one eats forbidden or permitted foods? "If you are wise, you are wise for yourself, and if you scoff you alone will bear the consequences" [Prov. 9:12]. The commandments have been given for the purpose of purifying men through them.[71]

The commandment concerning the killing of animals is necessary, because the natural food of man consists of vegetables and of the flesh of animals. . . . Since, therefore, the desire of procuring good food necessitates the slaying of animals, the Law enjoins that the death of the animal should be the easiest. It is not allowed to torment the animal by cutting the throat in a clumsy manner, by poleaxing, or by cutting off a limb while the animal is alive.

It is also prohibited to kill an animal and its young on the same day [Lev. 22:28], in order that people should be restrained and prevented from killing the two together in such a manner that the young is slain in the sight of the mother; for the pain of the animals under such circumstances is very great. There is no difference in this case between the pain of man and the pain of other living beings. . . .

The same reason applies to the law which enjoins that we should let the mother [bird] fly away when we take the young. . . . If the Law provides that such grief should not be caused to cattle or to birds, how much more careful must we be that we should not cause grief to our fellowmen.[72]

CHARITY

Caring for one's fellow man is not merely a generalized moral commandment in Judaism. It is spelled out in specific, legally binding obligations which each man must heed. In all ages Jews were supremely conscious of the need to aid and succor one another. This was especially emphasized for them by the innumerable persecutions they have suffered since the beginning of the Exile in the year 70 and which have not ceased even in our own generation, which has witnessed Nazism. The immense efforts of present-day Jewry through such agencies as the United Jewish Appeal, which labors for the helping of Jews in need all over the world, are in the line of this most ancient tradition.

For six years you shall sow your land and gather in its yield; but the seventh year you shall let it rest and lie fallow, that the poor of your people may eat; and what they leave the wild beasts may eat. You shall do likewise with your vineyard, and with your olive orchard.[73]

When you reap the harvest of your land, you shall not reap your field to its very border, neither shall you gather the gleanings after your harvest. And you shall not strip your vineyard bare, neither shall you gather the fallen grapes of your vineyard; you shall leave them for the poor and for the sojourner: I am the Lord your God.[74]

At the end of every three years you shall bring forth all the tithe of your produce in the same year, and lay it up within your towns; and the Levite, because he has no portion or inheritance with you, and the sojourner, the fatherless, and the widow, who are within your towns, shall come and eat and be filled; that the Lord your God may bless you in all the work of your hands that you do.[75]

If one of your brethren that dwells within the gates of your city in the land which the Lord your God gives you, should come to poverty, you shall not harden your heart nor close your hand, but you shall open your hand to him and you shall lend him that which you perceive he has need of. Beware that there be not a base thought in your heart, saying, "The seventh year, the year of release, draws near" and you turn away your eye from your poor brother, giving him nothing, lest he cry against you to the Lord, and it be a sin in you. But you shall give to him, and your heart shall not be grieved when you give to him, that the Lord your God may bless you at all times, and in all things to which you put your hand. For the poor shall never cease out of the land; therefore I command you to open your hand to your poor and needy brother that lives in the land.[76]

The ear that heard me blessed me, and the eye that saw me gave witness to me, because I had delivered the poor man that cried out, and the fatherless, that had no helper. The blessing of him that was ready to perish came upon me, and I comforted the heart of the widow. I was clad with justice, and I clothed myself with righteousness as with a robe and a diadem. I was eyes to the blind and feet to the lame. I was the father of the poor, and the cause which I knew not, I searched out most diligently. I broke the jaws of the wicked man, and out of his teeth I took away the prey.[77]

The passage below is a letter written by the the Jews of Alexandria in the eleventh century to a nearby community in Fostat, asking for help in the ransoming of captives.

You are the supporters of the poor and the aid of the men in need, you study diligently, you rouse the good against the evil impulse. You walk in the right way and practise justice. We let you know that we always pray for you. May God grant you peace and security.

We turn to you today on behalf of a captive woman who has been brought from Byzantium. We ransomed her for 24 denares besides the governmental tax. You sent us 12 denares; we have paid the remainder and the tax. Soon afterwards sailors brought two other prisoners, one of them a fine young man possessing knowledge of the Torah, the other a boy of about ten. When we saw them in the hands of the pirates, and how they beat them and frightened them before our own eyes,

we had pity on them and guaranteed their ransom. We had
hardly settled this when another ship arrived carrying many
prisoners. Among them were a physician and his wife. Thus
we are again in difficulties and distress. And our strength is
overstrained, as the taxes are heavy and the times criti-
cal. . . .[78]

Maimonides summarized the legal obligation to give
charity in his code of Jewish law, the *Mishneh Torah*, in
the section entitled "The Laws of Giving to the Poor."

If the poor asks of you and you have nothing in your hand
to give him, soothe him with words. It is forbidden to rebuke
a poor man or to raise one's voice against him in a shout,
for his heart is shattered and crushed and it is written, "A
broken and contrite heart, O God, You will not despise" [Ps.
51:19]. And it is written, "I dwell in the high and holy place
and also with him who is of a contrite and humble spirit, to
revive the spirit of the humble and to revive the heart of the
contrite" [Isa. 57:15]. Alas for anyone who has humiliated a
poor man, alas for him. He should rather be like a father both
with compassion and with words, as it is written, "I was a
father to the poor" [Job 29:16]. . . .
There are eight degrees in the giving of charity, each one
higher than that which follows it:

1. The highest degree, exceeded by none, is giving a gift or
   a loan or taking one as a partner or finding him employ-
   ment by which he can be self-supporting. . . .

2. Giving charity to the poor without knowing to whom one
   gives, the recipient not knowing the donor's identity, for
   this is a good deed of intrinsic value, done for its own
   sake. An example of this is the Hall of Secret Donations
   which was maintained in the Temple. The righteous would
   donate in secret and the poor would be supported from it
   in secret. Approximating this is giving to a charity fund.
   One should not give to a charity fund unless he knows the

collector is trustworthy and wise and conducts himself
properly, like Rabbi Hananiah ben Tradyon.

3. Giving to one whose identity one knows, although the
recipient does not know the donor's identity. An example
of this would be the action of those great sages who would
walk about in secret and cast coins at the doors of the
poor. It is fitting to imitate such a custom and it is a high
degree indeed, if the charity collectors [through whom
one can give impersonally] do not conduct themselves
properly.

4. Giving without knowing to whom one gives, although the
recipient knows the donor's identity. An example of this
would be the action of those great sages who would wrap
up coins in a bundle and throw it over their shoulder. The
poor would then come to take it without suffering any
embarrassment.

5. Giving before being asked.

6. Giving only after being asked.

7. Giving inadequately, though graciously.

8. Giving grudgingly.

The great sages would give a coin for the poor before each
prayer service and then pray, as it is written, "I shall behold
Your face in righteousness" [Ps. 17:5]. Giving food to one's
older sons and daughters (though one is not obligated to do
so) in order to teach the males Torah and to direct the fe-
males on the proper path, and giving food to one's father and
mother is considered to be charity. And it is a great degree of
charity, for relatives should have precedence. . . .

One should always press himself and suffer rather than be
dependent upon others; he should not cast himself upon the
community as a responsibility. Thus the sages commanded:
"Rather make your Sabbath like a week day than be dependent upon others" [*Pesahim* 112a]. Even if a man was
learned and respected and then became poor he should occupy himself with a trade, even a lowly trade, rather than be
dependent upon others. It is better to strip the hide of dead

animals than to say "I am a great sage, I am a Priest; support me." Among the great sages there were wood choppers, those who watered gardens and those who worked with iron and charcoal. They did not ask the community for money and they did not take it when it was offered to them.[79]

The paragraphs which follow are a selection from a more recent code of Jewish law, the *Shulkhan Arukh.* Its author was Rabbi Joseph Caro (1488–1575), of Safed in Palestine, and the code that he wrote is to this day the recognized authority in Jewish law for those who follow classical rabbinic Judaism.

The ransom of captives takes precedence over the act of supporting and clothing the poor, and there is no commandment which is as great as that of ransoming captives. Therefore, any religious object may be converted into cash for the purpose of using that money to ransom captives, even if this involves the use of monies designated for the restoration of the Temple. . . .

Whoever tarries in ransoming captives when it is possible to do so is considered as one who sheds blood.

Captives are not to be ransomed for exorbitant sums, for the sake of social order, lest enemies devote themselves to capturing. But one may ransom himself with whatever sum he desires. . . .

We should not help captives escape, for the sake of the social order, lest enemies make life more difficult for them and increase the regulations for guarding them. . . .

A woman is to be ransomed before a man; if the place of captivity is one where the practice of homosexuality is common, the men are to be ransomed first.

If one is in captivity along with his father and his teacher, he is to be ransomed before his teacher, and his teacher before his father. However, if his mother is also there, her being ransomed has first priority.

If a man and his wife are both in captivity, she is to be shown preference, and a court may take possession of and administer his property in order to ransom her, even if he strongly states that she should not be ransomed with his property. He is not to be obeyed in such a case.

If a man is in captivity and he has property but does not want to ransom himself, he is ransomed against his will.[80]

LOVE YOUR NEIGHBOR

The well-known passage from rabbinic teaching with which this section begins is expanded on in turn by Samuel Laniado, a rabbi in Aleppo in the second half of the sixteenth century, Moses Luzatto, and by four Hasidic teachers of the eighteenth and nineteenth centuries.

A heathen once came to Shammai and said, "I will become a proselyte on the condition that you teach me the entire Torah while I stand on one foot." Shammai chased him away with a builder's measuring stick. When he appeared before Hillel with the same request, Hillel said, "Whatever is hateful to you, do not do to your neighbor. That is the entire Torah. The rest is commentary; go and learn it."[81]

". . . you shall love your neighbor as yourself; I am the Lord . . . " [Lev. 19:18].

"I am the Lord." This explains two things. First, since the souls that are as they should be, are all a part of God, and since the soul of one man and the soul of his neighbor are both carved out of the same throne of Splendour, therefore "love for your neighbor as for yourself" is meant literally, for he is as you. Since I, God, am He who created your soul and the soul of your neighbor, he is as you. And, second, if your love for your neighbor is as the love for yourself, this is considered love for Me, because "I am the Lord." Since your love for him is like the love for yourself, even for him who is an infinitesimal part of Me—how much more will you love Me! For the love of your neighbor will be considered as if I, God, had myself received it.[82]

The practice of lovingkindness is essential to piety. The [Hebrew] word for piety or saintliness is derived from the same root as the word for kindness. According to our sages, the world is based upon three things, one of them being the practice of lovingkindness. . . . Raba preached that whoever possesses the following three traits is obviously a descendant of our father Abraham: compassion, modesty, and the practime of lovingkindness. . . . Our sages said, "In three respects lovingkindness is superior to giving charity. Charity entails the giving of one's property, while the practice of lovingkindness entails the giving of one's self. Charity is given only to the poor, while lovingkindness may be shown both the poor and the rich. Charity can be given only to the living, while lovingkindness can be shown to both the living and the dead" (*Sukkah* 49b). . . . Lovingkindness demands that we not cause pain to any human being, not even to an animal. We must be merciful and compassionate to animals. Thus is it written, "A righteous man has regard for the life of his beast" [Prov. 12:10].[83]

A minor saint is capable of loving minor sinners. A great saint loves great sinners. The Messiah will see the merit of every Jew.[84]

Falsehood imitates truth and it seems impossible to know which is which. What, therefore, is the difference between the upholders of truth and the champions of falsehood? This is the unfailing sign: men of truth are especially dedicated to the task of redeeming captives. They hate slavery. This is the test by which you can tell the difference.[85]

A disciple of Rabbi Mendel of Kotzk, a man of large affairs, once came to him and complained that he was so involved in business that he could find no time even to study a bit of the Torah. The master asked him: "How many people do you employ in your business?" "A hundred and fifty," was the answer. "So. You provide a living for a hundred and fifty families. This is worth while enough that you should suffer for it both in this world and in the world to come."[86]

It is written of Joseph's brothers that "They saw him afar off, and before he came near unto them, they conspired against him to slay him [Gen. 37:18]". The reason why the brothers wanted to kill Joseph is that they saw him only from afar. Had they seen him in true nearness, they would have understood his essence, and they would have loved him.

In every man there is a spark of the Divine Soul. The power of evil in man darkens this flame and almost puts it out. Brotherly love among men rekindles the soul and brings it closer to its source.[87]

CHAPTER FOUR

The Cycle of the Year

THE SABBATH

Man, in a central rabbinic image, is God's partner in the work of creation. God labored and then He rested; man labors to perform his creative tasks and he, too, must rest. The Five Books of Moses ordain absolute abstention from work. The Prophets emphasized that the ritual restrictions are necessary for the attaining of the spiritual state which is the purpose and meaning of the Sabbath.

The heavens and the earth were finished, and all their host. And on the seventh day God finished His work which He had done, and He rested on the seventh day from all His work which He had done. So God blessed the seventh day and hallowed it, because on it God rested from all His work which He had done in creation.[1]

Remember the Sabbath day, to keep it holy. Six days you shall labor, and do all your work; but the seventh day is a Sabbath to the Lord your God; in it you shall not do any work, you or your son, or your daughter, your manservant or your maidservant, or your cattle, or the sojourner who is within your gates; for in six days the Lord made heaven and earth, the sea and all that is in them, and rested the seventh day; therefore the Lord blessed the Sabbath day and hallowed it.[2]

Wherefore the children of Israel keep the Sabbath, to observe the Sabbath throughout their generations, for a perpetual covenant. It is a sign between Me and the children of Israel for ever, for in six days the Lord made heaven and earth, and on the seventh day He ceased from work and rested.[3]

Observe the Sabbath day to keep it holy, as the Lord your God commanded you. Six days you shall labor and do all your work; but the seventh day is a Sabbath to the Lord your God; in it you shall not do any work, you or your son, or your daughter or your manservant or your maidservant, or your ox or your ass or any of your cattle or the sojourner who is within your gates, that your manservant and your maidservant may rest as well as you. You shall remember that you were a servant in the land of Egypt, and the Lord your God brought you out thence with a mighty hand and an outstretched arm; therefore the Lord your God commanded you to keep the Sabbath day.[4]

Thus says the Lord: Keep judgment, and do righteousness, for My salvation is soon to come, and My justice to be revealed. Blessed is the man that does this, and the son of man that holds fast by it, that keeps the Sabbath from profaning it, that keeps his hands from doing any evil. Let not the alien that adheres to the Lord speak, saying, "The Lord will surely separate me from His people." . . . And the aliens that adhere to the Lord, to worship Him and to love His name, to be His servants, everyone that keeps the Sabbath from profaning it, and that holds fast to My covenant, will I bring to My holy mountain, and will I make joyful in My house of prayer. Their burnt offerings and their sacrifices shall be acceptable upon My altar, for My house shall be called a house of prayer for all peoples.[5]

If you turn away your foot from the Sabbath, from doing your business on My holy day, and call the Sabbath a delight, and the holy of the Lord glorious, and honor it, not going your own ways, nor pursuing your business, nor speaking thereof, then you shall be delighted in the Lord, and I will lift you up above the high places of the earth, and will feed you with the heritage of Jacob your father; for the mouth of the Lord has spoken it.[6]

And it shall come to pass, if you will hearken to Me, says the Lord, to bring in no burdens by the gates of this city on the Sabbath day, and if you will sanctify the Sabbath day, doing no work therein, then shall there enter in by the gates of this city kings and princes, sitting upon the throne of David, riding in chariots and on horses, they and their princes, the men of Judah, and the inhabitants of Jerusalem, and this city shall be inhabited for ever. . . . But if you will not hearken to Me, to sanctify the Sabbath day, and not to carry burdens, and not to bring them in by the gates of Jerusalem on the Sabbath day, then I will kindle a fire in its gates and it shall devour the houses of Jerusalem, and it shall not be quenched.[7]

In those days I saw in Judah some treading winepresses on the Sabbath, and carrying sheaves, and loading asses with wine and grapes and figs, and all manner of burdens, and bringing them into Jerusalem on the Sabbath day, and I warned them on the day when they sold food. Some men of Tyre also dwelled there, who brought fish, and all manner of wares, and they sold them on the Sabbaths to the children of Judah in Jerusalem. And I rebuked the nobles of Judah, and said to them, "What is this evil thing that you do, profaning the Sabbath day? Did not our fathers do these things and our God brought all this evil upon us and upon this city? And you bring more wrath upon Israel by violating the Sabbath."[8]

The Mishnah, the code of Jewish law edited by Rabbi Judah the Prince in the second century, is next to the Bible the most sacred of Jewish books. It is the kernel of the Talmud, which is the record of three centuries of exegesis of the Mishnah. The rules for the Sabbath that appear next are primarily from the Mishnah, with a comment or two included from its interpretation in the Talmud (the *Gemara*).

The rules about the Sabbath, Festal offerings and sacrilege are like mountains hanging by a hair, for there is scanty teaching about them in Scripture while the rules are many.[9]

The principal categories of work [which are forbidden on the Sabbath] are forty less one: sowing, plowing, reaping, binding sheaves, threshing, winnowing, cleansing crops, grinding, sifting, kneading, baking, shearing, washing, beating or dyeing wool, spinning, weaving, making two loops, weaving two threads, separating two threads, tying a knot, loosening a knot, sewing two stitches, ripping in order to sew two stitches, hunting a gazelle [or similar beast], slaughtering or flaying or salting it or curing its hide, scraping it or cutting it up, writing two letters, erasing in order to write two letters, building, pulling down, putting out a fire, lighting a fire, striking with a hammer and taking anything from one domain to another [e.g. from private domain to public domain or vice versa]. These are the principle categories of work: forty less one.[10]

They sat and pondered: We have learned that the principal categories of work [forbidden on the Sabbath] are forty less one. To what do these categories correspond [i.e. on what basis have they been selected]? Rabbi Hanina bar Hama told them that they correspond to the categories of work in the building of the Tabernacle. [NOTE: Because of the juxtaposition of the commandments not to work on the Sabbath, Ex. 35:1–3, and the description of the work involved in the construction of the Tabernacle, Ex. 35:4*ff*., it was derived that every type of work which went into the construction of the Tabernacle is the type of work which is forbidden on the Sabbath. The Hebrew word for "work" is the same in both passages: *melakhah*.] . . . It has been taught: Liability is incurred [for working on the Sabbath] only for work which comes under one of those categories which were involved in the construction of the Tabernacle. They sowed; therefore you must not sow on the Sabbath. They reaped; therefore you must not reap on the Sabbath. [NOTE: Certain crops had to be sown and reaped in the process of producing dyes for the hangings in the Tabernacle.] They lifted planks from the ground [public domain] to a cart [private domain]; therefore you must not carry from a public to a private domain on the Sabbath. They lowered planks from the cart to the ground; therefore you must not carry from a private to a public domain on the

Sabbath. They transferred planks from cart to cart; therefore you must not carry from one private domain to another on the Sabbath. But, you may ask, what wrong is done by that? Abaye and Rava, and some say Rav Adda bar Ahavah, explained that this would entail passing through public domain [the air between the carts is held to be public domain].[11]

Whenever there is doubt as to whether a life may be in danger, the laws of the Sabbath may be suspended.[12]

One may warm water for a sick person on the Sabbath. . . . We do not wait until the Sabbath is over, on the assumption that he will get better, but we warm the water for him right away, because whenever there is doubt as to whether or not a life may be in danger, the laws of the Sabbath may be suspended. . . . And this [violation of the Sabbath laws, whatever it might have to be] is not to be done by Gentiles or by minors [who are not obligated to observe the Sabbath law anyway] but by Jewish adults.[13]

"Call the Sabbath day a delight" [Isa. 58:13]. How do you make it a delight? Rav Judah, the son of Rav Samuel bar Shilat said in the name of Rav: With a dish of vegetables [spinach or beets] and a large fish and garlic. Rav Hiyya ben Ashai said, quoting Rav: Even something very small, if it was prepared specifically in honor of the Sabbath, is a delight. What is an example of this? Rav Papa said: A pie of fish-hash and flour.[14]

"God blessed the seventh day and He hallowed it" [Gen. 2:3]. He blessed it with man's countenance, for man's countenance on the Sabbath day is unlike that of any other day of the week.[15]

The Emperor asked Rabbi Joshua ben Hananiah, "What gives your Sabbath-meal such an aroma?" He replied, "We have a spice called Sabbath, which is added to each dish we serve." The Emperor said, "Give me some of this spice." Rabbi Joshua replied, "If you observe the Sabbath, the spice works; but if you do not observe it, the spice does not work."[16]

Rabbi Levi said: If the Jewish people would observe the Sabbath properly even once, the son of David [the Messiah] would come. Why? Because it is equal to all the other commandments in importance.[17]

This brief excerpt from Judah Halevi's *Kuzari* summarizes the classic themes of the Sabbath.

God commanded cessation of work on the Sabbath and holy days, as well as in the culture of the soil, all this "as a remembrance of the exodus from Egypt," and "remembrance of the work of creation." These two things belong together, because they are the outcome of the absolute divine will, but not the result of accident or natural phenomena. It is said, "For ask now of the days that are past . . . whether such a great thing as this has ever happened or was ever heard of. Did any people ever hear the voice of God speaking out of the midst of the fire, as you have heard, and still live? Or has any god ever attempted to go and take a nation for himself from the midst of another nation . . . " [Deut. 4:32 f.]. The observance of the Sabbath is itself an acknowledgment of His omnipotence, and at the same time an acknowledgment of the creation by the divine word. He who observes the Sabbath because the work of creation was finished on it acknowledges the creation itself. He who believes in the creation believes in the Creator. He, however, who does not believe in it falls prey to doubts of God's eternity and to doubts of the existence of the world's Creator. The observance of the Sabbath is therefore nearer to God than monastic retirement and asceticism.[18]

Rabbi Judah the Pious (1150–1207), one of the saintliest figures of medieval German Jewry, is the author of the *Sefer Hasidim* ("The Book of the Pious"), a compendium of spiritual practices and tales. The two paragraphs that follow are excerpted from his discussion of the Sabbath.

"Remember the Sabbath day, to keep it holy" [Ex. 20:8]. But is one liable to forget the Sabbath day? For it does recur every seventh day. The verse means to imply that one must remember to remove those things which would make him forget to remember the Sabbath. For example, one should not be sad on the Sabbath. . . . Each Sabbath, one should do those things which remind him that it is Sabbath: One should bathe on Sabbath eve and dress in his best clothes and arrange for an *oneg shabbat* ("joy of the Sabbath") celebration, and read those things which are suitable for the Sabbath day. . . .

"On the sixth day they shall prepare" [Ex. 16:5]. One must very diligently prepare for the Sabbath in advance. He must be diligent and quick in this as one who has heard that the Queen is going to lodge at his home, or as one who has heard that a bride and all her company are coming to his home. What would he do in such instances? He would greatly rejoice and say: "They do me great honor by staying under my roof." He would say to his servants: "Make the house ready, set it in order, sweep it out and make the beds in honor of those who are coming. I shall go to buy as much bread, meat and fish as I can, in their honor." What, for us, is greater than the Sabbath? The Sabbath is a bride, a Queen; the Sabbath is called a delight. Therefore, we surely must take pains to prepare for the Sabbath; each person himself must prepare, even though he has one hundred servants.[19]

The contemporary American religious philosopher, Abraham Joshua Heschel, is the author of this prose-poem about the Sabbath.

The Bible is more concerned with time than with space. It sees the world in the dimension of time. It pays more attention to generations, to events, than to countries, to things; it is more concerned with history than with geography. To understand the teaching of the Bible, one must accept its premise that time has a meaning which is at least equal to that of space; that time has a significance and sovereignty of its own. . . .

Judaism teaches us to be attached to *holiness in time*, to be attached to sacred events, to learn how to consecrate sanctuaries that emerge from the magnificent stream of a year. The Sabbaths are our great cathedrals; and our Holy of Holies is a shrine that neither the Romans nor the Germans were able to burn; a shrine that even apostasy cannot easily obliterate: the Day of Atonement. According to the ancient rabbis, it is not the observance of the Day of Atonement, but the Day itself, the "essence of the day," which, with man's repentance, atones for the sins of man. . . .

One of the most distinguished words in the Bible is the word *qadosh*, holy; a word which more than any other is representative of the mystery and majesty of the divine. Now what was the first holy object in the history of the world? Was it a mountain? Was it an altar?

It is, indeed, a unique occasion at which the distinguished word *qadosh* is used for the first time: in the Book of Genesis at the end of the story of creation. How extremely significant is the fact that it is applied to time: "And God blessed the seventh *day* and made it *holy*" [Gen. 2:3]. There is no reference in the record of creation to any object in space that would be endowed with the quality of holiness.

This is a radical departure from accustomed religious thinking. The mythical mind would expect that, after heaven and earth have been established, God would create a holy place—a holy mountain or a holy spring—whereupon a sanctuary is to be established. Yet it seems as if to the Bible it is *holiness in time*, the Sabbath, which comes first. . . .

The meaning of the Sabbath is to celebrate time rather than space. Six days a week we live under the tyranny of things of space; on the Sabbath we try to become attuned to *holiness in time*. It is a day on which we are called upon to share in what is eternal in time, to turn from the results of creation to the mystery of creation; from the world of creation to the creation of the world.[20]

The liturgy prescribes special prayers for the Sabbath, some of which find their place at this point in our volume. First, two paragraphs from the prescribed prayers for Sabbath day; then, the prayer over the wine, the symbol of joy, with which the Friday night meal, the feast of the Sabbath, begins; and then, the *Havdalah*, the prayer over wine, spices, and fire with which the end of the Sabbath is marked—wine in remembrance of the joy of the Sabbath that has just gone, spices to uplift the spirit which is saddened by its end and fire to mark the fact that now the workaday week begins, and fire may again be kindled.

Those that observe the Sabbath and call it a delight shall rejoice in Your kingdom. The people that hallows the seventh day shall all be sated and delighted with Your goodness, as You did find pleasure in the seventh day and hallowed it. You did call it the most desirable day, a remembrance of Creation.

Our God and God of our fathers, accept our rest. Hallow us with Your commandments and grant our portion in Your Torah. Sate us with Your goodness and gladden us with Your deliverance. Purify our hearts to serve You in truth. In love and favor, O Lord our God, let us inherit Your holy Sabbath. May Israel, who hallow Your name, rest thereon. Praised are You, O Lord, who hallows the Sabbath.[21]

Praised are You, O Lord our God, King of the universe, who creates the fruit of the vine.

Praised are You, O Lord our God, King of the universe, who has hallowed us with His commandments and has taken pleasure in us. In love and favor You have given us Your holy Sabbath as an inheritance, a memorial of Creation. This day is also the first of the holy convocations, in remembrance of the departure from Egypt. You have chosen us and have hallowed us above all nations, and in love and favor You have given us Your holy Sabbath as an inheritance. Praised are You, O Lord, who hallows the Sabbath.[22]

God is my deliverance, confident my trust in Him;
The Lord is my strength, my song, my deliverance.

Joyfully shall you drink from the fountains of deliverance;
The Lord will rescue; the Lord will bless His people.

The Lord of hosts is with us, the God of Jacob is our fortress.
O Lord of hosts, happy is the man who trusts in You.
O Lord and King, answer us when we call, and rescue us.

Grant us the blessings of light, of gladness and of honor,
Which the miracle of Your deliverance brought to our fathers.

I lift up the cup of deliverance; I call upon the Lord:

Praised are You, O Lord our God, King of the universe,
who creates the fruit of the vine.

Praised are You, O Lord our God, King of the universe,
who creates fragrant spices.

Praised are You, O Lord our God, King of the universe,
who creates the light of fire.

Praised are You, O Lord our God, King of the universe,
who has endowed all creation with distinctive qualities and
differentiated between light and darkness, between sacred
and profane, between Israel and the nations, and between
the seventh day and the other days of the week. Praised are
You, O Lord, who differentiates between the sacred and the
profane.[23]

THE FESTIVALS

The Sabbath is of course the most frequent of Jewish
holidays, but there are others. In Biblical times, when the
Temple still stood in Jerusalem, there were three pilgrim
festivals when all male adults were required to visit the
Temple, "to appear before the Lord." As we shall soon
see, historical explanations are given for these festivals
in the Bible, that is, each is related to a major event in
Jewish history. Biblical Judaism, however, knew their

agricultural origin as equally important. They marked the stages of the harvest, and were therefore celebrated with a special joy. In contemporary practice there are many reminiscences of their agricultural character.

You shall rejoice in your feast, you and your son and your daughter, your manservant and your maidservant, the Levite, the sojourner, the fatherless and the widow who are in your towns.[24]

Three times a year all your males shall appear before the Lord your God at the place which He will choose: at the feast of unleavened bread, at the feast of weeks and at the feast of booths. They shall not appear before the Lord empty handed. Every man shall give as he is able, according to the blessing of the Lord your God which He has given you.[25]

Everyone is required to fulfill the commandment to appear before the Lord [at the three festivals of the year; *see* Ex. 23:14–17] with the exceptions of a deaf-mute, and imbecile, and a child [none of whom is obliged to fulfill any of the commandments], a person of doubtful sex, a person of double sex, women, slaves that have not been completely freed, a man that is either lame, blind, sick, or aged and a person that can not go up to Jerusalem by foot.[26]

Rabbi Eliezer said: On a holiday a man can either eat and drink or sit and study. Rabbi Joshua said: He should divide the day, devoting half to eating and drinking and half to the House of Study. And Rabbi Johanan said: Both of them [Rabbi Eliezer and Rabbi Joshua] were expounding Scripture. One verse says "a solemn assembly for the Lord your God" [Deut. 16:8]. Another verse says "a solemn assembly for you" [Num. 29:35]. Rabbi Eliezer held that the day should be either completely "for the Lord" or completely "for you." And Rabbi Joshua held that it should be divided, one half "for the Lord" and one half "for you."[27]

Our sages taught: A man is obligated to see that his wife and the other members of his household enjoy the festivals, as it is written, "You shall rejoice in your festivals, you and your son and your daughter, your manservant and your maidservant . . . " [Deut. 16:14]. How do you see that they enjoy the festival? By giving them wine. But Rabbi Judah says that men and women should each be provided for according to what is suitable for them. Men should be provided for with wine. And what of women? Rav Joseph taught: In Babylonia they should be provided for with many-colored garments, and in Palestine with garments of polished flax.[28]

A non-Jew asked Rabbi Akiva in Sepphoris [in the upper Galilee]: Why do you celebrate the festivals, since God has told you "My soul despises your New Moons and your appointed festivals" [Isa. 1:14]? Rabbi Akiva answered him: Had He said "My New Moons and My appointed festivals" I would have to agree with you. However, He said "your New Moons and your appointed festivals," referring to festivals like those which Jeroboam ben Nevat celebrated, as it is written "Jeroboam celebrated a festival on the fifteenth day of the eighth month . . . that he had devised in his own heart, and he ordained a festival for the people of Israel . . . " [I Kings 12:32–33]. But those festivals and New Moons which are decreed in the Torah will never be abolished. How do I know? Because their source is the Holy One, praised be He, as it is written: "These are the appointed festivals of the Lord . . . " [Lev. 23:4].[29]

PASSOVER

The miracle of the exodus from Egypt is an event which Judaism has never ceased to remember. References to it pervade the prayer book. God Himself, personally and not through the agency of an angel, redeemed His people from bondage. They left Egypt so quickly at the moment of redemption that the Jews had no time to allow their dough to leaven. Hence they baked flat cakes, the matzoth which are eaten to this day during the Passover holiday in commemoration of the exodus.

And this day shall be for a memorial to you, and you shall keep it a feast to the Lord throughout your generations by ordinance for ever. Seven days shall you eat unleavened bread. In the first day there shall be no leaven in your houses; whoever eats anything leavened, from the first day until the seventh day, that soul shall be cut off from Israel. The first day shall be a holy convocation, and the seventh day shall be a holy convocation; you shall do no work in them, except those things to prepare for eating. And you shall observe the feast of unleavened bread, for in this same day I brought your hosts out of the land of Egypt. Therefore you shall observe this day throughout your generations by ordinance for ever. In the first month, on the fourteenth day of the month in the evening, you shall eat unleavened bread, until the twenty-first day of the same month in the evening. Seven days there shall not be any leaven in your houses. Whoever eats that which is leavened, his soul shall be cut off from the congregation of Israel, whether he be a stranger or one that is born in the land. You shall not eat anything leavened; in all your habitations you shall eat unleavened bread.[30]

On the night preceding the fourteenth of Nisan [Passover begins on the fifteenth] the *hametz** must be searched out by the light of a candle. Any place into which *hametz* is never brought need not be searched.[31]

Rabbi Meir says: *Hametz* may be eaten through the fifth hour [i.e. eleven A.M.] on the fourteenth of Nisan, but at the start of the sixth hour it must be burned. Rabbi Judah says: It may be eaten through the fourth hour, held [neither eaten nor burned] during the fifth hour, and it must be burned at the start of the sixth hour.[32]

So long as *hametz* may be eaten, a man may give it as fodder to cattle, wild animals and birds, or sell it to a non-

* *Hametz*—anything, edible or not, made from or containing grain, flour or bran of wheat, barley, spelt, goat-grass, or oats, which, due to contact with water or other liquid containing water, has fermented or is in the process of fermenting. Ex. 12:19 forbids *hametz* throughout the seven days of Passover (15–21 of Nisan).

Jew, and he is permitted to derive benefit from it in any fashion. But when the time is past [and *hametz* may no longer be eaten] it is forbidden to derive benefit from it, nor may one light an oven or stove with it. Rabbi Judah says: Removal of the *hametz* [Ex. 12:15] may be accomplished by burning. But the sages say: *Hametz* may be crumbled and scattered to the wind or thrown into the sea.[33]

If [on the fourteenth of Nisan] a man was on his way to slaughter his Passover offering or to circumcise his son or to participate in the wedding banquet at the home of his father-in-law and he remembered that he had left *hametz* in his house, he may return and remove it if he has time to do so and yet fulfill his religious obligation; otherwise, he may annul the *hametz* in his heart [thus decreeing that it be considered as dirt, and as not in his possession]. If he was on his way to help those endangered by soldiers, a flood, thieves, a fire, or a falling building, he should annul the *hametz* in his heart [and not try to return by any means, since his action may save a life]. However, if he was on his way to celebrate Passover at a place of his own choosing, he must return home at once to remove the *hametz*.[34]

Where it is the custom to do work until noon on the day before Passover, people may do so. Where it is the custom not to do work, people may not work. If a man went from a place where they do to a place where they do not, or from a place where they do not to a place where they do, we apply the more stringent custom of both the place which he has left [in case he should return] and the place to which he has gone. Let no man act in a manner different from local custom, lest it lead to conflict.[35]

Rabban Gamaliel used to say: Whoever has not said the verses concerning the following three things at Passover has not fulfilled his obligation: "Passover, unleavened bread and bitter herbs." "Passover," because God passed over the houses of our fathers in Egypt. "Unleavened bread," because our fathers were redeemed from Egypt. "Bitter herbs," because the Egyptians embittered the lives of our fathers in Egypt. In every generation each man must regard himself as though he himself came out of Egypt, for it is written "You shall tell your son on that day 'It is because of what the Lord did for me when I came out of Egypt' " [Ex. 13:8].[36]

Three references to rejoicing are found [in the Pentateuch] concerning the festival of Sukkot. "You shall rejoice in your festival" [Deut. 16:14], ". . . you shall be altogether joyful" [Deut. 16:15] and "you shall rejoice before the Lord your God seven days" [Lev. 23:40]. However, there is not one such reference concerning Passover. Why not? . . . Because that season of the year was a time of death for many Egyptians. [When Israel came out of Egyptian slavery, many Egyptians died at the Red Sea and, in addition, the Egyptian first-born had already died during the plagues.] Thus indeed is our practice: All seven days of Sukkot we recite the prayer of Hallel [joyous praise of the Lord] but on Passover we recite the prayer of Hallel in its entirety only on the first day. Why? Because of the verse, "Do not rejoice in the fall of your enemy, and let not your heart be glad when he stumbles" [Prov. 24:17].[37]

They mix him the second cup [of the four cups of wine which are drunk at the Passover table]. Then the son asks his father—and if the son does not understand the procedure, his father teaches him how to ask—"Why is this night different from other nights? On all other nights we may eat either leavened or unleavened bread, but on this night we eat only unleavened bread. On all other nights we may eat all types of herbs, but on this night we eat only bitter herbs. On all other nights we eat meat roasted, stewed or cooked, but on this night we eat only roasted meat. On all other nights we dip but once, but on this night we dip twice." The father instructs the son according to the understanding of the son. He begins with the disgrace and ends with the glory. And he expounds, beginning with "A wandering Aramean was my father . . . " [Deut. 26:5] and continuing until he finishes the entire section.[38]

On the night of Passover Jews sit down to a ceremonial meal at which the ritual symbols described just above, the bitter herb and the matzoth, are eaten as an act of symbolic remembering. A stylized version of the story of the exodus is told; it begins by having the youngest member of the family ask four ritualized questions (quoted above) about the meaning of the feast. Here are a few excerpts from the Passover ritual (the Haggadah), representing some of the "answers" that are given him.

We were slaves to Pharaoh in Egypt, but the Lord our God brought us out of there with a mighty hand and an out-stretched arm. If the Holy One, praised be He, had not brought our forefathers out of Egypt, then we, our children and our children's children would be slaves to Pharaoh in Egypt.

Though all of us might be wise, all of us learned and all of us elders, though all of us might know the Torah well, it is our duty to tell the story of the exodus from Egypt. And the more one tells of the exodus from Egypt, the more praiseworthy he is. . . .

At first our forefathers were idol-worshippers, but now God has brought us near to His service, as it is written, "Joshua said to all the people: Thus says the Lord, God of Israel, 'In olden times your fathers lived beyond the river [Terah, the father of Abraham and Nahor] and they served other gods. But I took your father Abraham from there and led him throughout the land of Canaan and I increased his descendants. I gave him Isaac, and to Isaac I gave Jacab and Esau. I gave to Esau Mount Seir as an inheritance while Jacob and his children went down to Egypt.' "

Praised is He who keeps His promise to Israel, praised is He. . . .

In every generation a person is obliged to see himself as though he personally came out of Egypt, as it is written, "You shall tell your son on that day saying: This is because of what the Lord did for *me* when I left Egypt." It was not our ancestors alone that the Holy One, praised be He, redeemed, but He redeemed us as well, along with them, as it is written, "He brought *us* out of there, in order to lead us to, and give us, the Land which He promised to our fathers."

Therefore are we obliged to thank, praise, laud, glorify and exalt, to honor, bless, extol and adore Him who performed all these wonders for our fathers and for us: He brought us out of slavery into freedom, out of sorrow into happiness, out of mourning into a holiday, out of darkness into daylight and out of bondage into redemption. Let us then sing Him a new song: Halleluyah![39]

SHABUOTH

In the ancient agricultural calendar this festival was marked by bringing the first fruits of the harvest to the Temple. In the cycle of Jewish historical memory, Shabuoth is the day of the encounter at Sinai, when God revealed Himself to Moses and the Jewish people. The Voice was heard speaking the Ten Commandments. Jewish piety has embroidered on the meaning of this encounter in a myriad of ways. One of the most imaginative and poetic among the many is the idea that at Sinai God and Israel were "married" (the essential image, as we have seen earlier, of the rabbinic commentary on the Song of Songs). There are a number of examples in Jewish literature of "marriage contracts" between God and Israel, with heaven and earth "signing" as witnesses.

You shall count seven weeks. Begin to count the seven weeks from the time you first put the sickle to the standing grain. Then you shall keep the Feast of Weeks to the Lord your God with the tribute of a freewill offering from your hand, which you shall give as the Lord your God blesses you. And you shall rejoice before the Lord your God, you and your son and your daughter.[40]

I am the Lord your God who brought you out of the land of Egypt, out of the house of bondage. You shall have no gods before Me.

You shall not make for yourself a graven image, nor the likeness of anything that is in heaven above or in the earth beneath, nor of those things that are in the waters under the earth. You shall not bow down to them, nor serve them, for I, the Lord your God, am a jealous God, visiting the iniquity of the fathers upon the children to the third and fourth generations of those that hate Me, and showing mercy to the thousandth generation of those that love Me and keep My commandments.

You shall not take the name of the Lord your God in vain, for the Lord will not hold him guiltless that takes His name in vain.

Remember the Sabbath day, to keep it holy. Six days shall you labor, and do all your work, but the seventh day is the Sabbath of the Lord your God; you shall do no work on it, you, nor your son, nor your daughter, nor your manservant, nor your maidservant, nor your beast, nor the stranger that is within your gates. For in six days the Lord made heaven and earth, the sea and all that is in it, and rested on the seventh day. Therefore the Lord blessed the seventh day and sanctified it.

Honor your father and your mother, that you may live long upon the land which the Lord your God gives you.

You shall not kill.

You shall not commit adultery.

You shall not steal.

You shall not bear false witness against your neighbor.

You shall not covet your neighbor's house; neither shall you covet his wife, nor his servant nor his handmaid, nor his ox, nor his ass, nor anything that is his.[41]

"Your two breasts are like two fawns, twins of a gazelle . . . " (Song of Songs 4:5). This alludes to the two tablets upon which were inscribed the Ten Commandments, each tablet the "twin" of the other. The five commandments on the first tablet correspond to the five commandments on the second tablet. "I am the Lord your God" corresponds to

"You shall not kill," for the murderer diminishes the image of the Holy One, praised be He, [as man is created in the image of God]. "You shall have no other gods" corresponds to "You shall not commit adultery," for one who whores after idolatrous worship is like an "adulterous wife, who receives strangers instead of her husband" [Ezek. 16:32]. "You shall not take the name of the Lord your God in vain" corresponds to "You shall not steal," for the thief will be led to taking a false oath. "Remember the Sabbath day" corresponds to "Do not bear false witness," for whoever desecrates the Sabbath bears false witness against his Creator, declaring [by his action] that He did not rest on the seventh day, after Creation. "Honor your father and your mother" corresponds to "You shall not covet," for one who is covetous [of his neighbor's wife] will in the end beget a son who will treat him with disrespect and who will honor one who is not his father.[42]

SUKKOTH

To discuss the Sukkoth festival here is to step somewhat out of chronological order, for in the calendar of the Jewish year this festival occurs after the High Holy Days, Rosh Hashanah and Yom Kippur. Nonetheless, Sukkoth belongs together with Passover and Shabuoth, for it is the last of the three "pilgrim festivals." Like them, it has a dual significance. In the ancient Palestinian agricultural calendar it was the end of the harvest, when everybody moved out into the field, living in tents, in order to complete the work before the winter rains began. The Bible also gives us a historical reason for prescribing that one must live in a temporary abode specially erected for the festival; it is a way of remembering the forty years of wandering by the Jews in the desert on their way to the Promised Land.

From the fifteenth day of this seventh month shall be kept the feast of tabernacles, seven days to the Lord. The first day

shall be a holy convocation; you shall do no servile work.
Seven days you shall bring an offering made by fire to the
Lord. On the eighth day shall be a holy convocation, and you
shall bring an offering made by fire to the Lord. It is a day of
solemn assembly; you shall do no servile work.[43]

From the fifteenth day of the seventh month, when you
shall have gathered in all the fruits of the land, you shall
celebrate the feast of the Lord seven days; on the first day
and on the eighth day there shall be a solemn rest. And you
shall take on the first day the fruit of goodly trees, and
branches of palm trees, and boughs of thick trees, and willows
of the brook, and you shall rejoice before the Lord your God
seven days. And you shall keep it a feast to the Lord seven
days in the year. It shall be a statute forever throughout your
generations. In the seventh month you shall celebrate this
feast. You shall dwell in booths seven days; all that are
native-born in Israel shall dwell in booths, that your posterity
may know that I made the children of Israel dwell in booths,
when I brought them out of the land of Egypt; I am the Lord
your God.[44]

A *Sukkah* [the temporary shelter erected for the Sukkoth
holiday] more than twenty cubits high is not valid; though
Rabbi Judah declares it valid. If it is not ten handbreadths
high or does not have three sides or if the unshaded area is
larger than the shaded area, it is not valid. The School of
Shammai declare an old *Sukkah* invalid, and the School of
Hillel declare it valid. What is deemed an "old" *Sukkah*?
One that was built thirty days before the holiday. However,
if it was made specifically for the holiday, even at the beginning of the year [i.e. immediately after the preceding Sukkoth
holiday], it is valid.[45]

Our sages taught: "You shall dwell in booths for seven
days" [Lev. 23:42]. This means that you should consider the
booth as a fixed dwelling for these days. This statement led
them to say that a man should consider his *Sukkah* [booth]
permanent and his house temporary for these seven days of
Sukkoth. How? He should transfer his finest furniture and

beds to the *Sukkah*, eat and drink in the *Sukkah* and study in the *Sukkah*.⁴⁶

If a palm branch [for a lulab*] was acquired by robbery or was withered, it is not valid. If it came from an *asherah* [a tree worshiped by idolaters] or from an apostate city [*see* Deut. 13:16], it is not valid. If its tip was broken off or if its leaves were split, it is not valid. If its leaves were spread apart, it is valid. Rabbi Judah says: It may be tied up at the end. The thorn-palms of the Oron Mount [near Jerusalem] are valid. A palm-branch three handbreadths in length is valid if it is long enough to shake.⁴⁷

Rabbi Eleazar said: Why were seventy bullocks offered in the Temple at Sukkoth? [This is a comment to Mishnah *Sukkah* 5:6. Biblical law in Num. 29:13–32 ordains that thirteen bullocks be offered on the first day of Sukkoth. During the remaining six days the number of bullocks was reduced by one each day.] Seventy were offered for the sake of the seventy nations of the world [to atone for them]. Why was a single bullock offered on the eighth day? For the single nation [i.e. Israel]. . . . Rabbi Johanan said: Alas for the idolaters! They have suffered a great loss without even knowing what they have lost. While the Temple stood, the altar could atone for them; but now [since the Temple has been destroyed] what will atone for them?⁴⁸

This interpretation of the meaning of the "four species" is from the *Sefer Hahinukh* ("The Book of Education"), the first medieval volume of Jewish religious instruction. It was composed by Aaron Halevi of Barcelona, a Spanish Talmudist who lived at the end of the thirteenth century.

. . . Since the rejoicing [on the holiday of Sukkoth] might cause us to forget the fear of God, He, praised be He, has

---

* Lulab consists of branches of palm, myrtle and willow bound together; they are held during part of the liturgy, along with an ethrog (citron) during holiday of Sukkoth [Lev. 23:40].

commanded us to hold in our hands at that time certain objects which should remind us that all the joy of our hearts is for Him and His glory. It was His will that the reminder be the four species . . . for they are all a delight to behold. In addition, the four species can be compared to four valuable parts of the body. The *ethrog* [citron] is like the heart, which is the temple of the intellect, thus alluding that man should serve his Creator with his intellect. The *lulav* is like the spinal cord, which is essential for the body, alluding that man should direct his entire body to His service, praised be He. The myrtle is like the eyes, alluding that man should not be led astray after his eyes on a day when his heart rejoices. The willow branch is like lips. Man completes his actions through speech, and thus the willow branch alludes to the fact that man should control his mouth and the words that issue from it, fearing God, praised be He, even at a time of rejoicing.[49]

Jonathan Eibschutz (1690–1764) was essentially a product of East European Jewry, though he served as rabbi in Metz, France, and Hamburg, Germany. A master of all fields of Jewish learning, including the cabala, he was particularly noted as a preacher.

On Sukkoth, the end of the Days of Repentance, the Torah advises us to accept the exile and to consider all the world as void, as a shadow. Therefore we are told to leave permanent dwellings for a temporary one, to teach that we are strangers on the earth, without permanence, and that our days are like a shadow lasting a night, blown away by a wind. What does man profit from all his labors under the sun? All his days let his eyes be on high to the One who dwells in the heavens. Therefore one must use twigs and branches for the roof of the *Sukkah* [booth], that the stars be clearly visible from inside it, that one might direct his heart to heaven. The Holy One praised be He will have compassion for the afflicted and the poor, for He knows man's low state. . . . What man can escape the afflictions and alterations of time? . . . It is profound advice to observe the seven days of Sukkoth, for the verdict of the judgment of the Day of Atonement is not definitely set until Shemini Atzereth [at the end of the Sukkoth holiday]. We must then rejoice, trusting in the lovingkindness of the Lord, that He will judge our cause. Thus for the seven days of the festival. But the man who fears the word of the King of the universe will have a booth [Sukkah] not only during the festival of Sukkoth. During the whole year, everything for him will be a temporary dwelling, and he will sleep in the shadow of the *Sukkah* and leave his permanent dwelling.[50]

A comparable thought is expressed in a contemporary sermon.

Sukkoth is the harvest festival. At the conclusion of the harvest in ancient Israel, the tithes were due. The Jewish farmer had then to exercise his generosity by setting aside a portion of the harvest for the priesthood and some of it for the support of the poor. Obviously, at the moment when the farmer found himself confronted by the commandment to give away some of his crop to charity, there was danger that the spirit of perversity would arise within him. He might reason: why should I give away that for which I have labored, which I have earned, to others? Therefore, it was ordained that men live in the *Sukkah*, in a temporary dwelling, during this festival. Its purpose was to suggest that man himself is but a temporary sojourner in this world, that his home is his but for a moment, that nothing really permanently belongs to anyone, for the earth is the Lord's. This sobering thought is a bar to selfishness and a spur to charity.[51]

The Sukkoth festival ends with an additional day "of solemn assembly." In contemporary Jewish practice this holiday is marked primarily by the festival of the Rejoicing in the Law. Throughout the year, in the prescribed ritual in the synagogue, the Five Books of Moses are read consecutively as the weekly lesson from the Bible. This cycle of readings ends and begins over again on this day. It is marked by joyous processions with the Scrolls of the Law, which are taken from the ark in which they rest, and by the calling of everyone in the synagogue to say a blessing at the reading desk over a passage from the Torah scroll.

Seven days [of Sukkoth] you shall present offerings by fire to the Lord. On the eighth day you shall hold a holy convocation and present an offering by fire to the Lord. It is a solemn assembly; you shall do no laborious work.[52]

"On the fifteenth day of the seventh month you shall have a holy convocation . . . you shall keep a feast to the Lord seven days. . . . On the eighth day you shall have a solemn assembly . . . " [Num. 29:12, 35]. This might be compared to a king who invited his children to a banquet for seven days. When it was time for them to leave, he said to them: My children, please, stay with me one more day. It is difficult for me to part with you.[53]

ROSH HASHANAH

Rosh Hashanah, the New Year, is the beginning of the annual cycle of the Jewish religious year. It falls on the first of the lunar month Tishri, which usually occurs some time in September. The ten days from Rosh Hashanah (literally, the "head of the year") through Yom Kippur (the Day of Atonement) are known as the "Ten Days of Repentance." These are the most solemn days of the year, for this is the period in which, in the image of the tradition, all the world is judged before God's heavenly throne. Nonetheless, solemn and serious as Rosh Hashanah is, it is not somber. It is the season of repentance —and of the faith that God accepts and forgives the contrite heart.

In the seventh month, on the first day of the month, you shall observe a day of solemn rest, a memorial proclaimed with blast of trumpets, a holy convocation. You shall do no laborious work and you shall present an offering by fire to the Lord.[54]

And Nehemiah, who was Tirshatha, and Ezra the priest and scribe, and the Levites who taught the people, said to all the people: "This is a holy day to the Lord your God; do not mourn, nor weep." For all the people wept when they heard the words of the law. And he said to them, "Go, eat fat meats and drink sweet wine, and send portions to him for whom nothing is prepared, for this day is holy to our Lord; be not sad, for the joy of the Lord is your strength." And the Levites stilled all the people, saying, "Hold your peace, for the day is holy; be not sorrowful." So all the people went to eat and drink, and to send portions, and to make great mirth, because they understood the words that he had taught them.[55]

Rabbi Abbahu said: Why is the horn of a ram sounded on Rosh Hashanah? The Holy One praised be He said, "Sound before Me the horn of a ram, that I might be reminded of the binding of Isaac, the son of Abraham, and thus consider your fulfillment of this commandment [of sounding a horn] as though you had bound yourselves upon an altar before Me. [See Gen. 22, where the ram is sacrificed in place of Isaac.][56]

Rabbi Kruspedai said, quoting Rabbi Johanan: On Rosh Hashanah [when the world is judged], three books are opened in the heavenly court; one for the wicked, one for the righteous, and one for those in between. The fate of the righteous is inscribed and sealed then and there: Life. The fate of the wicked is inscribed and sealed then and there: Death. The fate of those in between lies in doubt from Rosh Hashanah until Yom Kippur. If, during those days, they show their worth through their deeds, they are inscribed and sealed for Life; and if not, they are inscribed and sealed for death.[57]

Rabbi Pinhas and Rabbi Hilkiah said in the name of Rabbi Simon: Each year, all of the ministering angels appear before the Holy One, praised be He, and ask, "Lord of the Universe! When does Rosh Hashanah occur this year?" And He answers them, "Why do you ask Me? Let us inquire of the earthly court" [which in ancient times set the date of each new month and thus the entire calendar].

Rabbi Hoshayah taught: When the earthly court decrees "Today is Rosh Hashanah," the Holy One, praised be He, tells the ministering angels, "Set up the court room, and let the attorneys for defense and prosecution take their places, for My children have stated 'Today is Rosh Hashanah.' " But if the earthly court should reconsider and decide that the following day should be declared the first of the year, the Holy One, praised be He, tells the ministering angels "Set up the court room and let the attorneys for prosecution and defense take their places on the morrow, for My children have reconsidered and decided that tomorrow is to be declared the first of the year."

What is the reason for this? "For it is a statute in Israel, an ordinance of the God of Jacob" [Ps. 81:5]. However, if it is not a statute in Israel, it is not an ordinance of [for] the God of Jacob.[58]

Let not a repentant sinner imagine that he is remote from the estate of the righteous because of the sins and misdeeds that he has done. This is not true, for he is beloved and precious to God as if he had never sinned. Indeed, his reward is great, because he has tasted of sin and separated himself from it, having conquered his evil inclination. It is written in the Talmud, that "In the place where repentant sinners stand perfect saints cannot stand" (*Berakhot* 34b), i.e. their estate is higher than that of those who never sinned because they have had to struggle more fiercely to subdue their evil inclination.[59]

With the help of God, the eve of the holy Sabbath, 5591 [1831].

To my beloved son, Isaac, may his light shine;

I received your letter this very hour and I have no time at all to answer it properly. May the Almighty strengthen your heart and move you on the great and fearful day of Rosh Hashanah which is approaching, that you may make it your purpose henceforth to renew yourself each day for good. Do not lose a day without a period of solitary meditation, during which you will contemplate your ultimate purpose. Snatch each day as much study of Torah, prayer and good deeds as you will be able to steal from this passing shade, this vanity of vanities, this evanescent cloud. Remember well that all our days are nothing. Every man can snatch in them some piece of eternity on some level. More than this I am not free to write now.

The words of your father, who seeks your peace and prays for you,

Nathan of Nemirov[60]

The selections that follow, to the end of the section on Rosh Hashanah, are taken from the prescribed prayers of the Rosh Hashanah liturgy.

We will celebrate the mighty holiness of this day, a day of awe and anxiety. On this day Your kingdom is exalted, Your throne is established in grace, and You are enthroned in truth. Truly You alone are Judge, prosecutor, investigator and witness, recorder, sealer, scribe and teller. You remember all things forgotten; You open the book of records and it tells its own story, for it is signed by the hand of every man.

The great Shofar is sounded, and a still small voice is heard. Angels are seized with fear and trembling as they proclaim: "This is the Day of Judgment!" The hosts of heaven are to be arraigned in judgment, for in Your eyes even they are not free of guilt. All who enter this world pass before you as a flock of sheep. As the shepherd musters his flock, causing each one to pass beneath his staff, so You pass and number, record and visit every living soul, setting the measure of every creature's life and decreeing its destiny.

On New Year's Day the decree is inscribed and on the Day of Atonement it is sealed: How many shall pass away and how many shall be born, who shall live and who shall die, who shall attain the measure of his days and who shall not, who shall perish by fire and who by water, who by the sword and who by the beast, who by hunger and who by thirst, who by earthquake and who by plague, who by strangling and who by stoning, who shall have rest and who shall wander, who shall be at ease and who shall be afflicted, who shall be tranquil and who shall be disturbed, who shall become poor and who shall become rich, who shall be brought low and who shall be exalted.

But repentance, prayer and righteousness avert the severe decree.

For Your praise is like Your name, slow to anger and ready to forgive. You desire not the death of the sinner but that he turn from his way and live. And You wait for him until his dying day; perhaps he will repent and You will straightway receive him.

Truly, as Creator You know man's nature, for he is but flesh and blood. Man's origin is dust and he returns to dust. By the peril of his life he obtains his bread. He is like a fragile potsherd, like grass that withers and a flower that fades, like a fleeting shadow, a passing cloud, like the blowing wind and the floating dust, like a dream that vanishes.

But You are the eternal God and King.

There is no limit to Your years and no end to the length of Your days. No one can conceive Your glory or fathom Your mysteries. Your name befits You and You befit Your name; may our name be forever linked with Yours.[61]

This day the world was called into being; this day You cause all creatures of the universe to stand in judgment, as children or as servants. If as children, pity us as a father pities His children. If as servants, our eyes are turned to You, that You may deal graciously with us and declare our judgment, O revered and holy God.[62]

O Lord our God, grant that fear of You be set over all Your works and that reverence for You be manifest in all that You have created. May all Your creatures revere You and worship You. May they all unite into one fellowship to do Your will with a perfect heart. O Lord our God, we know that dominion, power and might are Yours. You are revered over all that You have created.

O Lord, grant glory to Your people, praise to those who revere You, hope to those who seek You and the courage to speak to those who yearn for You. Bring joy to Your land, gladness to Your city, renewed strength to David Your servant and light to the son of Jesse, Your anointed, speedily in our day.

Grant that the righteous see and be glad, that the just exult and that the pious rejoice in song. May iniquity close its mouth and all wickedness vanish like smoke, when You remove the dominion of tyranny from the earth.[63]

YOM KIPPUR

One day a year man attempts to serve God not as if he were man but as if he were an angel. The angels neither eat nor drink and their sole daily task is to praise God and live in His sight. So on Yom Kippur (the Day of Atonement) the Jew neither eats nor drinks anything at all, observing the strictest of fasts, and he spends all his waking hours in prayer. On that day, the conclusion of the "Ten Days of Repentance," the judgment of every man for the year to come is finally decided. It was legal procedure in the ancient Jewish law courts that the accused sat in the dock in an attitude of mourning; such an attitude is prescribed for all Jews on this most solemn day. But despite its solemnity, even on Yom Kippur the Jewish sense of at-homeness with God continues to exist. Note in particular the story of Rabbi Elimelekh of Lizhensk (died in 1787), one of the founders of Hasidism, in the section following.

On the tenth day of this seventh month shall be the Day of Atonement. There shall be a holy convocation to you, and you shall afflict your souls, and you shall bring an offering made by fire to the Lord. You shall do no servile work in this day, for it is a day of atonement, to make atonement for you before the Lord your God. Every soul that is not afflicted on this day shall be cut off from his people. And every soul that will do any work will I destroy from among his people. You shall do no work on that day; it is a statute forever throughout your generations, in all your dwellings. It is a sabbath of rest, and you shall afflict your souls beginning on the ninth day of the month, from evening until evening you shall keep your sabbath.[64]

Seven days before Yom Kippur, the High Priest was taken away from his household to a special chamber in the Temple court and another priest was prepared to take his place in the event that anything should happen to render him ineligible [by becoming ritually unclean or by suffering certain bodily defects] for fulfilling his duties.[65]

The High Priest placed both hands upon the bullock and made confession. And thus would he say: O God, I have committed iniquity, sinned and transgressed before You, I and my household. O God, forgive the iniquities, transgressions and sins of myself and of my house, as it is written in the Torah of Moses, Your servant, "On this day atonement shall be made for you, to cleanse you. You shall be clean of all your sins before the Lord" [Lev. 16:30]. And the people answered after him "Praised be the glory of His kingdom for ever and ever."[66]

[The High Priest then followed a similar procedure on behalf of the priestly House of Aaron (Mishnah *Yoma* 4:2) and on behalf of the entire House of Israel (Mishnah *Yoma* 6:2). —Ed.]

On Yom Kippur, eating, drinking, washing, anointing with oil, wearing of sandals and sexual intercourse are forbidden. A king or bride may wash their faces, and a woman after childbirth may wear sandals, according to Rabbi Eliezer. But the sages forbid it.[67]

Young children are not to fast on Yom Kippur. But one or two years before they come of age they should be trained [by fasting part of the day], that they may become well versed in the commandments.[68]

If a pregnant woman smells food and craves it on Yom Kıppur, she may be fed until she recovers. One who is ill may be fed at the word of experts [i.e. medical advisers]. If no experts are readily available, he may be fed at his own wish, until he says "Enough."[69]

The numerical value of the letters in the word "Satan" [Hebrew: *Hasatan*] is 364, the total number of days in a year, less one. Satan can accuse the Jewish people and lead them astray every day of the year, with the exception of Yom Kippur. On that day the Holy One, praised be He, says to Satan "You have no power over them today. Nevertheless, go and see what they are doing." When Satan finds them all fasting and praying, clothed in white garments like the angels, he immediately returns in shame and confusion. The Holy One asks him "How are My children?" Satan answers "They are like angels, and I have no power over them." Thereupon the Holy One, praised be He, puts Satan in chains and declares to His people "I have forgiven you."[70]

He who says "I will sin and repent, and sin again and repent again" will be given no chance to repent. If one says, "I will sin and Yom Kippur will effect atonement," then Yom Kippur effects no atonement for him. Yom Kippur effects atonement for a man's transgressions against God; but it effects atonement for a man's transgressions against his fellow man only if he has first appeased his fellow man.[71]

Rabbi Simeon ben Gamliel said: There were no happier days for the Jewish people than the fifteenth of Ab and Yom Kippur, on which the young girls of Jerusalem would venture forth. All of them would dress in simple white garments, borrowed from each other, so that not even the poorest among them need be embarrassed. . . . They would venture forth to dance in the vineyards. What would they sing as they danced?

"Lift up your eyes, young man, and look around, that you might make your choice. Look not for beauty, but look for family. 'Charm is deceitful and beauty is vain, but a God-fearing woman is much to be praised' [Prov. 31:30]."[72]

Rabbi Elimelekh of Lizhensk once sent his disciples on the eve of the Day of Atonement, to observe the actions of a tailor. "From him," he said, "you will learn what a man should do on this holy day." From a window they saw the tailor take a book from his shelf in which was written all the sins that he had committed throughout the entire year. Book in hand, the tailor addressed God: "Today, the day of forgiveness for all Israel, the moment has come for us—You, God, and myself—to settle our account. Here is the list of all my sins, but here also is another volume in which I have written down all the sins that You have committed, the pain, the woe and the heartache that You have sent me and my family. Lord of the universe, if we were to total the accounts exactly, You would owe me much more than I would owe You! But it is the eve of the Day of Atonement, when everyone is commanded to make peace with his fellow. Hence, I forgive You for Your sins if You will forgive me for mine." The tailor then poured himself a cup of wine, pronounced the blessing over it, and then exclaimed: "L'hayyim! [To life!], Master of the world. Let there now be peace and joy between us, for we have forgiven each other, and our sins are now as if they never were."

The disciples returned to Rabbi Elimelekh, recounted the tale of what they had seen and heard and complained that the tailor's words were overly impudent before Heaven. Their master answered that God Himself and His heavenly court had come to listen to what the tailor had said in great simplicity, and that the tailor's words had caused great joy in all the spheres.[73]

It is written in the liturgy of Rosh Hashanah:
"And the angels will hasten, and fear and trembling will seize them, and they will say, Behold it is the Day of Judgment, to judge the hosts of heaven in justice." Why quote the hosts of heaven? When God sits as Judge over Israel, he also

judges the angels. The angels themselves were created only so that they may raise the prayers of Israel on high. The Almighty desires that on this day they should be defenders of Israel before His judgment seat. He scrutinizes the angels to determine whether they are carrying out this responsibility of theirs perfectly. When Rosh Hashanah comes, the angels begin to tremble, for fear that they are not carrying out the will of their Creator.[74]

On the Day of Atonement it is the custom to wear a shroud, which is a white and clean garment used as the last raiment of the dead. This custom acts to implant in man's heart humility and submission to the Divine will. (Gloss of Rabbi Moses Isserlin, *Orah Hayyim*, 510).

Rabbi Moses Teitelbaum once commented on this passage on the night of Yom Kippur, as follows: "Brethren, heed well that these garments which we are now wearing will be our apparel when we go to the next world, to account to the King of kings. Let us therefore imagine that we are now standing in these robes before the heavenly throne. Would we not be completely repentant? But repentance does not help after death. It does help now; therefore let us be remorseful with all our heart for our sins, and truly resolve not to sin again."[75]

The most famous of Jewish prayers is the Kol Nidre, the prayer with which the evening service of Yom Kippur begins. (All Jewish holidays and the Sabbath begin at sundown, for the "day" of the religious calendar is from sundown to sundown.) It is a declared and unalterable view of Judaism that man's prayers even on Yom Kippur can atone only for the sins between him and God; the sins that he has committed to the hurt of other men he must repent for by getting their pardon. The Kol Nidre came into the ritual in the early Middle Ages as a form of annulling those vows that man had made to God, *not* whatever obligations a man might have assumed to another. In Jewish sentiment the Kol Nidre prayer has been associated with the secret synagogues of the Marranos in medieval Spain. These forced converts to Christianity supposedly made it possible for themselves to say the Yom Kippur prayers with clear conscience by first anulling the vows to another faith that they had taken under duress. The haunting melody of the Kol Nidre is perhaps the best known in all of Jewish liturgy.

By the authority of the heavenly court and the earthly court, with the sanction of God and the sanction of the congregation, we hereby declare it permissible to pray together with those who have transgressed.

Of all vows, bonds, promises, obligations and oaths wherewith we have avowed, sworn and bound ourselves from this Day of Atonement to the next Day of Atonement, may it come unto us for good;—of all these vows we hereby repent. They shall be absolved, released, annulled, made void, and of no effect; they shall not be binding, nor shall they have any power. Our vows shall not be vows; our bonds shall not be bonds; and our oaths shall not be oaths.[76]

Ten times on Yom Kippur the liturgy prescribes the saying of the "confession." It is characteristic of Judaism that the confession obviously includes more sins than perhaps the greatest of sinners could have committed and that it is said not in the singular but in the plural. In the deepest sense, we are each responsible for the sins of all men.

Our God and God of our fathers, let our prayer come before You. Hide not from our supplication, for we are neither so brazen nor so arrogant as to say before You, O Lord our God and God of our fathers, "We are righteous and have not sinned"; truly, we have sinned.

We have trespassed, we have betrayed, we have robbed, we have spoken slander. We have perverted what is right, we have wrought wickedness, we have been presumptuous, we have done violence, we have forged lies. We have given evil counsel, we have spoken falsely, we have scoffed, we have revolted, we have blasphemed, we have been rebellious, we have been perverse, we have transgressed, we have oppressed, we have been stiff-necked. We have acted wickedly, we have acted corruptly, we have committed abomination, we have gone astray, we have led others astray.

We have turned away from Your good commandments and judgments and it has not profited us. You are righteous in all that has befallen us, for You have acted truthfully while we have wrought unrighteousness.

What shall we say before You, who dwell on high, and what shall we recount before You, who abide in the heavens? You know all things, hidden and revealed.

You know the mysteries of the universe, and the hidden secrets of all living. You search out the innermosts reason and probe the heart and mind. Nothing is concealed from You, or hidden from Your sight.

May it therefore be Your will, O Lord our God and God of our fathers, to forgive us for all our sins, to pardon us for all our iniquities, and to grant us atonement for all our transgressions.[77]

We must mention here the more important minor festivals and fast days of the Jewish religious calendar. These are the eight days of Hanukkah, which commemorates the deliverance of the Maccabees from their Syrian and Greek oppressors; its chief ritual is the kindling of candles for eight days. Purim marks the triumph of Mordecai and Esther over the wicked Haman in Persia. The story of that event as told in the Book of Esther is read in the synagogue. The most solemn of non-Biblical fasts is the Ninth of Ab, which was ordained by the rabbis in memory of the destruction of the Temple. Indeed, according to rabbinic tradition, both the First and the Second Temples were destroyed on the Ninth of Ab. This fast is as complete as that of Yom Kippur. It is a day of mourning, and the Book of Lamentations is read. But on the Sabbath immediately following this somber fast the ecstatic words of Isaiah, "Comfort ye, comfort ye, My people . . . speak to the heart of Jerusalem and cry out to it . . . that its sin is forgiven," are read in the synagogue service.

CHAPTER FIVE

Land

THE HOLINESS OF THE LAND

There is hardly a major passage in the Five Books of Moses which fails to refer to and to reiterate the promise that God made to Abraham, that the land of Canaan would be his inheritance and that of his descendants. Judah Halevi expressed the classic view of Jewish faith that the people of Israel is the heart of humanity (*see above*, Chapter I); a few paragraphs below, in this section, there is a comparable image from rabbinic literature, that the Holy Land is the navel of the world. This land was fashioned by God for a particular service to Him, that its very landscape should help mold the character and spirit of His beloved people.

The Bible itself was already aware of the problem that the land was inhabited by others and that they might therefore claim ownership. It offers two answers: that the tribes living in the land were guilty of many sins, thus defiling it, and that no people could claim ultimate ownership in any land, for the earth is the Lord's. The comment of Rashi on the first verse of Genesis, with which we begin this section, expands on the second argument to "explain" why the Bible needed to begin with the story of creation. This argument has had a long history; it recurs in so modern a writer as Martin Buber in an answer two decades ago to Mahatma Gandhi: "It seems to me that God does not give any one portion of the earth away.

... The conquered land is, in my opinion, only lent even to the conqueror who has settled on it—and God waits to see what he will make of it."

God dwells particularly in the Holy Land, and yet He is present everywhere, for the heavens and the heavens of the heavens cannot contain Him. In other words, everything that can be said about the doctrine of the chosenness of Israel applies to His choice of the land. It is ultimately a mystery. Like the doctrine of the chosenness of the people, it has been and remains a powerful and impassioned motif of Jewish faith.

"In the beginning God created the heavens and the earth" [Gen. 1:1]. Rabbi Isaac said: The Torah [which is the book of Law for the Jewish people] should have commenced with the verse "This month shall be unto you the first of the months" [Ex. 12:2], for that is the first commandment in the Bible to the Jewish people as a whole. Why, then, does it commence with the account of Creation? Because of the following: "He has told His people the power of His works [i.e. an account of the work of Creation] in order that He might give them the heritage of the nations" [Ps. 111:6]. Should the people of the world tell the Jewish people, "You are robbers, because you took the land of the seven nations of Canaan by force," they could reply, "All the earth belongs to the Holy One, praised be He. He created it and gave it to whom He pleased. When He willed, he gave it [the Land] to them, and when He willed He took it from them and gave it to us."[1]

I will give to you, and to your descendants after you, the land of your sojournings, all the land of Canaan, for an everlasting possession; and I will be their God.[2]

And when the time drew near that Israel [Jacob] must die, he called to his son Joseph and said to him, "If now I have found favor in your sight, put your hand under my thigh, and promise to deal loyally and truly with me. Do not bury me in

Egypt, but let me lie with my fathers. Carry me out of Egypt and bury me in their burying place.[3]

Now when all these things shall have come upon you, the blessing and the curse, which I have set before you, and you shall be touched with repentance among all the nations among whom the Lord your God shall have scattered you, and shall return to the Lord your God, and obey His commandments, as I command you this day, you and your children, with all your heart and with all your soul, then the Lord your God will turn your captivity and will have mercy upon you, and will gather you again out of all the nations among whom he scattered you. If you be driven as far as the uttermost parts of heaven, the Lord your God will bring you back from there. And the Lord your God will bring you into the land which your fathers possessed, and you shall possess it, and blessing you He shall make you more numerous than your fathers were.[4]

Is it then to be thought that God shall indeed dwell upon earth? For if heaven and the heaven of heavens cannot contain You, how much less this house which I have built. But have regard for the prayer of Your servant and to his supplication, O Lord my God, to hearken to the cry and the prayer which Your servant prays before You this day: That Your eyes may be open upon this house night and day, upon the house of which You have said, "My name shall be there," to hearken to the prayer which Your servant shall pray toward this place; that You may hearken to the supplication of Your servant and of Your people Israel, whenever they shall pray toward this place. Hear them in Your dwelling place in heaven, and when You hear, forgive.[5]

Just as the navel is found at the center of a human being, so the Land of Israel is found at the center of the world, as it is stated: "Who dwell at the center of the earth" [Ezek. 38:12], and it is the foundation of the world. Jerusalem is at the center of the Land of Israel, the Temple is at the center of Jerusalem, the Holy of Holies is at the center of the Temple, the Ark is at the center of the Holy of Holies and the Foundation Stone is in front of the Ark, which point is the foundation of the world.[6]

Even after the destruction of the Temple in Jerusalem and the Exile of Jewry from the land, its holiness remained. The rabbis of the Talmud enacted this doctrine into law.

One may compel his entire household to go up with him to the Land of Israel, but none may be compelled to leave it. All of one's household may be compelled to go up to Jerusalem [from any other place in the Land of Israel], but none may be compelled to leave it.[7]

One should live in the Land of Israel, even in a city the majority of whose people are not Jews, rather than live outside of the Land, even in a city the majority of whose people are Jews. Whoever lives in the Land of Israel is considered to be a believer in God. . . . Whoever lives outside of the Land is considered to be in the category of one who worships idols. . . . Whoever lives in the Land of Israel lives a sinless life, as it is written, "The people who dwell there will be forgiven their iniquity" [Isa. 33:24]. . . . Whoever is buried in the Land of Israel is considered as though he were buried beneath the Altar. . . . Whoever walks a distance of four cubits in the Land of Israel is assured of a place in the world to come.[8]

Living in the Land of Israel equals in import the performance of all the commandments of the Torah.[9]

Rabbi Zeira said: Even the conversation of those who live in the Land of Israel is Torah.[10]

Ten measures of wisdom came into the world. The Land of Israel took nine, and the rest of the world took one.[11]

The Land of Israel is holier than all other lands.[12]

The atmosphere of the Land of Israel makes men wise.[13]

The Holy One, praised be He, said: A small group of men in the Land of Israel is dearer to Me than the Great Sanhedrin outside of the Land.[14]

A man may enter into a contract [verbally, with a non-Jew] for the purpose of acquiring a house in the Land of Israel, even on the Sabbath [on which day such a transaction is usually forbidden].[15]

Jerusalem is the light of the world, as it is stated: Nations shall walk by your light [Isa. 60:3]. Who is the light of Jerusalem? The Holy One, praised be He, as it is written: The Lord will be your everlasting light [Isa. 60:19].[16]

Ten measures of beauty came into the world; nine for Jerusalem and one for the rest of the world.[17]

In every age, even during the dangerous days of the Crusades, there were pietists who obeyed the commandment to dwell in the Holy Land. The Jewish community in Palestine was often few in number, but some always came to replenish it. The prayer book abounds in expressions of longing for the Land, but the tie through the ages was not merely emotional. Even in the unlikeliest circumstances it remained the continuing tale of "ascents" (for to go to the Holy Land meant to the Jew to ascend in degree). Here is a letter written by one such pietist who went to Palestine, Isaiah Hurwitz (1555–1630), a distinguished Talmudist who was born in Prague and ended his days in Safed.

Although Jerusalem lies in ruins now, it is still the glory of the whole earth. There is peace and safety, good food and delicious wine. . . . The Sephardim also increase much in Jerusalem, even in the hundreds, and they build big houses here. We consider all this a sign of deliverance, may it come speedily. Within a short time, you will hear, with the help of the Lord, that the community of the Ashkenazim is great indeed and venerable. For I know that many will come there who are desirous of joining me. May the Lord grant me life and health. I shall develop a wonderful activity for the study of the Torah which so far has been without a right guidance. That is why, because of our sins, ruin came. I wish to become a faithful shepherd to them. It is also my intention to report the state of affairs here to the leaders of our people in Poland, to the sages among the leaders in Bohemia and to spread truth and confidence in every respect. . . .

My beloved children, tell everybody who intends to go to the Holy Land to settle in Jerusalem. Let nobody assume that I give this advice because I shall settle there. Far be this from me! But I give this advice in all sincerity because all is good there and nothing is lacking. The city is enclosed and surrounded by a wall. It is as big as Lwow, but the most important point is that it is particularly holy and the gate of heaven. I have firm confidence that the Lord will let much knowledge of Torah spread through me, so that the word may be fulfilled that out of Zion shall go forth the Law.[18]

Among the Hasidim, a sect which was founded in the eighteenth century, the Baal-Shem Tov himself attempted to go to the Holy Land, but failed. Legend has it that Satan opposed the plan, fearing that the encounter between the holiest man of the generation and the sacred soil of the Promised Land would produce such holiness that the Messiah would come. The Baal-Shem Tov's great-grandson, Rabbi Nahman of Bratslav, did succeed in reaching the Holy Land, but did not stay there more than a few months. The story of his journey, too, has been embellished with many legends. Upon his return Rabbi Nahman told his disciples that he had been reborn and that his true teaching could only be that which he would say after the refreshment of his soul in the Holy Land. The version below is from the authorized account of Rabbi Nahman's teachings written by his faithful disciple, Rabbi Nathan of Nemerov.

Rabbi Nahman of Bratslav lived in the Land for only six months, and most of this time he spent in Tiberias, engaged in the study of *kabbalah* and mystic discipline. He made haste to return to his disciples, in order to bring the message of the Land to them. From this time forth, Rabbi Nahman was another man.

His disciples have borne witness that all the life which he possessed came only from his having lived in the Land of Israel. Every thought and opinion which was his came only from the power of his having lived in the Land of Israel, for the root of all power and wisdom is in the Land of Israel. It was his wish that all teachings which he had disclosed before he was in the Land of Israel not be recorded in his books. It was necessary to record only those new teachings which he propounded after he was in the Land of Israel, and it was necessary to write all of these, every single word.[19]

GALUTH (EXILE)

The Jewish people was exiled from the Holy Land into Babylonian captivity in Biblical days. Why did this happen? The Bible has a simple answer, that it was punishment for the sins of the people. Even less than the original inhabitants of the land did the chosen people have a right to defile the soil that God had given it. Would God forsake them utterly on foreign soil? No, is the answer of prophets and psalmists. The God of all the world is present in Babylonia, too. After the term of their punishment is over they will be restored. But the exile wore on, especially the Second Exile after the year 70, and the most self-critical of peoples could not really believe that its suffering was entirely the result of its own sins. The doctrine of the "suffering servant" was invoked and expanded, that the people of Israel in the mysterious will of God was bearing not only its own sins but the sins of others. The Exile was a time of testing, a prolonged corporate trial, like God's trial of Abraham. The task of the people was to remain faithful and to remember Zion.

Who is the wise man that may understand this? Who is he to whom the mouth of the Lord has spoken, that he may declare it? Why is the land perished, and burnt up like a wilderness, so that no one passes through? And the Lord said: Because they have forsaken My law which I gave them, and have not heard My voice, and have not walked in it, but have gone after the perverseness of their own heart, and after Baalim, which their fathers taught them. Therefore thus says the Lord of hosts, the God of Israel: Behold I will feed this people with wormwood, and give them water of gall to drink. And I will scatter them among the nations, which they and their fathers have not known, and I will send the sword after them, until they be consumed.[20]

By the rivers of Babylon, there we sat and wept
When we remembered Zion.
On the willows in the midst thereof
We hung up our instruments.
For there they that led us into captivity
Asked of us words of song,
And those that carried us away said:
"Sing us one of the songs of Zion."

How shall we sing the Lord's song
In a foreign land?
If I forget you, O Jerusalem,
Let my right hand forget her cunning,
Let my tongue cleave to the roof of my mouth
If I remember you not,
If I set not Jerusalem above my chiefest joy.[21]

The wicked emperor Hadrian, who conquered Jerusalem, boasted, "I have conquered Jerusalem with great power." Rabbi Johanan ben Zakkai said to him, "Do not boast. Had it not been the will of Heaven, you would not have conquered it." Rabbi Johanan then took Hadrian into a cave

and showed him the bodies of Amorites who were buried
there. One of them measured eighteen cubits [approximately
thirty feet] in height. He said, "When we were deserving, such
men were defeated by us, but now, because of our sins, you
have defeated us."²²

Whenever Israel is enslaved, the *Shekhinah*, as it were, is
enslaved with them. . . . For it says "In all their affliction, He
was afflicted" [Isa. 63:10]. This teaches that He shares in the
affliction of the group, but what of the affliction of the individual? Scripture states, "He will call upon Me and I will answer him; I will be with him in trouble" [Ps. 91:15]. . . . It is
written, "From before Your people, whom You did redeem
to Yourself out of Egypt, the nation and its God" [after II
Sam. 7:23]. . . . Rabbi Akiva said: Were it not written in
Scripture, it would be impossible to say such a thing. Israel
said to God: You have redeemed Yourself, as it were. Likewise, you find that whenever Israel was exiled, the *Shekhinah*,
as it were, went into exile with them, as it is written, "I exiled
Myself to the house of your fathers when they were in Egypt"
[after I Sam. 2:27]. When they were exiled to Babylon, the
Shekhinah went into exile with them as it is written, "For your
sake I was sent to Babylon" [*after* Isa. 43:14]. When they
were exiled to Elam, the *Shekhinah* went into exile with them,
as it is written, "I will set My throne in Elam" [Jer. 49:38].
. . . And when they return in the future, *the Shekhinah*, as it
were, will return with them, as it is written, "Then the Lord
your God will return with your captivity" [Deut. 30:3]. This
verse does not state "The Lord will bring back" [Hebrew:
v'heshiv], but "He will return" [Hebrew: *v'shav*].²³

Judah Halevi lived in Spain and longed for Zion, to
which he went toward the end of his life. This poem is
part of the liturgy for the fast of the Ninth of Ab, which
commemorates the destruction of the Temple.

My heart is in the east, and I in the uttermost west.
How can I savour food? How shall it be sweet to me?

How shall I render my vows and my bonds, while yet
Zion lies beneath the fetters of Edom, and I in Arab
chains?
A light thing would it seem to me to leave all the good
things of Spain—
Seeing how precious in mine eyes it is to behold the dust
of the desolate sanctuary.[24]

Hasdai ibn Shaprut (915–970) was the principal minister in the court of the Caliph of Cordova and the leader of all Jewry in the Iberian peninsula. The letter below to the king of the Khazars is remarkable in its longing for the Holy Land, and equally remarkable is the answer that he received, which is here printed right after Hasdai's letter.

I, Hasdai, son of Isaac, may his memory be blessed, son of Ezra, may his memory be blessed, belonging to the exiled Jews of Jerusalem, in Spain, a servant of my Lord the King, bow to the earth before him and prostrate myself towards the abode of your Majesty, from a distant land. I rejoice in your tranquillity and magnificence, and stretch forth my hands to God in heaven that He may prolong your reign in Israel. . . . We, indeed, who are of the remnant of the captive Israelites, servants of my Lord the King, are dwelling peacefully in the land of our sojourning, for our God has not forsaken us. . . . He who tries the heart and searches the reins knows that I did none of these things [in trying to communicate with you] for the sake of my own honor, but only to know the truth, whether the Israelitish exiles anywhere form one independent kingdom and are not subject to a foreign ruler. If, indeed, I could learn that this was the case, then, despising all my glory, abandoning my high estate, leaving my family, I would go over mountains and hills, through seas and lands, till I should arrive at the place where my lord the King resides, that I might see not only his glory and magnificence, and that of his servants and ministers, but also the tranquility of the Is-

raelites. On beholding this my eyes would brighten, my reins
would exult, my lips would pour forth praises to God who
has not withdrawn His favor from His afflicted ones. Now,
therefore, let it please your Majesty, I beseech you to have
regard to the desires of your servant, and to command your
scribes who are at hand to send back a reply from your distant
land to your servant and to inform me fully concerning the
condition of the Israelites and how they came to dwell
there. . . .

One thing more I ask of my lord, that he would tell me
whether there is among you any computation concerning the
final redemption [i.e. Messianic redemption] which we have
been awaiting so many years, while we went from one captivity to another, from one exile to another. How strong is the
hope of him who awaits the realization of these events, and
Oh! how can I hold my peace and be restful in the face of the
desolation of the house of our glory and remembering those
who, escaping the sword, have passed through fire and water,
so that the remnant is but small. We have been cast down
from our glory, so that we have nothing to reply when they
say daily unto us, "Every other people has its kingdom, but
of yours there is no memorial on the earth." Hearing, therefore, the fame of my lord the King, as well as the power of his
dominions, and the multitude of his forces, we were amazed,
we lifted up our head, our spirit revived, and our hands were
strengthened, and the kingdom of my lord furnished us with
an argument in answer to this taunt. May this report be sub-
stantiated, for that would add to our greatness. Blessed be the
Lord of Israel who has not left us without a kinsman as defender nor suffered the tribes of Israel to be without an independent kingdom. May my lord prosper for ever.[25]

The Reply:

With reference to your question concerning the miraculous
end of days, our eyes are turned to the Lord our God and to
the wise men of Israel who dwell in Jerusalem and Babylon.
Although we are far from Zion, we have heard that because of
our iniquities the computations are erroneous; nor do we
know aught concerning this. But if it please the Lord, He will
do it for the sake of His great name; nor will the desolation

of His house, the abolition of His service and all the troubles
that have come upon us be lightly esteemed in His sight. He
will fulfil His promise, and "the Lord whom you seek shall
suddenly come to His temple, even the messenger of the
Covenant whom you delight in: behold, he shall come, saith
the Lord of hosts" [Mal. 3:1]. . . . May God hasten the redemption of Israel, gather together the captives and dispersed,
you and me and all Israel that love His name, in the lifetime
of us all.[26]

Each of the documents that follow, from various centuries, expresses the theme of mourning for Zion and the
desire to return. The first is from a letter of Rabbi Obadiah of Bartinoro, a distinguished Italian Talmudist of
the second half of the fifteenth century, who left his home
to settle in the Holy Land. He is here writing to his father
in Italy.

On Tuesday morning . . . we left Hebron, which is a day's
journey distant from Jerusalem, and came on as far as
Rachel's tomb, where there is a round, vaulted building in the
open road. We got down from our asses and prayed at the
grave, each one according to his ability. On the right hand of
the traveller to Jerusalem lies the hill on which Bethlehem
stands. . . .
From Bethlehem to Jerusalem is a journey of about three
miles. The whole way is full of vineyards and orchards. The
vineyards are like those in Romagna, the vines being low, but
thick. About three-quarters of a mile from Jerusalem, at a
place where the mountain is ascended by steps, we beheld the
famous city of our delight, and here we rent our garments, as
was our duty. A little farther on, the sanctuary, the desolate
house of our splendour, became visible, and at the sight of it
we again made rents in our garments.[27]

The next piece dates from the eleventh century. It is
part of a letter of recommendation written by the com-

munity of Salonica and addressed to the Jewish communities on the route to Palestine.

. . . We send greetings to you and feel it is our duty to inform you about the request of Mr. N. N. He is a Jew from Russia and stayed with us here in Salonica, where he met his relative, Mr. X. Y., who returned recently from the holy city of Jerusalem, may it be restored by the Lord for ever. When he was told about the splendor of Palestine, Mr. N. N. too became very desirous of going there and prostrating himself on the sacred spot. He asked us to give him these few lines in order to use them as a means of introduction.

Please help him to reach his goal by the proper route, with the support of reliable men, from town to town, from island to island. For he knows neither Hebrew nor Greek nor Arabic but only Russian, the language of his homeland.

At all times the house of Israel, our brethren . . . excelled in the strength of righteousness and the power of charity, and you know their reward.[28]

Here is another letter, written around 1550, by Jews of Salonica.

The two Hebrew men, the two good messengers whom you have sent to seek out a refuge for you, have arrived here, and we rejoiced when we saw them, but we were deeply afflicted in our hearts on hearing of the yoke which the nations are about to let fall on you, and of the sufferings of exile which have been heaped up and placed upon your neck. And even this does not satisfy the nations, their hand is stretched out to strike at you once more, as they say: "Let us drive out the Jews!" Because of this our heart is faint, and we are sorry for you because the enemy has prevailed. The only thing which comforts us by the mercy of the Lord, the Master of pity, praise to Him and to His gracious deeds, is that He has made us come hither to this vast place where we eat bread which

has not been given in pledge, to a land which the Lord cares
for from the beginning of the year even unto its end, and
where nothing is lacking. . . .

Therefore, our esteemed brethren, who combine judgment
with energy, do not hesitate to come hither and to enjoy the
best of this land, and do not wait until the Count-Palatine
tells you: "Rise up, and get you forth from among my people"
[Ex. 12:31], lest the Egyptians become urgent upon you and
send you out of the land in haste. You might not be able to
spare the time necessary for the preparation of the departure,
and the name of the Lord might, unfortunately, be profaned,
as happened with the painful expulsion of the unfortunate
Jews, descendants of Jacob, driven from Castile and Portugal,
who, pressed by time, were forced to change their faith, on
account of our great sins.

May the supreme Lord reunite the whole of Israel in the
one place which has been elevated from the beginning, the
place of our sanctuary; may your eyes and ours see Zion,
the peaceful abode, when the Lord will bring back the captives of Jacob, and when it will again be said: "The Lord will
be magnified from the border of Israel" [Mal. 1:5], because
He will break the yoke of the nations which weighs heavily
on your neck according to the desire of your heart, full of
the fear of God, and according to the desire of us who are
making vows for your welfare and for your deliverance, and
who invoke the Lord every day in favor of the remnant of
Israel.[29]

This prayer about the Exile is very famous indeed. It
was composed late in the eighteenth century by a great
Hasidic master, Rabbi Levi Isaac of Berditshev (1740-
1810).

Good morning to You, Lord of the world!
I, Levi Isaac, son of Sarah of Berditshev, am coming to you
     in a legal matter concerning Your people of Israel.
What do You want of Israel?

It is always: Command the children of Israel!
It is always: Speak unto the children of Israel!
Merciful Father! How many peoples are there in the world?
Persians, Babylonians, Edomites!
The Russians—what do they say?
 Our emperor is the emperor!
The Germans—what do they say?
 Our kingdom is the kingdom!
The English—what do they say?
 Our kingdom is the kingdom!
But I, Levi Isaac, son of Sarah of Berditshev, say:
 "Glorified and sanctified be His great name!"
And I, Levi Isaac, son of Sarah of Berditshev, say:
I shall not go hence, nor budge from my place
until there be a finish
until there be an end of exile—
"Glorified and sanctified be His great name!"[30]

Why the pain of the Exile? Spanish Jewry in the fifteenth century, the community which suffered intense persecution and, finally, expulsion in 1492, faced this question with particular sharpness. Solomon ibn Verga, a Spanish Jew who lived through the expulsion, gives poignant expression to the mood of that generation.

Surely from of old You are my holy God. We shall not die though fire consume us. With regularity our troubles appear, the latter in their severity causing the former to be forgotten. The happy of heart moan, the joy of our proudly exulting ones has ceased. In days to come, Jacob shall take root, all our enemies shall march forth to scatter us; the light is darkened by the clouds of our time; they have driven us to the final border; we have not retained strength and there is no breath left.

O God, You have expelled me time after time, but I have said that I shall bear the wrath of the Lord, for I have sinned. Defend, now, my cause, bring me out into light. Behold, new

troubles I declare; we look for brightness but we walk in gloom. Lions roar at us, fiercer than the evening wolves.
. . . answer me, O Lord my God; preserve our remnant, for if You oppose us, what can our latter end be? . . .

I remember days of old. You set our nest among the stars and the splendor of Your glory was upon us, but now You have brought us down from there. . . .

Send forth Your hand from on high, O Lord God, for there is no worm on earth as low as we are in our humiliation, like one forsaken among the dead. . . . If they increase the weight of his tombstone, he will not know it and if they attempt to trouble him, he will not understand. But the living takes his own continual troubles and confusions to heart; his soul is bitter day and night, like ours at this time. If our transgressions have increased . . . pray increase Your power as You have promised, shepherd Your people with Your staff; do not deliver up our survivors with mortal staff, merciful and compassionate God.

How can You tolerate more when You have witnessed the evil which has befallen Your people, how can You, when you have witnessed the destruction of the homeland of Your servants' children? Belittle not our troubles; regard us from Your holy habitation. In spite of all the persecutions we have followed You. Speedily robe Yourself with lovingkindness and deliver us, for Your sake.[31]

Rabbi Jacob Emden (1697-1776) and Rabbi Jonathan Eibshutz were fierce antagonists, but they agreed on the hope of the return to Zion as a central theme of Jewish piety. The first paragraph just below is by Emden, and the second, by Eibshutz.

We do not mourn properly over Jerusalem. Were we guilty of this transgression alone, it would be sufficient reason for the extension of the period of our Exile. In my opinion this is the most likely, most apparent and the strongest reason for all of the dreadful terrifying persecutions which have befallen us in Exile, in all the places of our dispersion. We have been hotly pursued. We have not been granted rest among the nations with our humiliation, affliction and homelessness, because this sense of mourning has left our hearts. While being complacent in a land not ours, we have forgotten Jerusalem; we have not taken it to heart. Therefore, "Like one who is dead have we been forgotten," from generation to generation sorrow is added to our sorrow and our pain.[32]

One must weep ceaselessly over the rebuilding of Jerusalem and the restoration of the glory of King David, for that is the object of human perfection. If we do not have Jerusalem and the kingdom of the House of David, why should we have life? . . . Since our many transgressions have led to the Destruction and to the desolation of our glorious Temple and the loss of the kingdom of the House of David, the degree to which we suffer the absence and the lack of good is known to all. Surely have we descended from life unto death. And the converse is also true: "When the Lord restores the captivity of Zion," we shall ascend from death unto life. Certainly the heart of anyone who possesses the soul of a Jew is broken when he recalls the destruction of Jerusalem.[33]

TENSION BETWEEN GALUTH AND RETURN

After the destruction of the First Temple, Jeremiah was convinced that the Exile would not end immediately. He therefore counseled the Jewish people to make peace with the condition that would last some generations by settling down into the civic life of Babylonia. Six centuries later, after the destruction of the Second Temple, Babylonia soon became a greater center of Jewish population and of Jewish learning than Palestine. There are therefore echoes in rabbinic writings of the notion that Babylonia is as good a place for the Jew to live in as Palestine. Medieval rabbis quieted their conscience for failing to fulfill the commandment to go to the Holy Land by emphasizing the difficulty of the journey and the fact that the laws of tithing and other such obligations which applied in the Holy Land could no longer be obeyed there.

Thus says the Lord of hosts, the God of Israel, to all that are carried away captives, whom I have caused to be carried away from Jerusalem to Babylon: Build houses, and dwell in them; plant orchards, and eat the fruit of them. Take wives, and beget sons and daughters, and take wives for your sons and give your daughters to husbands, and let them bear sons and daughters, and multiply there and be not diminished. And seek the peace of the city to which I have caused you to be carried away captives, and pray to the Lord for it, for in its peace shall be your peace. . . .

For thus says the Lord: After seventy years are accomplished for Babylon I will visit you, and I will perform My good word toward you, to bring you again to this place. For I know the thoughts that I think toward you, says the Lord, thoughts of peace and not of affliction, to give you a future and a hope. And you shall call upon Me, and you shall go; and you shall pray and I shall hear you. You shall seek Me and shall find Me, when you shall seek Me with all your heart. And I will be found by you, says the Lord, and I will turn your captivity, and I will gather you out of all nations, and from all the places to which I have driven you, says the Lord. And I will bring you back from the place to which I caused you to be carried away captive.[34]

Whoever lives in Babylon is considered as though he lived in the Land of Israel.[35]

Rabbi Berokia and Rabbi Eliezer were once walking by a gate outside of Tiberias, when they saw a coffin being brought into Israel from outside the Land. Rabbi Berokia said: Of what use is this? He lived and died outside of the Land, and now he has come to be buried in it! I would quote Scripture to him: In your life "you made My heritage an abomination" [Jer. 2:7] and in your death "you have come to defile My land" (*ibid*). Rabbi Eliezer said to him: Since he will be buried in the Land of Israel, the Holy One, praised be He, will grant him atonement, as it is written, "He makes expiation for the land of His people" [Deut. 32:43].[36]

This law [emphasizing the importance of living in the Land of Israel] is no longer enforced due to the risks inherent in a journey to the Land of Israel. Rabbenu Hayyim maintains that living in the Land of Israel is no longer a religious obligation because of the difficulty and impossibility of fulfilling many of the precepts involving the soil.[37]

Mordecai Kaplan here presents a widely accepted contemporary view. He argues that those Jews living in lands of freedom are not in Exile, while maintaining that the state of Israel has a particular importance for a present-day revival of Jewish culture and spiritual values. For him Israel is a social, political and cultural necessity for the creative survival of his very much this-worldly version of Judaism. Absent from his thinking is the mystery of the divine choice of a people and of the land for it. Peace, freedom and Jewish survival are his Messiah, not the Messiah of the traditional vision, who will appear in the world as the dramatic culmination of human history.

Jews in the Diaspora will continue to owe exclusive political allegiance to the countries in which they reside. The tie that binds Diaspora Jewry to Eretz Israel is a cultural and religious one. Culture and socioeconomic life are so closely interrelated that it is difficult for Diaspora Jewry to create new Jewish cultural values, since there is no possibility in the Diaspora of an autonomous Jewish social and economic life.

American Judaism is needed, and will long continue to be needed as a force to inspire and motivate our participation in the establishment of a Jewish commonwealth. . . .

. . . We have a part in the social, economic, and cultural life of America, and, unless we give to the common welfare of the American people the best that is in our power to give, we are not doing our full duty to our country. But as Jews, the very best we have to give is to be found in Judaism, the distillation of centuries of Jewish spiritual experience. As convinced Jews and loyal Americans, we should seek to incorporate in American life the universal values of Judaism, and to utilize the particular sancta of Jewish religion as an inspiration for preserving these universal values. To fail to do so would mean to deprive Judaism of universal significance and to render Jewish religion a mere tribalism that has no relevance to life beyond the separate interests of the Jewish group. The attitude of Jewish isolationists or the negators of the Diaspora, which would keep American Jewry with its loins perpetually girt for a hasty departure for Eretz Israel, is not likely to inspire our neighbors with confidence in the Jew, or with respect for Judaism.

Those of our young people who possess the abilities that are needed now in Eretz Israel to build there a productive economy for the rising Jewish Commonwealth, an economy based on the socialized exploitation of natural resources instead of on the exploitation of the weak by the strong, should by all means be encouraged to go to Eretz Israel. The colonizing and constructive effort in Eretz Israel should enlist those of our youth who possess the kind of pioneer spirit essential to nation-building. Our Jewish young men and women ought to be made to feel that their going to Eretz Israel to serve their own people would be as legitimate and noble an adventure as for other Americans to serve the various peoples in the Far East in a missionary or cultural capacity. But students who plan to go to Eretz Israel, with the expectation of engaging in some white-collar profession, would not render any specially needed service there, and only deprive American Jewish life of some needed service they might render here. We American Jews need desperately every available person who has the ability to transmute the cultural and religious values of our tradition into a living creative force.

. . . Those who despair of Jewish survival in the Diaspora, by maintaining that only in Eretz Israel can Judaism survive, evade the urgent task of rendering Judaism viable in America. Long-distance building of Eretz Israel is no less important than building it on the spot, but it cannot serve as a substitute for living a Jewish life here. Until Jews realize that the Jewish problem in the Diaspora and the Jewish problem in Eretz Israel are one, they are running away from reality and defeating their own purpose. Only as we assume the responsibility for having Judaism live wherever Jews are allowed to live are we likely to succeed in any of our Jewish undertakings.

There can be no question that in the Diaspora we Jews lack the spirit of dedication that goes with our people's renascence in Eretz Israel. We are without the magic power that comes with the spoken and creative Hebrew word. We are far from the land where the Jewish spirit is being reborn. But given the will, the intelligence and the devotion, it is feasible so to relive and to re-embody, within the frame of a democratic American civilization, the vital and thrilling experience of our people in Eretz Israel that, in the long run, we might achieve in our way as great and lasting a contribution to human values as they are achieving in theirs.[38]

THE RETURN

The ultimate return of Jewry to the Holy Land and the Messianic age are related to each other. The faith in God's promise is the ground for the sure and certain hope that the return will take place.

Thus says the Lord: Keep your voice from weeping and your eyes from tears; for your work shall be rewarded, says the Lord, and they shall come back from the land of the enemy. There is hope for your future, says the Lord, and your children shall come back to their own country.[39]

An ancient tradition states that Jerusalem will not be rebuilt until the ingathering of all the exiles. If anyone should tell you that all the exiles have been gathered but Jerusalem is not rebuilt, do not believe it. For the Psalmist first stated "The Lord builds up Jerusalem" and then "He gathers the dispersed of Israel" [Ps. 147:2].[40]

As for the principle of the redemption itself, that is something that must be accepted for several reasons. Among these are the validation presented by the miracles performed by Moses, who was the first to speak of these things. There are also the signs produced for the prophet Isaiah and other prophets who announced the redemption as well as the fact that He that sent them would undoubtedly carry out His promise, as is stated by Scripture: "That confirms the word of His servant, and performs the counsel of His messengers" [Isa. 44:26].

Another (reason why Israel's ultimate redemption must be accepted as a matter of course) is that God is just, doing no injustice, and He has already subjected this nation to a great and long-protracted trial, which undoubtedly serves partly as punishment and partly as a test for us. Whichever happens to be the case, however, there must be a limitation of time, for (such operations) cannot proceed endlessly. . . .

A (third) reason is that God is trustworthy in His promise, His utterance standing firm and His command enduring forever, as it is said in Scripture: "The grass withers, the flower fades, but the word of our God shall stand forever" [Isa. 40:8].

A (fourth) reason (for believing in our people's final redemption) is the parallel we can make between the promises concerning it and God's first promise, the one He had made to us at the time when we were in Egypt. He had then promised us only two things; namely, that He would execute judgment upon our oppressor and that He would give us great wealth. That is the import of His statement: "And also that nation, whom they shall serve, will I judge; and afterward they shall come out with great substance" [Gen. 15:14]. Yet our eyes have seen what He has done for us besides that; namely, the cleaving of the sea, and the Manna and the quail, and the assembly at Mount Sinai, and the arresting of the sun and other such things. All the more certain, therefore, (must the ultimate redemption be). For God has made us great and liberal promises of the well-being and bliss and greatness and might and glory that He will grant us twofold (in return) for the humiliation and the misery that have been our lot. Thus it is said in Scripture: "For your shame which was double

. . . therefore in their land they shall possess double" [Isa. 61:7].

Furthermore, what has befallen us has been likened by Scripture to a brief twinkling of the eye, whereas the compensation God will give us in return therefore has been referred to as His great mercy. For it says: "For a small moment have I forsaken you; but with great compassion will I gather you" [Isa. 54:7]. . . .

Therefore, also, do you find us patiently awaiting what God has promised us, not entertaining any doubts concerning it, nor worrying or despairing. On the contrary, our courage and tenacity increase constantly, as is expressed in Scripture: "Be strong, and let your heart take courage, all you that wait for the Lord" [Ps. 31:25].[41]

Everyone in Israel must in his heart steadfastly resolve to go to Eretz Yisrael and to remain there. But if he cannot go himself, he should, if his circumstances permit—whether he be a craftsman or a merchant—support some person in that country, and so do his part in restoring the Holy Land, which has been laid waste, by maintaining one of its rightful inhabitants.

He must feel the desire to pray there before the King's palace, to which the Divine Presence still clings, even in destruction. Therefore he who does not live in that country cannot give perfect service to God.

You shall not plan, God forbid, to settle in a place not in that country. The mistake our parents made was that of ignoring this precious land, and thereby they caused much suffering in the generations that came after them. The thought of this land was our solace in our bitter exile, when not one alone rose against us, for never could we find peace and rest. But when we forgot our yearning for that land, we ourselves were forgotten like the dead. Not one in a thousand fared forth to settle there, perhaps only one from a whole country, and two out of a whole generation. No heart longed for its love or was concerned with its welfare and no one yearned to behold it. Whenever we found a little rest, we thought we had come upon a new land of Israel and a new Jerusalem. And misfortune befell us because Israel lived in peace and enjoyed honors in Spain and in other countries, for more than a thousand years after the destruction of the Temple, and no son of Israel remained in the Holy Land. God is just. They were no longer aware that exile is their lot, and they mixed with the people among whom they lived, and learned their ways. No one at all yearned for Zion; it was abandoned and forgotten. We did not think of returning to our home. The city that contained the graves of our fathers was not our goal. We shared the joys of others.

We asked, "Who is the wise man that he may understand this? Wherefore is the land perished and laid waste like a wilderness?" And the Lord said: "Because they have forsaken My law" [Jer. 9:11–12]. For Israel is called God's heritage, and the land is His heritage, and the Torah [Law] is connected with both, with the people of God and the heritage of God, and whoever leaves the one has also abandoned the other.[42]

Eretz Israel and the Torah are one and the same thing. And had the land not previously been in the hands of the Canaanites, it would have spewed out Israel, those who sinned against the Torah, and never would they have been allowed to return. That was why the sheath had to be in existence before the core of the fruit, and the land had to remain in the hands of the Canaanites, for many years. But in reality, it was holy even then, for holiness was innate in it from time immemorial, save that then it was well hidden and none knew of it until our father Abraham came and began to reveal the holiness of the land. For he was a man of love. Love that seeks no return was the quality with which he sustained the world before the Torah was given, and it was this very love that was hidden in Eretz Israel: it was the hidden Torah, for Eretz Israel and the Torah are one and the same thing. Then, when Israel received the Torah, and came to Eretz Israel, they were able to continue in the revelation of holiness, and to lift hidden holiness into the open. And so, even though later on they offended the holiness that had been made apparent, and were lacking in the fulfillment of the Torah, they could still long endure in Eretz Israel, because of the strength of that love which seeks no returns, and that hidden Torah.

And even now that we are exiled from our land for the vast
number of our transgressions, Eretz Israel still persists in
holiness because of the strength of the hidden Torah and the
love that seeks no returns, the love that was hidden in the
land even when it was still in the hands of the Canaanites.
That is why we are always waiting to return to our land,
for we know that in secret it is ours.[43]

Modern Zionism was nurtured in the soil of the religious doctrines about the Holy Land and the return to it.
In its contemporary expression, however, it represents on
the surface a blending of three other things: the pain of
the Exile, in its modern manifestation in anti-Semitism;
the example of the national revivals in Europe and the
world as a whole in the past century or so and a secular-
ized version of the Messianic ideal, either by making an
end to the peculiarities of the situation of the Jew in the
world by gathering Jews into a nation of their own or,
after the creation of that state, by setting for it tasks of
larger importance for humanity than those a small people
would normally set for itself.

The passages below are from Leo Pinsker (1821–
1891), an early figure of Russian Zionism; from Theodor
Herzl (1860–1904), the greatest figure of modern Zionism and from Solomon Schechter. The first two were
primarily secular thinkers; the third, a modern religionist
of conservative bent.

The Jews are not a living nation; they are everywhere
aliens; therefore they are despised. The civil and political
emancipation of the Jews is not sufficient to raise them in the
estimation of the peoples.

The proper and the only remedy would be the creation of
a Jewish nationality, of a people living upon its own soil, the
auto-emancipation of the Jews; their emancipation as a nation
among nations by the acquisition of a home of their own.

We should not persuade ourselves that humanity and enlightenment will ever be radical remedies for the malady of our people. The lack of national self-respect and self-confidence, of political initiative and of unity, are the enemies of our national renaissance.

In order that we may not be constrained to wander from one exile to another, we must have an extensive and productive place of refuge, a gathering place which is our own.

The present moment is more favorable than any other for realizing the plan here unfolded.

The international Jewish question must receive a national solution. Of course, our national regeneration can proceed only slowly. *We* must take the first step. Our *descendants* must follow us with a measured and unhurried pace.

A way must be opened for national regeneration of the Jews by a congress of Jewish notables.

No sacrifice would be too great in order to reach the goal which will assure our people's future, everywhere endangered.

The financial accomplishment of the undertaking can, in the nature of the situation, encounter no insuperable difficulties.

Help yourselves, and God will help you![44]

I have been occupied for some time with a work which is of immeasurable greatness. I cannot tell today whether I shall bring it to a close. It has the appearance of a gigantic dream. But for days and weeks it has filled me, saturated even my subconsciousness; it accompanies me wherever I go, broods above my ordinary daily converse, looks over my shoulder and at my petty, comical journalistic work, disturbs me, and intoxicates me.

What it will lead me to it is impossible to surmise as yet. But my experience tells me that it is something marvelous, even as a dream, and that I should write it down—if not as a memorial for mankind, then for my own delight or meditation in later years. And perhaps for something between both these possibilities: for the enrichment of literature. If the romance does not become a fact, at least the fact can become a romance. Title: The Promised Land![45]

. . . Zionism is an ideal, and as such is indefinable. It is thus subject to various interpretations and susceptive of different aspects. . . . That each of its representatives should emphasize the particular aspect most congenial to his way of thinking, and most suitable for his mode of action, is only natural. On one point, however, they all agree, namely, that it is not only desirable, but absolutely necessary, that Palestine, the land of our fathers, should be recovered with the purpose of forming a home for at least a portion of the Jews, who would lead there an independent national life. . . . . The great majority of Zionists remain loyal to the great idea of Zion and Jerusalem, to which history and tradition, and the general Jewish sentiment, point. It is "God's country" in the fullest and truest sense of the words. It is the "Promised Land" still maintaining its place in every Jewish heart, excepting those, perhaps, with whom Jewish history commences about the year 1830.

. . . Zionism declares boldly to the world that Judaism means to preserve its life by *not* losing its life. It shall be a true and healthy life, with a policy of its own, a religion wholly its own, invigorated by sacred memories and sacred environments, and proving a tower of strength and of unity not only for the remnant gathered within the borders of the Holy Land, but also for those who shall, by choice or necessity, prefer what now constitutes the Galut.

. . . I belong to that class of Zionists that lays more stress on the religious-national aspects of Zionism than on any other feature peculiar to it. The rebirth of Israel's national consciousness, and the revival of Israel's religion, or, to use a shorter term, the revival of Judaism, are inseparable. When Israel found itself, it found its God. When Israel lost itself, or began to work at its self-effacement, it was sure to deny its God. The selection of Israel, the indestructability of God's covenant with Israel, the immortality of Israel as a nation, and the final restoration of Israel to Palestine, where the nation will live a holy life on holy ground, with all the wide-reaching consequences of the conversion of humanity and the establishment of the Kingdom of God on earth—all these are the common ideals and the common ideas that permeate the whole of Jewish literature extending over nearly four thousand years.[46]

The concluding selection is from Rabbi Abraham Isaac Kook. He was very aware of the announced secular ideals in the name of which most of modern Zionism was conceived. Kook, the greatest of contemporary Jewish thinkers in the classical mold, was at once enough of a believer and enough of a radical thinker to assert that Jewish destiny yet proceeded in the ancient categories of divine election, sin, exile and redemption. It was clear to Kook that laboring for Zion was holy and part of the divine plan, the necessary human preparations for the coming of the Messiah. Men might think that they were laboring for socialism or secular nationalism but they were doing God's holy work, for whatever contributed to making an end to the Exile was a divinely appointed preamble to the Messiah.

Eretz Yisrael is not something apart from the soul of the Jewish people; it is no mere national possession, serving as a means of unifying our people and buttressing its material, or even its spiritual, survival. Eretz Yisrael is part of the very essence of our nationhood; it is bound organically to its very life and inner being. Human reason, even at its most sublime, cannot begin to understand the unique holiness of Eretz Yisrael; it cannot stir the depths of love for the land that are dormant within our people. What Eretz Yisrael means to the Jew can be felt only through the Spirit of the Lord which is in our people as a whole, through the spiritual cast of the Jewish soul, which radiates its characteristic influence to every healthy emotion. This higher light shines forth to the degree that the spirit of divine holiness fills the hearts of the saints and scholars of Israel with heavenly life and bliss.

To regard Eretz Yisrael as merely a tool for establishing our national unity—or even for sustaining our religion in the

Diaspora by preserving its proper character and its faith, piety and observances—is a sterile notion; it is unworthy of the holiness of Eretz Yisrael. A valid strengthening of Judaism in the Diaspora can come only from a deepened attachment to Eretz Yisrael. The hope for the return to the Holy Land is the continuing source of the distinctive nature of Judaism. The hope for the Redemption is the force that sustains Judaism in the Diaspora; the Judaism of Eretz Yisrael is the very Redemption.

Jewish original creativity, whether in the realm of ideas or in the arena of daily life and action, is impossible except in Eretz Yisrael. On the other hand, whatever the Jewish people creates in Eretz Yisrael assimilates the universal into characteristic and unique Jewish form, to the benefit of the Jewish people and of the world. . . .

Deep in the heart of every Jew, in its purest and holiest recesses, there blazes the fire of Israel. There can be no mistaking its demands for an organic and indivisible bond between life and all of God's commandments; for the pouring of the spirit of the Lord, the spirit of Israel which completely permeates the soul of the Jew, into all the vessels which were created for this particular purpose; and for expressing the word of Israel fully and precisely in the realms of action and idea. . . .

An outsider may wonder: How can seeming unbelievers be moved by this life force, not merely to nearness to the universal God but even toward authentic Jewish life—to expressing the divine commandments concretely in image and idea, in song and deed. But this is no mystery to anyone whose heart is deeply at one with the soul of the Jewish people and who knows its marvelous nature. The source of this Power is the Power of God, in the everlasting glory of life.[47]

CHAPTER SIX

Doctrine

When God resolved upon the creation of the world, He took counsel with the Torah—that is Divine Wisdom. She was skeptical about the value of an earthly world on account of the sinfulness of man, who would be sure to disregard her precepts. But God dispelled her doubts. He told her that Repentance had been created long before and sinners would have the opportunity to mend their ways. Besides good work would be invested with atoning power and Paradise and Hell were created to dispense reward and punishment. Finally, the Messiah was appointed to bring salvation, which would put an end to all sinfulness.[1]

The preceding quotation is from the *Sefer Raziel*, a volume of secret mystic writings of uncertain date and authorship. The themes mentioned above are the major foci of doctrinal concern in Judaism. It should be added here again, for emphasis, that Judaism knows no accepted catechism. It is nonetheless untrue to maintain that the Jewish religion is a set of legal commandments divorced from faith. Jewish faith is indefinable in Western theological categories, which are alien to its essence, and by nature it permits variation in belief. There is, however, an immanent logic of its own that will appear to the careful reader of this volume and especially of the selections that follow in this section.

MAN: HIS DIGNITY AND POSSIBILITIES

Man is created in the image of God—this is the essential Biblical doctrine of man. God loves justice and mercy;

man must therefore be true to his divinely ordained character by practicing these virtues. To be like God in the Jewish view means to be His partner in ruling the world and in carrying forward the work of making order, i.e. a just order, in the world. Man can descend to great depths, but he is not by nature irretrievably sinful. There are temptations to evil in the world but the path of piety is not in the renunciation of the world of the here and now. Man's task is to hallow life, to raise the workaday world in which he eats, labors and loves, to its highest estate so that his every act reflects the divine unity of all being. Note in particular the last three selections in this section, by Judah Halevi and Nahman of Bratslav.

God created man in His own image, in the image of God He created him.[2]

Thus says the Lord: "Let not the wise man glory in his wisdom, let not the mighty man glory in his might, let not the rich man glory in his riches; but let him who glories glory in this, that he understands and knows Me, that I am the Lord who practices kindness, justice, and righteousness in the earth; for in these things I delight, says the Lord."[3]

When I look at Your heavens, the work of Your fingers, the moon and the stars which you have established, what is man that You are mindful of him, and the son of man that You care for him? Yet You have made him but little lower than the angels, and have crowned him with glory and honor. You have made him to have dominion over the works of Your hands; You have put all things under his feet. . . .[4]

Long ago when the world with its inhabitants was not yet in existence, You conceived the thought, and commanded with a word, and at once the works of creation stood before You. You said that You would make for Your world man

an administrator of Your works, that it might be known that
he was not made for the sake of the world, but the world for
his sake.[5]

How are the witnesses admonished in capital cases? They
would bring them in and admonish them as follows: Perhaps
you will offer mere assumption or hearsay or second hand
information; or you might say to yourselves that you heard
it from a man that is trustworthy. Or perhaps you do not
know that we shall test your statements with subsequent ex-
amination and inquiry. Know, therefore, that capital cases
are not like civil cases. In civil cases, a man may make atonement by paying a sum of money, but in capital cases the
witness is answerable for the blood of any person that is
wrongfully condemned and for the blood of his descendants
that would have been born to him to the end of time. For
thus have we found it to be with Cain, who slew his brother.
It is written, "The bloods of your brother cry to Me from the
ground" [Gen. 4:10]. It says not "the blood of your brother"
but "the *bloods* of your brother"—his blood and the blood
of his descendants.

Therefore a single man was first created in the world, to
teach that if any man causes a single soul to perish, Scripture
considers him as though he had caused an entire world to
perish; and if any man saves a single soul, Scripture considers
him as though he had saved an entire world.

And a single man was first created for the sake of peace
among mankind, that no man could say to another, "My
father was greater than yours."

And a single man was first created to proclaim the greatness of the Holy One, praised be He, for man casts many
coins with one die and they are all alike, while the King of
kings, the Holy One, praised be He, patterns every man after
Adam and every man is unique. Therefore every man is
obliged to say: For my sake was the world created.[6]

Man is dear to God, for he was created in the divine image.
Man is especially dear to God in that he has been made aware
that he was created in the divine image, as it is written, "In
the image of God He made man" [Gen. 9:6].[7]

Let all your deeds be for the sake of heaven. They once asked Hillel where he was going. He answered, "I am going to perform a religious act (*mitzvah*)." "Which one?" "I am going to the bath house." "Is that a religious act?" "Yes. . . . Those who are in charge of the images of kings which are erected in theaters and circuses scour them and wash them and are rewarded and honored for it. How much more should I take care of my body, for I have been created in the image of God, as it is written, 'In the image of God He created man' " [Gen. 5:1].[8]

Why was man created on the sixth day [after the creation of all other creatures]? So that, should he become overbearing, he can be told "The gnat was created before you were."[9]

"Consider the work of God; who can make straight what He has made crooked?" [Eccles. 7:13]. When the Holy One, praised be He, created Adam, he showed him all of the trees in the Garden of Eden, telling him "Behold, My works are beautiful and glorious; yet everything which I have created is for your sake. Take care that you do not corrupt or destroy My world."[10]

Rabbi Simon said: When the Holy One, praised be He, was about to create Adam, the angels were divided into two different groups. Some said, "Let him not be created," while others said, "Let him be created." "Love and Truth met together; Righteousness and Peace kissed each other" [Ps. 85:10]. Love said, "Let him be created, for he will do loving deeds" but Truth said, "Let him not be created, for he will be all lies." Righteousness said, "Let him be created, for he will do righteous deeds", but Peace said "Let him not be created, for he will be all argument and discord." What did the Holy One, praised be He, do? He seized Truth and cast it to the ground, as it is written, "Truth was cast down to the ground" [Daniel 8:12]. Then the angels said to the Holy One: Lord of the Universe! How can You despise Your angel Truth? Let Truth rise from the ground, as it is written, "Truth will spring up from the ground" [Ps. 85:11].[11]

One day Elijah the prophet appeared to Rabbi Baruka in the market of Lapet. Rabbi Baruka asked him, "Is there any one among the people of this market who is destined to share in the world to come?" . . . Two men appeared on the scene and Elijah said, "These two will share in the world to come." Rabbi Baruka asked them, "What is your occupation?" They said, "We are merry-makers. When we see a man who is downcast, we cheer him up. When we see two people quarrelling with one another, we endeavor to make peace between them."[12]

When the Holy One, praised be He, was about to create men, the angels said, " 'What is man, that You are mindful of him?' [Ps. 8:5.] Why do You need man?" The Holy One, praised be He, answered, "Who, then, shall fulfil My Torah and commandments?" The angels said, "We shall." God answered, "You cannot, for in it is written 'This is the law when a man dies in a tent . . . ' [Num. 19:14], but none of you die. In it is written 'If a woman conceives, and bears a male child . . . ' [Lev. 12:2], but none of you give birth. It is written 'This you may eat . . . ' [Lev. 11:21], but none of you eat."[13]

According to our view a servant of God is not one who detaches himself from the world, lest be he a burden to it, and it to him; or hates life, which is one of God's bounties granted to him. . . . On the contrary, he loves the world and a long life, because it affords him opportunities of deserving the world to come. The more good he does the greater is his claim to the next world. . . .

The pious man is nothing but a prince who is obeyed by his senses, and by his mental as well as his physical faculties, which he governs corporeally, as it is written, "He who rules his spirit is better than he who takes a city" [Prov. 16:32]. He is fit to rule, because if he were the prince of a country he would be as just as he is to his body and soul. He subdues his passions, keeping them in bonds, but giving them their share in order to satisfy them as regards food, drink, cleanliness, etc.[14]

The capacity to see is a high and lofty power. The eyes always see great and marvelous things. If man would only

attain the merit of having pure eyes, he would know important things by the power of his eyes alone. His eyes are always
seeing but they do not know what they are seeing.[15]

There are unbelievers who maintain that the world is eternal, but this view is baseless. The truth is that the world and
all that it contains can exist, but it need not necessarily; only
God *must* exist and He creates all the worlds *ex nihilo*. When
Israel obeys the will of God, it becomes rooted in the Highest
Source which is eternal and thereby the whole world is raised
into the realm of eternal existence.

Man can become part of God's unity, which is eternal, only
by forgetfulness of self; he must forget himself completely in
order to partake of the Divine Unity. One cannot reach such
an estate except in aloneness. By withdrawing into intimate
dialogue with God, man can attain the complete abandon-
ment of his passions and evil habits, i.e. he can free himself
from the claims of his flesh and return to his Source. The best
time for such withdrawal is at night, when the world is free
of the claims of earthly existence. During the day men chase
after the concerns of this world. This atmosphere is disturb-
ing even to the man who is personally detached from such
concerns, for the worldly bustle of others makes it harder for
him to attain to the state of self-forgetfulness. Such withdrawal is best attained in a place which people do not pass by.

When man attains this level, his soul becomes an existential
necessity, i.e. he ascends from the realm of the possible to
that of the eternal. Once he himself has become eternal, he
sees the whole world in the aspect of its eternity.[16]

MAN'S RESPONSIBILITY

God is omnipotent and yet man is responsible. Everything
is foreseen and yet man has free will. These are the classic
contradictions of theistic faith, and they appear very early
in Judaism. There is no attempt at philosophic resolution,
only the assertion that man knows that he has choices to
make and that he is morally responsible for those choices.

He cannot help but know that there is a God who judges him and upon whom he cannot place the responsibility for his own misdeeds.

Man is not responsible for himself alone. He is responsible to society for the well-being of all men. There must therefore be law in society and respect for government, unless society itself transgresses the moral law. The rights of individuals are absolute, for every man is created in the divine image. Each has his particular virtue and capacity for service.

Man's proper response to life is piety and reverence not only before God but before other men.

I call heaven and earth to witness against you this day, that I have set before you life and death, blessing and curse; therefore, choose life, that you may live, you and your descendants.[17]

Behold, I set before you this day a blessing and a curse: A blessing if you obey the commandments of the Lord your God which I command you this day; a curse if you do not obey the commandments of the Lord your God, but turn aside from the way which I command you this day, to go after other gods, which you know not.[18]

> There are six things which the Lord hates,
> Seven which are an abomination to Him:
> Haughty eyes, a lying tongue,
> Hands that shed innocent blood,
> A heart that devises wicked plots,
> Feet that are swift to run to mischief,
> A false witness that utters lies,
> And one that sows discord among brethren.[19]

Hasten to perform the slightest commandment, and flee from sin; for the performance of one commandment leads to another and one transgression leads to another. The reward

of a commandment is another to be fulfilled and the reward
of one transgression is another.[20]

Everything is foreseen by God, and freedom of choice is
given to man; the world is judged with goodness, and all depends upon the preponderance of good or evil deeds.[21]

Everything is in the hands of heaven, except the fear of
heaven.[22]

The world is judged according to the preponderance of
good or evil, and the individual is judged in the same way.
Therefore, if a man fulfils one commandment, he is truly
blessed, for he has tipped the balance to the side of merit for
himself and for the entire world. However, if he commits one
transgression, woe is he, for he has tipped the balance to the
side of guilt for himself and for the entire world, as it is said,
"One sinner destroys much good" [Eccles. 9:18]. One sin of
an individual destroys much good for himself and for the
entire world.[23]

"And the Lord spoke to Moses and Aaron, saying, 'Separate yourselves from this congregation, that I may consume
them in a moment.' And they fell upon their faces and said, 'O
God, the God of the spirit of all flesh, shall one man sin and
will You be wroth with all the congregation?' " [Num. 16:20–
22]. Rabbi Simeon ben Johai said: Several men were sitting
in a boat. One of them began boring a hole beneath him with
an auger. His companions said, "What are you doing?" He
replied, "What business is it of yours? Am I not boring a
hole under myself?" They answered, "It is our business because the water will come in and swamp the boat with all of
us in it."[24]

For two and one half years the Schools of Hillel and Shammai debated the question whether it would have been better
had man never been created. Finally they agreed that it would
have been better had man not been created. However, since
man had been created, let him investigate his past deeds, and
let him give due consideration to what he is about to do.[25]

When Rabbi Johanan ben Zakai was ill, his disciples visited him. . . . They said to him, "Bless us, master! He said to them, "May it be His will that the fear of heaven be as great to you as the fear of flesh and blood." His disciples asked, "Only as great?" He answered, "If it only *would* be as great! You know that when a man commits a sin he says, 'No one will see me.' "[26]

"You make men like the fish of the sea" [Hab. 1:14]. Just as in the sea the larger fish swallow up the smaller fish, so it is among men. Were it not for fear of the government, every man greater than another would swallow him up. This is what Rav Hanina said: Pray for the welfare of the government, for were it not for fear of the government, a man would swallow up his neighbor alive.[27]

Rabbah bar bar Hana had a litigation against some laborers who, during their work, broke a cask of wine. He took away their clothing, whereupon they complained against him to Rav, who told him to return their clothing to them. When Rabbah asked "Is this the law?" Rav answered "Yes, as it is written 'That you may walk in the way of the good' " [Prov. 2:20]. He returned their clothing to them. The laborers then said "We are poor men and have worked all day and have nothing to eat." Rav said "Pay them their wages." When Rabbah asked again "Is this the law?" Rav answered "Yes, as it is written 'Keep the path of the righteous' " (*ibid.*).[28]

RULES OF CONDUCT

The essential rule of conduct is *imitatio Dei*, the imitation of God. No matter what his circumstances, man can so organize his life that this is the basic principle of his conduct. The rule does not require asceticism, but it does ask that man live every waking moment in the awareness that he is not alone, for God is present.

The selections below in this section span the centuries, from early rabbinic writings of the second century through various medieval and early modern "rules" laid down by distinguished fathers for their children to the concluding passages of insights from the classic early generations of Hasidim in the eighteenth century.

Rabbi Hama ben Rabbi Hanina said: What does this verse mean?—"You shall walk after the Lord your God" [Deut. 13:5]. Is it possible for man to walk after the *Shekhinah*? Is it not written, "The Lord your God is a consuming fire" [Deut. 4:24]?—It means that we should walk after the attributes of the Holy One, praised be He.

He clothes the naked, as it is written "The Lord God made for Adam and for his wife garments of skins and clothed them" [Gen. 3:21]. Thus you should clothe the naked.

The Holy One, praised be He, visited the sick, as it is written, "The Lord appeared to him [Abraham] by the oaks of Mamre" [Gen. 18:1]. [According to rabbinic tradition, the elderly Abraham was recuperating from his circumcision, narrated in the seventeenth chapter.] Thus you should visit the sick.

The Holy One, praised be He, comforted mourners, as it is written, "After the death of Abraham, God blessed Isaac his son" [Gen. 25:11]. Thus you should comfort mourners.

The Holy One, praised be He, buried the dead, as it is written, "He buried him [Moses] in the valley in the lamb of Moab" [Deut. 34:6]. Thus you should bury the dead. . . .

Rabbi Simlai expounded: The Torah begins with an act of lovingkindness and it ends with an act of lovingkindness. It begins with an act of lovingkindness, as it is written, "The Lord God made for Adam and for his wife garments of skin and clothed them" [Gen. 3:21]. It ends with an act of lovingkindness, as it is written, "He buried him [Moses] in the valley in the land of Moab" [Deut. 34:6].[29]

This was a favorite saying of the rabbis of Javneh: I am a creature of God and my neighbor is also His creature; my work is in the city and his in the field; I rise early to my work and he rises early to his. As he cannot excel in my work, so I cannot excel in his. You might say that I do great things while he does small things. However we have learned that it matters not whether a man does much or little, if only he directs his heart toward Heaven.[30]

The Holy One, praised be He, daily proclaims the virtues of a bachelor who lives in a large city and does not sin, a poor man who restores a lost object to its owners and a rich man who gives a tithe of his profits in secret.[31]

The Holy One, praised be He, loves three: Whoever does not become angry, whoever does not become drunk, and whoever does not stand on his rights. The Holy One, praised be He, hates three: Whoever says one thing with his mouth and another thing in his heart, whoever knows of evidence in favor of someone but does not testify, and whoever sees a disgraceful thing in someone and testifies against him alone [since a minimum of two witnesses is needed to bring about a formal conviction, one witness merely gives the defendant a bad reputation].[32]

Rav said: At judgment day every man will have to give account for every good thing which he might have enjoyed and did not.[33]

He who refrains from wine is called a sinner [the Nazirite was required to bring a sin offering]. All the more, then, is he who painfully refrains from everything to be called a sinner. Also it was derived that he who habitually fasts is called a sinner.[34]

Akavya ben Mahalalel attested to four things [which he held in opposition to the majority of the contemporary sages]. The sages told him "Akavya! Reverse your opinion on these four matters and we will appoint you President of the Court of Israel." He answered "I prefer to be called a fool all my life rather than become wicked for one hour before God."[35]

These rabbinic values find expression in medieval and early modern "ethical wills."

. . . My son, be zealous in visiting the sick, for a visitor lightens pain. Urge the patient to return in repentance to his Maker. Pray for him, and go. Do not burden him with a long visit, for the burden of his illness is enough to bear. When you enter a sick-room, enter cheerfully, for his heart and eyes are on those who enter to visit him.

My son, be zealous in participating in the burial of the dead, delivering them into the hand of your Maker, for this is an important duty. Whoever performs a kind act with the knowledge that he who benefits cannot repay, will receive unmerited kindness from the Holy One, praised be He.

My son, be zealous in comforting mourners and speak to their heart. Job's companions were deserving of punishment because they reproached him when they should have consoled him. . . .

. . . My son, be zealous in helping to bring the bride to the bridal canopy and in gladdening the groom. . . .

My son, do not crush the poor with your words, for the Lord will plead his cause. Such sinful conduct would cause many accusers to rise on high, to reveal your sins to your detriment, and there will be no one to defend you. But whoever treats the poor with generosity acquires intercessors on high who will proclaim his cause to his benefit.[36]

Devote yourself to science and religion; habituate yourself to moral living, for "habit is master over all things." As the Arabian philosopher holds, there are two sciences, ethics and physics. Strive to excel in both. . . .

Show respect to yourself, your household, and your children, by providing decent clothing, as far as your means allow; for it is unbecoming for any one, when not at work, to go shabbily dressed. . . .

If the Creator has mightily displayed His love to you and me, so that Jew and Gentile have thus far honored you for my sake, endeavor henceforth so to add to your honor that they may respect you for your own self. This you can effect by good morals and by courteous behavior; by steady devotion to your studies and your profession. . . .

Let your countenance shine upon the sons of men: tend their sick, and may your advice cure them. Though you take fees from the rich, heal the poor gratuitously; the Lord will requite you. Thereby shall you find favor and good understanding in the sight of God and man. Thus you will win the respect of high and low among Jews and non-Jews, and your good name will go forth far and wide. You will rejoice your friends and make your foes envious. . . .

Examine your Hebrew books at every new moon, the Arabic volumes once in two months, and the bound codices once every quarter. Arrange your library in fair order, so as to avoid wearying yourself in searching for the book you need. Always know the case and chest where it should be. . . .

Never refuse to lend books to anyone who has not means to purchase books for himself, but only act thus to those who can be trusted to return the volumes. . . . Cover the bookcases with rugs of fine quality; and preserve them from dampness and mice, and from all manner of injury, for your books are your good treasure. . . .

Make it a fixed rule in your home to read the Scriptures and to peruse grammatical works on Sabbaths and festivals, also to read Proverbs and the Ben Mishle. . . .

My son, honor your comrades, and seek opportunities to benefit them by your wisdom, in counsel and deed.[37]

"Hear, my son, your father's instruction, and forsake not your mother's teaching" [Prov. 1:8]. Become accustomed to speaking gently to all men, at all times. Thus you will be delivered from anger, which causes man to sin. . . . When you are delivered from anger, there will arise in your heart the quality of humility, the best of all good things, for it is written, "The reward of humility is the fear of the Lord" [Prov. 22:4]. Reverence results from humility, for humility makes you to consider always whence you came and where you are going. Humility reminds you that you are a worm in life and all the more so in death. Humility reminds you before whom you must give account in the future—the King of glory.

So I will explain how you should accustom yourself to the quality of humility and how to practice it continually. Let all your words be gentle and let your head be bowed; let your eyes be directed to the ground and your heart on high. Do not look at the face of one with whom you speak. Let every man be greater than you in your eyes. If he be wise or wealthy you must honor him. If he is poor and you are rich or if you are wiser than he, take it to your heart that you are the guiltier and he the more innocent. If he sins, it is in error but if you sin it is with intent to do so.

In all your actions, words and thoughts, and at all times, think of yourself as standing before God, with His *Shekhinah* resting upon you, for His glory fills the universe. Speak in reverence and in respect, as a servant addressing his master. Conduct yourself with modesty in dealing with every man. If a man should call to you, do not answer him in a loud voice, but gently and in a subdued voice, as one standing before his superior.

Be zealous to read in the Torah regularly, so you will be able to fulfil its precepts. After you study, examine in your mind what you have learned, to ascertain if it contained some principle which you can fulfil. Examine your deeds in the morning and in the evening, and thus all your days will be spent in repentance.

When you pray, remove all worldly matters from your heart. Set your heart right before God. Cleanse your thoughts and meditate before uttering a word. Act in this way all the days of your life, in all things, and you will not sin. Thus will all your deeds be upright, and your prayer pure, clean, devout and accepted before God. For it is written "Lord, You will hear the desire of the humble; You will strengthen their heart, You will incline Your ear" [Ps. 10:17].[38]

These are the things which a man must do to escape the snares of death and to bask in the light of life:

Do not rush into an argument. Beware of oppressing other men, whether by money or by word; neither envy nor hate them. Keep far from oaths and from the iniquity of vows, from frivolity and anger which confuse both the spirit and the mind of man. Do not use the name of God for vain purposes or in foul places. Do not rely upon the broken reed of human support and do not set up gold as your hope, for that is the beginning of idolatry. Distribute your money according to God's will. He is able to cover your deficit. It is good and upright to belittle your good deeds in your own sight and to magnify your transgressions; to increase the mercies of your Creator, who formed you in the womb and gives you food in due season. Do not serve for the sake of being rewarded when you perform His commandments, and do not avoid sin out of fear of punishment. Serve in love. Let expenditure of your money be of less value to you than utterance of your words. Do not rush to utter a bad word until you have weighed it in the scales of your judgment. Bury in the walls of your heart whatever is said to you even though it is not said in secrecy. If you hear the same thing from someone else, do not say "I already heard it."

Accustom yourself to awaken at dawn and to rise from your bed at the song of the birds. Do not rise as a sluggard, but with eagerness to serve your Creator. Do not be a drunkard or a glutton, lest you forget your Creator and thus be led to sin. Do not set your eyes upon one who is richer than you but upon one who is poorer. Do not look to one who is your inferior in the service and fear of Heaven, but to one who is your superior. Rejoice when you are reproved; listen to advice and accept instruction. Do not be haughty, but be humble and like dust upon which everyone treads. Do not speak with insolence, and do not raise your forehead, rejecting the fear of Heaven. Never do privately what you would be ashamed to do publicly. Do not say "Who will see me?"

Do not raise your hand against your neighbor. Neither slander nor give false reports of any person. Do not rush to give an insolent answer to those who say unpleasant things to you. Do not shout in the street, do not bellow like an animal; let your voice be soft. Do not make your neighbor blush in public. The first of all precautions is the avoidance of covetousness. Do not consider it a small matter if you have but one enemy. Do not tire of seeking a faithful friend; do not lose him. Do not try to make your friendship attractive through flattery and hypocrisy and do not speak with a double heart. Do not maintain your anger against your neighbor for a day, but humble yourself and ask forgiveness. Do not be haughty, saying "He has harmed me. Let him ask forgiveness of me." Every night, before you retire, forgive whoever has harmed you with words. If men curse you, do not answer. Be counted among the insulted (and not among the insulters).

Keep your feet on the path, firmly maintaining yourself in the middle of the road in regard to eating and drinking. Be neither accessible to all nor a recluse from all. Turn neither to the left nor to the right. Do not rejoice too much; remember that your life is a breath. You are formed from the dust and your end is the worm. Do not be easily offended, lest you gather needless enemies. Do not pry into the secrets of others. Do not be overbearing to the people of your city, and yield to the will of others. Will that which your Creator wills. Rejoice in your lot, whether it be large or small. Pray continually before Him to incline your heart toward His testimonies. Do not be an ingrate. Honor everyone who opened a door for you to earn life's necessities. Do not speak falsehoods. Be faithful to every man. Do not be slow in greeting every man, whether Jew or Gentile. Do not anger another person. . . .

Pursue justice [i.e. in this context, contribute to charity]. Do not give less than a half a shekel each year and at one time. Every month and every week give what you can. On every day let there not be lacking a small donation before prayer. Contribute the "continual offering" each Friday. When your income reaches a titheable amount, set aside the tithe. Thus you will have something at hand whenever you would give, whether to the living or the dead, whether to the poor or the rich.

Enjoy neither food nor drink without reciting a blessing before and after. Be zealous to praise your Creator for satisfying you. Cover your head when you mention God. Let your innermost self be stirred when you speak of Him. Do not be among those of whom Scripture says "They honor Me with their lips, while their hearts are far from Me" [Isa. 29:13]. Wash your hands before praying and before eating. Sanctify yourself in all things. Do not behave with levity; let the fear of Heaven be upon you. Before eating and before sleeping set regular times for studying the Torah. Speak of its words at your table. Direct the members of your household according to the Torah, in all matters which need direction.

Be of proper intent when you pray, for prayer is service of

the heart. If your child speaks to you and does not speak from his heart, will you not be angry? How, then, insignificant droplet, should you act in the presence of the King of the universe? Do not be like a servant who was given an important object for his own good and spoiled it. How could such a one face the King? How good it would be to ask forgiveness for saying "Forgive us" without sincere intent. Do not be lax in confessing your sins morning and evening, or in mentioning Zion and Jerusalem with a broken heart and in tears. When you recite the verse "You shall love the Lord your God with all your heart, with all your soul, and with all your might," speak as one who is ready to offer his life and his wealth to sanctify Him. Thus will you fulfill the verse "For Your sake we are slain every day" [Ps. 44:23]. Yet trust in the Lord with all your heart and have faith in His providence, for His eyes scan the entire earth and He sees all the ways of each man. Make mention of Him day and night. When you lie down, think of His love and in your dreams you will find it. When you awake, you will delight in Him and He will set your paths straight. Fulfill your good deeds in the spirit of humbly walking before Him, for this is the preferred service of the Lord, the service acceptable to Him.[39]

The sin of taking interest is so great that whoever commits it is considered as though he denied the God of Israel, God forbid. "If he lends at interest, and takes increase, shall he live? He shall not live" [Ezek. 18:13]. In commenting upon this verse our sages said that "He shall not live" means that such a man will not be resurrected, for usury and the like are abominable in the sight of the Lord. I see no need in elaborating upon this, since every Jew already dreads it.[40]

Most people are not outright thieves, taking their neighbors' property and putting it in their own premises. However, in their business dealings most of them have a taste of stealing, whenever they permit themselves to make a profit at the expense of someone else, claiming that profit has nothing to do with stealing. . . .

Rabbi Judah forbade merchants to distribute parched corn and nuts to children as an inducement for them to come to his shop. The other sages permitted it, but only because his competitors could do the same [*Baba Metzia* 60a]. Our sages said, "Defrauding a human being is a graver sin than defrauding the Sanctuary" [*Baba Batra* 88b]. . . . When Abba Hilkiah was working for an employer, he would not even return the greetings of men of learning, considering it wrong to use the time belonging to his employer for his own purposes [*Ta'anit* 23a-b]. . . . Even if a man should perform a commandment during the time when he should be working, it is not accounted to his credit, but it is accounted as a transgression. . . . If a man should steal some wheat, grind it, bake it and then recite a benediction over it, he blasphemes, as it is written, "The greedy, though he bless, condemns the Lord" [Ps. 10:3].[41]

If you will delve into the matter, you will realize that the world was created for man's use. Surely the fate of the world depends upon the conduct of man. If a man is attracted by things of this world and is estranged from his Creator, he is corrupted and he can corrupt the entire world along with him. However, if he controls himself, cleaves to his Creator and makes use of the world only to the degree that it helps him in serving His creator, he raises himself to a higher level of existence and the world rises with him. For it is of great significance to all things created when they serve the perfect man who is sanctified with the holiness of God, praised be He.[42]

The wise man who is completely detached from the masses cannot ever raise the level of his generation. If a man is lying in a ditch, he who would drag him out must come close to him and get a bit dirty. It is impossible to get someone else out of a ditch by standing still in your own proper place.

A teacher of public morality is like a broom which can only sweep the dirt out of the house if it becomes somewhat soiled itself.[43]

"Who is wise? He who learns from every man" [Mishnah *Avot* 4:1], even from the lowest of the low. Even in such a man there is a spark of the good which can serve as an example. So, when Jethro came to his son-in-law Moses, he said to him: "Indeed, you are a prophet and a sage, but you may still learn something from me." This was an example for all future generations.⁴⁴

SIN AND REPENTANCE

Sin is rebellion against God, but more seriously yet, Judaism considers it the debasement of man's proper nature. Punishment is therefore not primarily retribution; it is chastisement, as a father chastises his children, to remind them of their proper dignity and character. Repentance is therefore in Hebrew *teshuvah*, returning, man's turning back to his truest nature.

The evil inclination is to be compared to a conjurer who runs around among people with a closed hand daring them to guess what is in it. At that moment each one thinks that the conjurer has what each one desires for himself hidden in the clenched hand. Everyone therefore runs after him. Once the conjurer stops for a moment and opens his hand, it becomes clear to everyone that it is completely empty; there is nothing in it.

Exactly so the evil inclination fools the whole world. Everyone rushes after him, for all imagine, in their error, that he has in his hand what they want and desire. In the end the evil inclination opens his hand and everyone sees that there is nothing in it. The very one who said to each man "open your mouth and I will fill it," he himself is completely empty.⁴⁵

Regret is a great art in which few are expert. The chief purpose of regret is not to feel sorry for evil actions but to uproot evil from its very source. Whoever is not expert in this art tends to use his power of regret to strengthen the evil within him and not to weaken it.

The wicked are as full of regrets as a pomegranate is full of seeds; nonetheless they do not know what regret is. Precisely because they have so many regrets, they tend to grow hardened in their wickedness. What I mean is best expressed by the image of two wrestlers: when one sees that the other is about to subdue him, he summons up strength with which to withstand the attack—and so it goes from round to round. By the same token, improper regrets, which are based in the human passion for conquest, represent a form of wrestling with evil and can therefore become a way of evoking redoubled efforts by the "Evil One."[46]

There is no righteous man on earth whose deeds are good and who does not sin.[47]

Therefore I will judge every man according to his own ways, O house of Israel, says the Lord God. Return, and repent for all your transgressions, so that they shall not be your ruin. Cast away from you all your transgressions by which you have transgressed, and make yourselves a new heart and a new spirit, for why will you die, O house of Israel? For I desire not the death of anyone, says the Lord God; therefore, return and live.[48]

The righteous descendants of Adam upon whom death has been decreed . . . approach Adam and say, "You are the cause of our death." Adam replies: "I was guilty of one sin, but there is not a single one among you who is not guilty of many sins."[49]

The First Temple was destroyed because of the sins of idolatry, adultery and murder. . . . But during the time of the Second Temple, the people were engaged in the study of Torah, and the performance of commandments and deeds of lovingkindness. Why, then, was the Second Temple destroyed? Because the people were guilty of groundless hatred. And this teaches that the sin of groundless hatred is considered to be as grave as the sins of idolatry, adultery and murder.[50]

Rav Immi said "There is no death without sin, and there is no suffering without transgression. There is no death without sin, as it is written, 'The soul that sins, it shall die. The son shall not bear the iniquities of the father, nor shall the father bear the iniquities of the son. The righteousness of the righteous shall be upon him and the wickedness of the wicked shall be upon him" [Ezek. 18:20]. And there is no suffering without transgression, as it is written, 'I will punish their transgressions with the rod and their iniquity with scourges [i.e. suffering]' " [Ps. 89:33].

The angels said to the Holy One, praised be He, "Lord of the universe! Why did You punish Adam with death?" He answered them: "I gave him one simple commandment to observe, and he transgressed it." The angels said, "But Moses and Aaron fulfilled the entire Torah and they died!" He said to them, "One fate comes to all, to the righteous and to the wicked . . . as is the good man so is the sinner" [Eccles. 9:2]. . . .

Rabbi Simeon ben Eleazar said: "Moses and Aaron also died because of their sin, as it is written 'because you did not believe in Me, to sanctify Me in the eyes of the people of Israel' [Num. 20:12]. Had you believed in Me, you would still be alive." . . .

On the other hand, there is death without sin, and there is suffering without transgression.[51]

"There was a small city with few men in it, and a great king came against it and besieged it, building great siege-works against it. But there was found in it a poor wise man, and he by his wisdom saved the city" [Eccles. 9:14–15]. Rabbi Ammi bar Abba explained these verses in the following way: "There was a small city"—this is the body. "With few men in it"—these are the parts of the body. "And a great king came against it and besieged it"—this is the evil impulse. "He built great siegeworks against it"—these are sins. "But there was found in it a poor wise man"—this is the good impulse. "And he by his wisdom saved the city"— this refers to repentance and good deeds.[52]

May it be Your will, O Lord my God and God of my fathers, to shatter and bring to an end the yoke of the evil impulse from our heart; for You have created us to do Your

will and we are under obligation to do Your will. You desire
it and we desire it. What, then, hinders? The leaven in the
dough [i.e. the evil impulse]. It is well-known to You that
there is in us no power to resist it; but may it be Your will,
my God and God of my fathers, to cause it to cease from
ruling over us and to subject it. Then we shall do Your will
as our own will, with a perfect heart.[53]

"Open to me, my sister, my love, my dove" (Song of
Songs 5:2). Rabbi Issi said: The Holy One, praised be He,
said to the Israelites, "Open to Me the gate of repentance as
much as the eye of a needle, and I will open for you gates
wide enough for carriages and wagons to pass through
them."[54]

Repentance is greater than prayer, for Moses' prayer to
enter the land of Canaan was not accepted while the repentance of Rahab the harlot was accepted.[55]

"Teach us to number our days" [Ps. 90:12]. Rabbi Joshua
said: If we knew the exact number of our days, we would
repent before we die. Rabbi Eleazar said: Repent one day
before your death. His disciples asked him, "Who knows
when he will die?" Rabbi Eleazar answered, "All the more
then should a man repent today, for he might die tomorrow.
The result of this will be that all his life will be spent in repentance."[56]

Scripture states, "Let the wicked man forsake his way and
the bad man his plans, and let him return to the Lord [i.e.
repent] and He will have mercy upon him" [Isa. 55:7]. God
desires repentance. He does not desire to put any creature to
death, as it is said, "I do not desire the death of the wicked
man, but that the wicked man turn from his evil way and
live" [Ezek. 33:11].[57]

How do we know that he who repents is regarded as if he
had gone up to Jerusalem, built the Temple and the altar and
offered upon it all the sacrifices mentioned in the Torah? It
is written, "The sacrifice acceptable to God is a broken
spirit, a broken and contrite heart" [Ps. 51:17].[58]

Five categories of men will not be forgiven: Those who repent repeatedly, those who sin repeatedly, those who sin in a righteous generation, those who sin with the intention of repenting and those who profane God's name.[59]

Judaism does have, as this passage reflects, a minor tendency to stress the sinfulness of man's nature, but this is never made into an absolute. There is a divinely appointed remedy which each man can and must apply to himself: the life of Torah.

The Torah is the only remedy for the impulse to evil. Whoever thinks that he can be helped without it is mistaken and will realize his error when he dies for his sins. Man's impulse to evil is truly very strong and unbeknown to him it gradually prevails over and dominates him.[60]

SUFFERING

Why do the righteous suffer? The question was asked in its most famous and searing form by Job. Job's friends attempted to provide him with answers, but he rejected them all. In the end Job could only affirm, in the image of God's speaking to him out of the whirlwind, that God's plans are beyond man's knowing and that man could not condemn God in order to justify himself. The believer cannot really stretch his faith to the uttermost limit and condemn himself so utterly as to assert that all his sufferings are direct punishment for his sins. Some are; some suffering is borne by men carrying part of the burden of the sin of their generation, or of past generations. But ultimately the believer can only say, in the words of a poignant Hasidic prayer, "God, do not tell me why I suffer, for I am no doubt unworthy to know why, but help me to believe that I suffer for Your sake." That suffering is not meaningless, though its meaning is often hidden from us, and that it is not wasted is the response of faith to tragedy.

Rava said: If a man sees suffering come upon him, let him scrutinize his past deeds, as it is written, "Let us search and examine our ways and return to the Lord" [Lam. 3:10]. If he has scrutinized his past deeds without discovering the cause of his suffering, let him attribute it to the neglect of Torah, as it is written, "Blessed is the man whom You chasten, O Lord, and whom You teach out of Your Torah" [Ps. 94:12]. If he has attributed his suffering to the neglect of the Torah without discovering any justification, it is certain that his suffering is a chastening of love, as it is written, "For whom the Lord loves He chastens, as a father the son in whom he delights" [Prov. 3:12].[61]

A calf led to slaughter buried its head between the knees of Rabbi Judah. He said to the calf "Go! For this you have been created." Since he was not compassionate, he was visited with great sufferings. . . . Once, when Rabbi Judah's housemaid was about to sweep away some newborn kittens, he said to her "Don't harm them! It is written, 'The Lord is good to all, and His compassion is over all that He has made' " [Ps. 145:9]. Since he now showed compassion, compassion was extended to him [and his sufferings ceased].[62]

Rav Judah said in the name of Rav: When Moses ascended on high, he found the Holy One, praised be He, engaged in adding coronets to the letters of the Torah [three small strokes are added to the tops of certain Hebrew letters when written in a Torah scroll]. Moses said, "Lord of the universe! Does the Torah lack anything, that these additions are necessary?" He answered, "After many generations, a man by the name of Akiva ben Joseph will arise, and he will expound heaps and heaps of laws based upon each jot and tittle." Moses said, "Permit me to see him." God replied, "Turn

around." Moses went and sat down behind eight rows of
Rabbi Akiva's disciples and listened to the discourses upon
the Torah. He was ill at ease, for he was unable to follow
their arguments. However, during a discussion of a certain
subject, when the disciples asked the master, "How do you
know that to be so?" and Rabbi Akiva replied, "It is a law
given to Moses at Sinai," he was comforted. When he returned to the Holy One, praised be He, he said, "Lord of the
universe! You have such a man and yet You give the Torah
through me?!" God replied: "Be silent. Such is My decree."
Moses then said, "Lord of the universe! You have shown me
his Torah; show me his reward." "Turn around," He said.
Moses turned around and saw merchants weighing out Rabbi
Akiva's flesh in a market place. [Rabbi Akiva died the death
of a martyr during the Hadrianic persecutions at the hands
of the Romans.] Moses cried out, "Lord of the universe!
Such Torah and such a reward?!" God replied, "Be silent.
Such is My decree."[63]

Rabbi Gamaliel, Rabbi Eleazar, Rabbi Joshua and Rabbi
Akiva were once travelling, and they heard the great tumult
of the city of Rome in the distance. The first three wept, but
Rabbi Akiva laughed. When they asked "Why do you
laugh?" he asked "Why do you weep?" They said, "These
heathen, who worship and burn incense to idols, live here in
peace and security, while our Temple, the footstool at the
Throne of God, is destroyed by fire. How should we not
weep?" Rabbi Akiva replied, "That is why I laugh. If this is
the lot of those who transgress His will, how much more
glorious shall be the lot of those who perform His will."[64]

God has also informed us that during our entire sojourn
in this workaday world He keeps a record of everyone's
deeds. The recompense for them, however, has been reserved by Him for the second world, which is the world of
compensation. This latter world will be brought into being
by Him when the entire number of rational beings, the creation of which has been decided upon by His Wisdom, will
have been fulfilled. There will He requite all of them according to their deeds. This is borne out by the statement of the

saint, "I said in my heart: 'The righteous and the wicked God will judge" [Eccles. 3:17]. He said also, "For God shall bring every work into judgment concerning every hidden thing, whether it be good or whether it be evil" [Eccles. 12:14]. . . .

Notwithstanding this, however, God does not leave His servants entirely without reward in this world for virtuous conduct and without punishment for iniquities. For such requitals serve as a sign and an example of the total compensation which is reserved for the time when a summary account is made of the deeds of God's servants. . . .

It is, therefore, only a specimen and a sample of these rewards and punishments that is furnished in this world, while the totality of their merits is stored for the virtuous like a treasure. Thus Scripture says: "O how abundant is Your goodness, which You have laid up for them that fear You" [Ps. 31:20]. Similarly the totality of their demerits is laid up and sealed for the wicked, as Scripture says elsewhere: "Is not this laid up in store with Me, sealed up in My treasuries?" [Deut. 32:34].[65]

The good is that which is closer to God and the evil is that which is farther from Him. Evil is therefore a lower degree of good.

Evil is the footstool of good, and there is no absolute evil.

"Open for us the treasury of the good" [from the Liturgy]. There no doubt is good in all the bitter woes that come upon us, because evil cannot proceed from God. We, however, do not understand the good that is hidden within it. Therefore we beg of you, our Creator, "Open for us the treasury of the good, that is, open our eyes that we may understand the good that is hidden within evil."[66]

Know that man has to walk on a very narrow bridge. The chief rule is that he should never fear. A spiritually mature person does not fear.

The truth is that the world is full of woes. There is no one who really possesses this world. Even the greatest magnates and princes do not truly possess this world, because their days are filled with upsets and pain, with disturbances and sadness, and every one has his own particular woe.

It is strange that everyone says that there exists both this world and the world to come. In respect to the world to come, yes, we believe that it exists. Perhaps there is even a this world in some universe, but here on earth it is clearly hell itself, for all men are ever laden with great woe.[67]

A man once came to Rabbi Mendel to pour out his bitter heart. His wife had died in childbirth leaving him with seven young children including the newly-born infant. He had other woes too and did not know where to turn.

Rabbi Mendel listened to him, but while listening the Rabbi kept his eyes lowered. After a moment of deep meditation Rabbi Mendel raised his head, looked straight into the eyes of the petitioner and said: "I am not equal to the task of consoling you after such cruel suffering. Only the true Master of mercy is equal to that. Turn to Him."[68]

Postbiblical thinkers have pondered how the freedom of the human will and the resultant indetermination of the future can be reconciled with divine foresight and predetermination. Outstanding among all that has been said in the effort to overcome this contradiction is the well-known saying of Akiva's ("All is surveyed, and the power is given"), whose meaning is that to God, Who sees them together, the times do not appear in succession but in progress-less eternity, while in the progression of times, in which man lives, freedom reigns, at any given time, in the concrete moment of decision; beyond that, human wisdom has not attained. In the Bible itself, there is no pondering; it does not deal with the essence of God but with His manifestation to mankind; the reality of which it treats is that of the human world, and in it, the immutable truth of decision applies.

For guilty man, this means the decision to turn from his wrong way to the way of God. Here we see most clearly what it means in the biblical view that our answering-for-ourselves is essentially our answering to a divine address. The two great examples are Cain and David. Both have murdered (for so the Bible understands also David's deed, since it makes God's messenger say to him that he "slew Uriah the Hittite with the sword"), and both are called to account by God. Cain attempts evasion: "Am I my brother's keeper?" He is the man who shuns the dialogue with God. Not so David. He answers: "I have sinned against the Lord." This is the true answer: whomsoever one becomes guilty against, in truth one becomes guilty against God. David is the man who acknowledges the relation between God and himself, from which his answerability arises, and realizes that he has betrayed it.

The Hebrew Bible is concerned with the terrible and merciful fact of the *immediacy* between God and ourselves. Even in the dark hour after he has become guilty against his brother, man is not abandoned to the forces of chaos. God Himself seeks him out, and even when He comes to call him to account, His coming is salvation.[69]

This passage concludes *The Last of the Just*, Andre Schwarz-Bart's novel about Jewish suffering through the ages, culminating in the Nazi death camps.

The building resembled a huge bathhouse. To left and right large concrete pots cupped the stems of faded flowers. At the foot of the small wooden stairway an S.S. man, mustached and benevolent, told the condemned, "Nothing painful will happen! You just have to breathe very deeply. It strengthens the lungs. It's a way to prevent contagious diseases. It disinfects." Most of them went in silently, pressed forward by those behind. Inside, numbered coathooks garnished the walls of a sort of gigantic cloakroom where the flock undressed one way or another, encouraged by their S.S. cicerones, who advised them to remember the numbers carefully. Cakes of stony soap were distributed. Golda begged Ernie not to look at her, and he went through the sliding door of the second room with his eyes closed, led by the young woman and by the children, whose soft hands clung to his naked thighs. There, under the showerheads embedded in the ceiling, in the blue light of screened bulbs glowing in recesses of the concrete walls, Jewish men and women, children and patriarchs were huddled together. His eyes still closed, he felt the press of the last parcels of flesh that the

S.S. men were clubbing into the gas chamber now, and his
eyes still closed, he knew that the lights had been extin-
guished on the living, on the hundreds of Jewish women suddenly shrieking in terror, on the old men whose prayers rose
immediately and grew stronger, on the martyred children,
who were rediscovering in their last agonies the fresh inno-
cence of yesteryear's agonies in a chorus of identical exclama-
tions: *"Mama! But I was a good boy! It's dark! It's dark!"*
And when the first waves of Cyclon B gas billowed among
the sweating bodies, drifting down toward the squirming car-
pet of children's heads, Ernie freed himself from the girl's
mute embrace and leaned out into the darkness toward the
children invisible even at his knees, and he shouted with all
the gentleness and all the strength of his soul, "Breathe
deeply, my lambs, and quickly!"

When the layers of gas had covered everything, there was
silence in the dark room for perhaps a minute, broken only
by shrill, racking coughs and the gasps of those too far gone
in their agonies to offer a devotion. And first a stream, then
a cascade, an irrepressible, majestic torrent, the poem that
through the smoke of fires and above the funeral pyres of
history the Jews—who for two thousand years did not bear
arms and who never had either missionary empires nor col-
ored slaves—the old love poem that they traced in letters of
blood on the earth's hard crust unfurled in the gas chamber, enveloped it, vanquished its somber, abysmal snicker-
ing: "SHEMA YISRAEL ADONOI ELOHENU ADONOI
ECHOD . . . Hear, O Israel, the Lord is our God, the Lord
is One. O Lord, by your grace you nourish the living, and by
your great pity you resurrect the dead, and you uphold the
weak, cure the sick, break the chains of slaves. And faithfully you keep your promises to those who sleep in the dust.
Who is like unto you, O merciful Father, and who could be
like unto you . . . ?"

The voices died one by one in the course of the unfinished
poem. The dying children had already dug their nails into
Ernie's thighs and Golda's embrace was already weaker, her
kisses were blurred when, clinging fiercely to her beloved's
neck, she exhaled a harsh sigh: "Then I'll never see you
again? Never again?"

Ernie managed to spit up the needle of fire jabbing at his throat, and as the woman's body slumped against him, its eyes wide in the opaque night, he shouted against the unconscious Golda's ear, "In a little while, *I swear it!*" And then he knew that he could do nothing more for anyone in the world, and in the flash that preceded his own annihilation he remembered, happily, the legend of Rabbi Chanina ben Teradion, as Mordecai had joyfully recited it: "When the gentle rabbi, wrapped in the scrolls of the Torah, was flung upon the pyre by the Romans for having taught the Law, and when they lit the fagots, the branches still green to make his torture last, his pupils said, 'Master, what do you see?' And Rabbi Chanina answered, 'I see the parchment burning, but the letters are taking wing.' " ... *"Ah, yes, surely, the letters are taking wing,"* Ernie repeated as the flame blazing in his chest rose suddenly to his head. With dying arms he embraced Golda's body in an already unconscious gesture of loving protection, and they were found that way half an hour later by the team of *Sonderkommando* responsible for burning the Jews in the crematory ovens. And so it was for millions, who turned from *Luftmenschen* into *Luft.* I shall not translate. So this story will not finish with some to be visited in memoriam. For the smoke that rises from crematoriums obeys physical laws like any other: the particles come together and disperse according to the wind that propels them. The only pilgrimage, estimable reader, would be to look with sadness at a stormy sky now and then.

And praised. *Auschwitz.* Be. *Maidanek.* The Lord. *Treblinka.* And praised. *Buchenwald.* Be. *Mauthausen.* The Lord. *Belzec.* And praised. *Sobibor.* Be. *Chelmno.* The Lord. *Ponary.* And praised. *Theresienstadt.* Be. *Warsaw.* The Lord. *Vilna.* And praised. *Skarzysko.* Be. *Bergen-Belsen.* The Lord. *Janow.* And praised. *Dora.* Be. *Neuengamme.* The Lord. *Pustkow.* And praised ...

Yes, at times one's heart could break in sorrow. But often too, preferably in the evening, I can't help thinking that Ernie Levy, dead six million times, is still alive somewhere, I don't know where. .... Yesterday, as I stood in the street trembling in despair, rooted to the spot, a drop of pity fell from above upon my face. But there was no breeze in the air, no cloud in the sky. . . . There was only a presence.[70]

DEATH AND THE WORLD TO COME

In the Bible itself the arena of man's life is this world. There is no doctrine of heaven and hell, only a growing concept of an ultimate resurrection of the dead at the end of days. The doctrine of the resurrection was debated in post-Biblical times and the normative view became that held by the Pharisees, that there would be a resurrection of the dead. Concurrently the notion of judgment of the individual in the afterlife beyond the grave, his consignment to heaven or to hell, began to arise.

A tree has hope; if it be cut, it grows green again and the boughs may sprout. Though its root be old in the earth and its stock be dead in the dust, at the scent of water it shall bud and bring forth leaves, as when it was first planted. But man dies, and lies low; man perishes, and where is he? As the waters fail from the sea, and the river is drained dry, so man, when he falls asleep, shall not rise again. Until the heavens are no more he shall not awake, nor rise up out of his sleep.[71]

In death there is no remembrance of You; in Sheol, who can give You praise?[72]

And there shall be a time of trouble, such as never has been since there was a nation until that time; but at that time your people shall be delivered. . . . And many of those that sleep in the dust of the earth shall awake, some to everlasting life and some to shame and everlasting contempt.[73]

All of Israel has a share in the world to come, for it is written, "Your people shall all be righteous; they shall possess the land [interpreted here as referring to the world to come] forever, the shoot of My planting, the work of My hands, that I might be glorified" [Isa. 60:21]. The following have no share in the world to come: He that says resurrection of the dead is not derived from the Torah, he that says that the Torah is not from Heaven and an Epicurean.[74]

How do I know that the resurrection of the dead is derived from the Torah? It is written, "The Lord said to Moses, you shall say to the Levites 'When you take the tithe from the people of Israel . . . you shall give the Lord's offering to Aaron the priest. . . .' " [Num. 18:25–28]. Did Aaron live forever? He did not even enter the land of Israel; how then could this verse apply? Therefore, we must infer that this verse teaches that Aaron will live in the future and Israel will then give him the offering. This teaches that the resurrection of the dead is derived from the Torah. . . . Rabbi Simlai said: How do we know that the resurrection of the dead is derived from the Torah? It is written "I established My covenant with them [the patriarchs], to give them the land of Canaan . . ." [Ex. 6:4]. The verse states not "to give you" but "to give them" [the patriarchs themselves]. This teaches that the resurrection of the dead is derived from the Torah.

The Sadducees asked Rabban Gamaliel: What evidence do you have that the Holy One, praised be He, revives the dead? He answered: I have proof from the Torah, the Prophets and the Writings; but they did not accept his proof. In the Torah it is written "Then the Lord said to Moses: You will sleep with your fathers, and will rise . . ." [Deut. 31:16]. The Sadducees objected: It may mean that this people will rise up and go whoring after the strange gods of the land. In the Prophets is is written, "Your dead shall live, your [my] dead bodies shall rise. Awake and sing, you that sleep in the dust, for your dew is a dew of light, and on the land of the shades you will let it fall" [Isa. 26:19]. But the Sadducees replied that this may refer to the dead that Ezekiel revived [Ezek. 37]. In the Writings it is written, "Your palate is like finest wine that glides down smoothly for my beloved, moving gently the lips of those that are asleep [i.e. in the tomb]" [Song of Songs 7:10]. The Sadducees replied that this may refer to an ordinary movement of the lips while one sleeps. . . . Finally, Rabban Gamaliel quoted the verse ". . . the land which the Lord swore to give to your fathers, to give to them . . ." [Deut. 11:9]. It is not said "to you" but "to them." This proves the resurrection of the dead [for since the patriarchs died before the occupation of the land, God's promise could be fulfilled only by raising them from the dead]. Others say that he cited the verse "You who hold fast to the Lord your God are all alive this day" [Deut. 4:4].[75]

Rabbi Eliezer said: The nations [i.e. non-Jews] will have no share in the world to come, as it is written "The wicked shall depart to Sheol, and all the nations that forget God" [Ps. 9:17]. The first part of the verse refers to the wicked among Israel. However, Rabbi Joshua said to him: If the verse had stated "The wicked shall depart to Sheol, and all the nations," I would agree with you. But the verse goes on to say "that forget God." Therefore it means to say that there are righteous men among the other nations of the world who do have a share in the world to come.[76]

When Rabbi Johanan ben Zakai was ill, his disciples visited him. When he saw them, he began to weep. They said to him, "Lamp of Israel, right hand pillar, mighty hammer! Why do you weep?" He answered them, "If I were being led before a king of flesh and blood, I would weep, even though his anger, if he were angry with me, would not be everlasting, though his prison, if he imprison me, would not hold me for eternity, though he could not sentence me to eternal death and though I could appease him with words and bribe him with money. And now I am being led before the Kings of kings, the Holy One, praised be He, who lives and endures to all eternity. If He is angry with me, His anger is eternal. If He imprisons me, His prison will hold me eternally. He could sentence me to eternal death. And I cannot appease Him with words nor bribe Him with money. And furthermore, two paths lie before me, one to the Garden of Eden, and one to Gehinnom, and I know not in which I will be led. Should I then not weep?"[77]

We have learned that the judgment of the wicked in Gehinnom lasts twelve months. Rabbi Eliezer asked Rabbi Joshua, "What should a man do to escape the judgment of Gehinnom?" He replied, "Let him occupy himself with good deeds." . . . "Better is a poor man who walks in integrity . . ." [Prov. 19:1]. Whoever walks in blamelessness before his Creator in this world will escape the judgment of Gehinnom in the world to come.[78]

Everything which the Holy One, praised be He, caused to be injured in this world will be healed in the world to come. The blind will be healed, as it is written "Then the eyes of the blind shall be opened" [Isa. 35:5]. The lame shall be healed, as it is written "Then shall the lame man leap as the hart" [Isa. 35:6]. The dumb shall be healed, as it is written "The tongue of the dumb shall sing" [Isa. 35:6]. Everyone shall be healed. However, each man shall rise with the defects he had in life. The blind shall rise blind, the deaf shall rise deaf, the lame shall rise lame and the dumb shall rise dumb. They shall rise clothed as they were in life. . . . Why shall each man rise with those defects which he had in life? That the wicked of the world might not say "After they died God healed them and then brought them here," implying that these were actually others. The Holy One, praised be He, said, "Let them rise with the defects they had in life, and then I shall heal them, as it is written, 'That you may know and believe Me and understand that I am He. Before Me there was no God formed, neither shall any be after Me' " [Isa. 43:10]. Later, even the animals shall be healed, as it is written "The wolf and the lamb shall feed together, and the lion shall eat straw like the ox" [Isa. 65:25]. However, the one that brought injury to everyone shall not be healed, as it is written "And dust shall be the serpent's food" [*ibid.*]. Why? Because he brought everything to dust.[79]

Rav used to say: In the world to come, there is neither eating nor drinking nor procreation, nor business dealings nor jealousy nor hate nor competition. But righteous men sit with their crowns on their heads and enjoy the splendor of the *Shekhinah*.[80]

Rabbi Hiyya bar Abba said, quoting Rabbi Johanan: All of the prophecies of consolation and of good things to come delivered by the prophets apply only to the days of the Messiah, but as for the world to come, "no eye has even seen, O God, only You have seen" [*after* Isa. 64:3].[81]

"You shall keep My statutes and ordinances, by doing which a man shall live; I am the Lord" [Lev. 18:5]. This implies that man shall live in the world to come. In this world, man's end is death. How, then, can it be said "by doing which a man shall live"? This "living" must refer to the world to come. "I am the Lord"; faithful to reward.[82]

Saadia in the ninth century concluded that the doctrine of resurrection was accepted by all Jews, most of whom identified that event with the end of time, when the Messianic redemption will come.

The author of this book declares that, as far as the doctrine of the resurrection of the dead is concerned—which we have been informed by our Master will take place in the next world in order to make possible the execution of retribution —it is a matter upon which our nation is in complete agreement. The basis of this conclusion is a premise mentioned previously in the first treatises of this book: namely, that man is the goal of all creation. The reason why he has been distinguished above all other creatures is that he might serve God, and the reward for his service is life eternal in the world of recompense. Prior to this event, whenever He sees fit to do so, God separates man's spirit from his body until the time when the number of souls meant to be created has been fulfilled, whereupon God brings about the union of all bodies and souls again. . . .
We consequently do not know of any Jew who would disagree with this belief. Nor is it hard for him to understand how his Master can bring the dead to life, since he has already accepted as a certainty the doctrine of *creatio ex nihilo*.

The restoration by God of aught that has disintegrated or decomposed should, therefore, present no difficulty to him.

Furthermore God has transmitted to us in writing the fact that there would be a resurrection of the dead at the time of the Messianic *redemption*, which has been borne out by means of miraculous proofs. It is in regard to this point that I have found a difference of opinion to exist: namely, as to whether there will be a resurrection of the dead in this world. For the masses of our nation assert that it will come about at the time of the *redemption*. They namely interpret all verses of the Bible in which they find references to the resurrection of the dead in their exoteric sense and set the time to which they refer as being unquestionably that of the *redemption*.

I have noted, moreover, that some few of the Jewish nation interpret every verse in which they find mention made of the resurrection of the dead at the time of the *redemption* as referring to the revival of a Jewish government and the restoration of the nation. Whatever, on the other hand, is not dated as taking place at the time of the *redemption* is applied by them to the world to come. . . .

I have inquired and investigated and verified the belief of the masses of the Jewish nation that the resurrection of the dead would take place at the time of the *redemption*.[83]

Maimonides defines the world to come, i.e. the world beyond the grave, as a place where pure spirits engage in purely spiritual exercise.

The good which is stored up for the righteous is life in the world to come, life unaccompanied by death, good unaccompanied by evil. This is written in the Torah: "That it may be good with you and that you may live long" [Deut. 22:7]. We learn from tradition that the phrase "that it may be good with you" refers to the world which is all good, and that the phrase "that you may live long" refers to the world which is certainly long, i.e. the world to come. The reward of the righteous is that they will merit this pleasantness and goodness. The punishment of the wicked is that they will not merit such life but will be utterly cut off in their death. Whoever does not merit such life is a dead being who will never live but is cut off in his wickedness and perishes like an animal. . . .

In the world to come there are no bodies, but only the souls of the righteous alone, without bodies, like the angels. Since there are no bodies in the world to come, there is neither eating nor drinking nor anything at all which the bodies of men require in this world. Nothing occurs in the world to come which would involve bodies, such as sitting and standing, sleep and death, sadness and laughter, etc. Thus the early sages said: There is no eating, drinking or sexual intercourse in the world to come, but the righteous sit there with their crowns on their heads, enjoying the splendor of the *Shekhinah* (*Berakhot* 17a). Clearly there are no bodies there, for there is neither eating nor drinking there, and the statement of the sages that "the righteous sit there" was stated as a parable. The righteous there neither work nor strain. The statement that their crowns are on their heads means to say that the knowledge they possessed, on account of which they merited life in the world to come, is there with them and this knowledge is their crown. . . . ". . . enjoying the splendor of the *Shekhinah*." This means that they know and derive from the Truth of the Holy One, praised be He, what they do not know in this world, confined by a dull and lowly body.[84]

Whatever may be the doctrine of heaven and hell, the central emphasis of Judaism has remained, from the beginning, on this world. It is here and not in any world to come that man has the possibility to choose and to justify his life by choosing the good.

King Solomon said: "Whatever your hand finds to do, do it with your might, for there is no work or thought or knowledge or wisdom in Sheol, where you are going" [Eccles. 9:10]. Whatever a man does not do while he has the power granted him by his Creator, the power of freedom of the will, which is his all the days of his life, during which he is free and responsible, he will not be able to do in the grave or in Sheol, where he will not have this power. Whoever does not perform many good deeds during his lifetime can not perform them after his death. Whoever has not taken account of his deeds will not have time to do so in the world to come. Whoever has not gained wisdom in this world will not gain wisdom in the grave.[85]

On the deathbed, if one is conscious, this is the prayer which is prescribed for his recitation. The pious have always regarded it as a mark of particular mercy from God if a man dies uttering the last two lines of the confession.

My God and God of my fathers, accept my prayer; do not ignore my supplication. Forgive me for all the sins which I have committed in my lifetime. I am abashed, and ashamed of those wicked deeds and sins which I committed. Please accept my pain and suffering as atonement and forgive my wrongdoing, for against You alone have I sinned.

May it be Your will, O Lord my God and God of my fathers, that I sin no more. With Your great mercy cleanse me of my sins, but not through suffering and disease. Send a perfect healing to me and to all who lie sick in their beds.

Unto You, O Lord my God and God of my fathers, I acknowledge that both my healing and death depend upon Your will. May it be Your will to heal me. Yet if You have decreed that I shall die of this affliction, may my death atone for all sins and transgressions which I have committed before You. Shelter me in the shadow of Your wings and grant me a share in the world to come.

Father of orphans and Guardian of widows, protect my beloved family, with whose soul my soul is bound.

Into Your hand I commit my soul. You have redeemed me, O Lord God of truth.

Hear O Israel, the Lord our God, the Lord is One.

The Lord, He is God. The Lord, He is God.[86]

This prayer is prescribed to be said at synagogue service for eleven months immediately after the death of a parent, immediate blood relative, or spouse. It is the Kaddish, the sanctification of God's name. What is noteworthy and characteristic is that the departed is not mentioned nor is his soul prayed for. Its theme is praise of the glory of God.

> Magnified and sanctified be the glory of God
> In the world created according to His will.
>
> May His sovereignty soon be acknowledged,
> During our lives and the life of all Israel.
> Let us say: Amen.
>
> May the glory of God be eternally praised,
> Hallowed and extolled, lauded and exalted,
> Honored and revered, adored and worshiped.
>
> Beyond all songs and hymns of exaltation,
> Beyond all praise which man can utter
> Is the glory of the Holy One, praised is He.
> Let us say: Amen.
>
> Let there be abundant peace from heaven,
> And life's goodness for us and for all Israel.
> Let us say: Amen.
>
> He who ordains the order of the universe
> Will bring peace to us and to all Israel.
> Let us say: Amen.[87]

THE MESSIAH

There are two countertendencies in the Jewish vision of the Messiah. The ecstatic poetry of the prophets tended to suggest that the Messiah would come as the result of cataclysms and cosmic miracles. There are, however, more sober views in the Bible, which identify the Messiah

with real political events, like the restoration of the Jews
from Babylonian captivity by their deliverer, the Persian
King Cyrus. Each of these notions has continued throughout the history of Jewish faith. Rabbi Akiva in the second
century hailed Bar Kochba, the leader of the revolt
against Rome in 132–5, as the Messiah; other rabbis held
to the ecstatic view.

> And it shall come to pass in the end of days
> That the mountain of the Lord's house
> Shall be established as the top of the mountains,
> And it shall be exalted above the hills,
> And all nations shall flow unto it.
> And many people shall go, and say:
> "Come, let us go up to the mountain of the Lord,
> To the house of the God of Jacob,
> And He will teach us His ways,
> And we will walk in His paths."
> For the law shall come forth from Zion,
> And the word of the Lord from Jerusalem.
> And He shall judge the nations,
> And shall decide for many peoples;
> And they shall beat their swords into ploughshares
> And their spears into pruning-hooks.
> Nation shall not lift up sword against nation,
> Neither shall they learn war anymore.[88]

Behold, the days are coming, says the Lord, when I will
raise up for David a righteous scion, and he shall reign as
king and deal wisely, and shall execute justice and righteousness in the land. In his days Judah will be saved and Israel
will dwell securely. . . .[89]

Behold, I will send you Elijah the prophet before the coming of the great and terrible day of the Lord. And he will
turn the heart of the fathers to the children and the heart of
the children to their fathers, lest I come and smite the land
with a ban.[90]

Rabbi Joshua ben Levi came upon Elijah the prophet while he was standing at the entrance of Rabbi Simeon ben Yohai's cave. . . . He asked Elijah, "When will the Messiah come?"

Elijah replied, "Go and ask him yourself."

"Where is he?"

"Sitting at the gates of the city."

"How shall I know him?"

"He is sitting among the poor covered with wounds. The others unbind all their wounds at the same time and then bind them up again. But he unbinds one at a time and binds it up again, saying to himself, 'Perhaps I shall be needed; if so I must always be ready so as not to delay for a moment.' "

Rabbi Joshua ben Levi went to the Messiah and said to him, "Peace unto you, my master and teacher."

The Messiah answered, "Peace unto you, son of Levi."

He asked, "When is the master coming?"

"Today," he answered.

Rabbi Joshua returned to Elijah, who asked, "What did he tell you?" . . .

"He indeed has deceived me, for he said 'Today I am coming,' and he has not come."

Elijah said, "This is what he told you: '*Today*—if you would hearken to His voice' " [Ps. 95:7].[91]

Rabbi Johanan ben Zakai said: If you should have a sapling in your hand when they tell you that the Messiah has arrived, first plant the sapling and then go to greet the Messiah.[92]

Here are some echoes in the writings of Saadia of the proliferating legends about the cataclysms and wars that would usher in the coming of the Messiah.

. . . it has been transmitted by the traditions of the prophets that God would cause misfortunes and disasters to befall us that would compel us to resolve upon repentance so that we would be deserving of redemption. That is the sense of the remark of our forbears: "If the Israelites will repent, they will be redeemed. If not, the Holy One will raise up a king whose decrees will be even more severe than those of Haman, whereupon they will repent and thus be redeemed" (*Sanhedrin* 97b).

Our forbears also tell us that the cause of this visitation will be the appearance in Upper Galilee of a man from among the descendants of Joseph, around whom there will gather individuals from among the Jewish nation. This man will go to Jerusalem after its seizure by the Romans and stay in it for a certain length of time. Then they will be surprised by a man named Armilus, who will wage war against them and conquer the city and subject its inhabitants to massacre, captivity and disgrace. Included among those that will be slain will be that man from among the descendants of Joseph.

Now there will come upon the Jewish nation at that time great misfortunes, the most difficult to endure being the deterioration of their relationship with the governments of the world who will drive them into the wilderness to let them starve and be miserable. As a result of what has happened to them, many of them will desert their faith, only those purified remaining. To these Elijah the prophet will manifest himself and thus the redemption will come.[93]

Maimonides reflects the more realistic tendency. The Messiah will indeed be a king from the house of David who will gather the scattered of Israel together, but the order of the world will not be radically changed by his coming. There will be a world of peace and justice, a world perfected to the level that Jewish teaching imagined for a humanity that is truly obedient to the teachings of the Torah, but there will be no radical change in the order of creation.

The Anointed King [the Messiah] will in time arise and establish the kingdom of David in its former position and in the dominion it originally had. He will build up the sanctuary and gather the scattered of Israel. In his day, the laws will become what they were in olden times. . . .

Do not think, however, that the Anointed King must give signs and miracles and create new things in this world, or bring the dead back to life, and the like. It will not be so. For see: Rabbi Akiva, who was a great sage among the sages of the Mishnah, it was he who carried arms for ben Koziba, the king, and it was he who said of him that he was the Anointed King. He and all the sages of his generation thought that this was the Anointed King, until he was slain in his guilt. And after he was slain they all knew that he was not the Anointed King. But never had the sages asked him for a sign or for miracles. The root of these things is the following: This Torah, its statutes and its laws are for all times. There is nothing one could add to it, and nothing one could take away. . . .

Do not think in your heart that in the days of the Anointed something will be changed in the ways of the world, or that an innovation will appear in the work of creation. No. The world will go its ways as before, and that which is said in Isaiah, "The wolf shall dwell with the lamb, and the leopard shall lie down with the kid" [Isa. 11:6], is but a parable, and its meaning is that Israel will dwell in safety with the wicked among the heathen, and all will turn to the true faith; they will not rob nor destroy, and they will eat only what is permitted, in peace, like Israel, as it is written, "The lion shall eat straw like the ox" [Isa. 11:7]. And everything else like this that is said concerning the Anointed, is also a parable. In the days of the Anointed all will know what the parable signified and what it was meant to imply.

The sages said: "Nothing, save the cessation of the servitude to the nations, distinguishes the days of the Anointed from our time" (*Sanhedrin* 91b). From the words of the prophets, we see that in the early days of the Anointed a battle will take place "against Gog and Magog," and that before this battle against Gog and Magog, a prophet will arise who will make straight the people of Israel and prepare their hearts, as it is written, "Behold, I will send you Elijah the prophet before the coming of the great and terrible day of the Lord" [Mal. 3:23]. But he comes only to bring peace into the world, as it is written, "And he shall turn the hearts of the fathers to the children" [Mal. 3:24].

Among the sages there are some who say Elijah will come before the Anointed. But concerning these things and others of the same kind, none knows how they will be until they occur. For the prophets veil these things, and the sages have no tradition concerning them, save what they have deduced from the Scriptures, and so herein their opinion is divided. At any rate, neither the order of this event nor its details are the root of faith. A man must never ponder over legendary accounts, nor dwell upon interpretations dealing with them or with matters like them. He must not make them of primary importance, for they do not guide him either to fear or to love God. Nor may he seek to calculate the end. The sages said: "Let the spirit of those breathe its last, who seek to calculate the end" (*Sanhedrin* 97b). Rather let him wait and trust in the matter as a whole, as we have expounded.

The sages and the prophets did not yearn for the days of the Anointed in order to seize upon the world, and not in order to rule over the heathen, or to be exalted by the peoples, or to eat and drink and rejoice, but to be free for the Torah and the wisdom within it, free from any goading and intrusion, so that they may be worthy of life in the coming world.

When that time is here, none will go hungry, there will be no war, no zealousness and no conflict, for goodness will flow abundantly, and all delights will be plentiful as the numberless motes of dust, and the whole world will be solely intent on the knowledge of the Lord. Therefore those of Israel will be great sages, who know what is hidden, and they will attain what knowledge of their Creator it is in man's power to attain, as it is written, "For the earth shall be full of the knowledge of the Lord, as the waters cover the sea" [Isa. 11:9].[94]

Rabbi Zvi Hirsch Kalischer (1795–1874), a rabbi in the classic mold who is one of the forerunners of modern Zionism, reiterates the view of Maimonides in order to justify human effort as preparation for the day of the Messiah.

The redemption of Israel, for which we long, is not to be imagined as a sudden miracle. The Almighty, praised be His name, will not suddenly descend from on high and command His people to go forth. He will not send His Messiah from heaven in a twinkling of an eye, to sound the great trumpet for the scattered of Israel and gather them into Jerusalem. He will not surround the Holy City with a wall of fire or cause the Holy Temple to descend from the heavens. The bliss and the miracles that were promised by His servants, the prophets, will certainly come to pass—everything will be fulfilled—but we will not run in terror and flight, for the redemption of Israel will come by slow degrees and the ray of deliverance will shine forth gradually.

My dear reader! Cast aside the conventional view that the Messiah will suddenly sound a blast on the great trumpet and cause all the inhabitants of the earth to tremble. On the contrary, the Redemption will begin by awakening support among the philanthropists and by gaining the consent of the nations to the gathering of some of the scattered of Israel into the Holy Land. . . .

Can we logically explain why the Redemption will begin in a natural manner and why the Lord, in His love for His people, will not immediately send the Messiah in an obvious miracle? Yes, we can. We know that all our worship of God is in the form of trials by which He tests us. When God created man and placed him in the Garden of Eden, He also planted the Tree of Knowledge and then commanded man not to eat of it. Why did He put the Tree in the Garden, if not as a trial? . . . When Israel went forth from Egypt, God again tested man's faith with hunger and thirst along the way. . . . Throughout the days of our dispersion we have been dragged from land to land and have borne the yoke of martyrdom for the sanctity of God's name; we have been dragged from land to land and have borne the yoke of exile through the ages, all for the sake of His holy Torah and as a further stage of the testing of our faith.

If the Almighty would suddenly appear, one day in the future, through undeniable miracles, this would be no trial. What straining of our faith would there be in the face of miracles and wonders attending a clear and heavenly command to go up and inherit the land and enjoy its good fruit? Under such circumstances, what fool would not go there, not because of his love of God, but for his own selfish sake? Only a natural beginning of the Redemption is a true test of those who initiate it. To concentrate all one's energy on this holy work and to renounce home and fortune for the sake of living in Zion before "the voice of gladness" and "the voice of joy" are heard—there is no greater merit or trial than this. . . .

For all this to come about there must first be Jewish resettlement in the Land; without such settlement, how can the ingathering begin?[95]

The thirteen articles of faith defined by Maimonides in his commentary to the Mishnah are as close as Judaism ever came to a catechism. Despite the author's immense prestige, they have never been completely accepted. These articles appear in the Daily Prayer Book in rhymed form, and serve as an introduction to the morning service. Nonetheless, they are not binding on the conscience of the believing Jew.

I believe with perfect faith that the Creator, praised be He, is the Creator and the Guide of all creation, and that He alone has made, does make and will make all things.

I believe with perfect faith that the Creator, praised be He, is a Unity, and that there is no unity like His in any manner, and that He alone is our God, who was, is, and will be.

I believe with perfect faith that the Creator, praised be He, is not a body, and that He is free from all attributes of a body, and that He has no form whatsoever.

I believe with perfect faith that the Creator, praised be He, is the first and the last.

I believe with perfect faith that to the Creator, praised be He, and to Him alone is it proper to pray, and that it is not proper to pray to any besides Him.

I believe with perfect faith that all the words of the prophets are true.

I believe with perfect faith that the prophecy of Moses our great teacher, may he rest in peace, was true, and that he was the father of the prophets, both those who preceded and who followed him.

I believe with perfect faith that the entire Torah now in our possession is the same that was given to Moses our teacher, may he rest in peace.

I believe with perfect faith that this Torah will never be replaced, and that there will never be another Torah from the Creator, praised be He.

I believe with perfect faith that the Creator, praised be He, knows every deed of men and all their thoughts, as it is written, "He fashions the hearts of them all and observes all their deeds" [Ps. 33:15].

I believe with perfect faith that the Creator, praised be He, rewards those who keep His commandments and punishes those that transgress His commandments.

I believe with perfect faith in the coming of the Messiah, and though he tarry I will wait daily for him.

I believe with perfect faith that there will be a revival of the dead at a time when it shall please the Creator, praised be He, and exalted His fame for ever and ever.[96]

passkeys, for with it one can break through all the doors and all the gates.

Each prayer has its own proper meaning and it is therefore the specific key to a door in the Divine Palace, but a broken heart is an axe which opens all the gates.[6]

Prayer is an act of daring. Otherwise it is impossible to stand in prayer before God. When man imagines the greatness of the Creator, how else could he stand in prayer before Him?

Prayer is a mystery, directed in its essence towards changing the order of the world. Every star and sphere is fixed in its order, yet man wants to change the order of nature, he asks for miracles. Hence, at the moment of prayer man must lay aside his capacity for shame. If men had shame, they would, God forbid, lose the faith that prayer is answered.[7]

PRAYER AS COMMANDMENT

To worship God is a spiritual necessity for the believer; to speak to his Maker, to beseech Him, to experience His nearness, and to express gratitude and wonder at His beneficence. It is the nature of Judaism not to leave prayer for man's spontaneous enthusiasm alone. Man must pray with true inwardness, with freshness of feeling, but he must pray regularly at stated times and occasions.

You shall revere the Lord your God. You shall serve Him and cleave to Him.[8]

And you shall eat and be sated, and you shall bless the Lord your God for the good land He has given you.[9]

The first section of the Mishnah is *Berakhot* ("Blessings"). It is devoted to the laws of prayer, and the passages that follow here are taken almost entirely from it, with the addition of a few passages from other rabbinic literature.

A note on technical terms: Shema refers to the passages from Deuteronomy 6:4–9, 11:13–21, and Numbers 15:37–41, which were prescribed in earliest times as the core of the daily morning and evening prayer. *Tefilah* (or *Amidah*) was composed during the rabbinic period and was prescribed to be said, along with the Shema, morning and evening. The full text of the version of this prayer that is said every weekday is reproduced later in this section.

If a man was reading the section of the Shema in the Torah and the time came to recite the Shema, if he read the passage with the full intention of fulfilling his duty to recite the Shema, he has fulfilled his obligation; otherwise he has not.[10]

Craftsmen may recite the Shema at the top of a tree or on top of a stone wall, but they may not recite the Tefilah in this manner.[11]

A bridegroom is exempt from reciting the Shema on the first night, or until the close of the following Sabbath if he has not yet consummated the marriage.

When Rabban Gamliel married, he recited the Shema on the first night. His disciples asked him: "Master, have you not taught us that a bridegroom is exempt from reciting the Shema on the first night?" He said to them: "I will not let your statements influence me to cast off the yoke of the kingdom of heaven even for a moment."[12]

He whose dead lies unburied before him is exempt from reciting the Shema, from saying the Tefilah and from wearing Tefillin. Concerning the pall bearers and all those that relieve them, those that walk in front of the coffin and those that walk behind it: those that are required for bearing the coffin are exempt but those that are not actually required are not

exempt from reciting the Shema. All of them are exempt
from saying the Tefilah.[13]

The morning Tefilah may be said any time until noon.
Rabbi Judah says: until the fourth hour [i.e. midmorning].
The afternoon Tefilah may be said any time until sunset.
Rabbi Judah says: until midway through the afternoon. The
evening Tefilah has no set time. The additional Tefilah may
be said any time during the day. Rabbi Judah says: until the
seventh hour [i.e. one o'clock].[14]

How many times is man obliged to pray each day? Our
rabbis taught that one is not to pray more than the three
times daily initiated by the patriarchs. Abraham initiated
morning prayer, as it is written "Abraham went early in the
morning to the place where he had stood before the Lord"
[Gen. 19:27]. Isaac initiated afternoon prayer, as it is written "Isaac went out to meditate in the field toward evening"
[Gen. 24:63]. Jacob initiated evening prayer, as it is written
"And he [Jacob] came to a certain place [Hebrew word for
"place" is also used, in rabbinic literature, as a synonym for
God], and stayed there that night, because the sun had set"
[Gen. 28:11]. And concerning Daniel, too, it is written
". . . he [Daniel] got down upon his knees three times a day
and prayed and gave thanks before his God . . . " [Daniel
6:11]. However, this verse does not give the times for prayer.
David came to explain "Evening and morning and at noon
I utter my complaint and moan, and He will hear my voice"
[Ps. 55:18]. Therefore, one is not allowed to pray more than
three times a day. However, Rabbi Johanan said: If only
man *would* pray the entire day. The emperor Antoninus
asked Rabbi Judah the Prince: Is one permitted to pray every
hour? When he answered: It is forbidden, Antoninus asked
him: Why? He answered: Lest one act irreverently with the
Almighty. Antoninus did not accept this as a satisfactory
answer. What did Rabbi Judah do? He arose early the next
morning to visit Antoninus and upon his arrival said: Does
it go well with the emperor? One hour later, he entered the
royal chamber to say: O Great Caesar! And with the passing
of another hour he said: I bring you greetings, emperor.

Antoninus asked him: Why must you degrade royalty? Rabbi
Judah answered: Let your ears hear what your mouth is
saying. You are but a mortal king, and when I greet you
every hour you accuse me of degrading you. Is this not truer
still for the King of kings? All the more so one should not
disturb Him every hour.[15]

If one is riding on an ass, he should dismount to say the
Tefilah. If he cannot dismount, he should turn his head toward Jerusalem. And if he cannot turn his head, he should
direct his heart toward the Holy of Holies.[16]

If one is travelling on a ship or a raft, he should direct his
heart toward the Holy of Holies.[17]

If one sees a place where miracles had been wrought for
Israel, he should say: "Praised be He who wrought miracles
for our fathers in this place." If one sees a place from which
idolatry had been rooted out, he should say: "Praised is He
who rooted out idolatry from our land."[18]

If one sees shooting stars, earthquakes, lightnings, thunders
and storms, he should say: "Praised is He whose power and
might fill the world." If one sees mountains, hills, seas, rivers
or deserts, he should say: "Praised be the Author of Creation." Rabbi Judah says: If one sees the Great Sea [the
Mediterranean], he should say: "Praised be He who made
the Great Sea." But only if he sees it at intervals of time.
Upon seeing rain or receiving good tidings, one should say:
"Praised is He, the Good, and the doer of good." Upon receiving bad tidings, one should say: "Praised be the true
Judge."[19]

One who has built a new house or purchased new utensils
should say: "Praised is He who has given us life." One
should say the benediction for misfortune when it occurs,
regardless of any consequent good, and for good fortune
when it occurs, regardless of any consequent evil. One who
cries out to God over what is past utters a prayer in vain.
Thus if a man's wife is pregnant and he says: "May it be His

will that my wife shall bear a male," his prayer is in vain.
If a man is returning from a journey and hears a sound of
lamentation in the city and he says: "May it be His will that
those who mourn be not from my house," his prayer is in
vain.[20]

Rav Judah said: Whoever walks out of doors during the
month of Nisan and sees trees which are beginning to bud
should say: Praised be He whose world lacks nothing, who
created in it goodly creatures and goodly trees for the benefit of man.

Mar Zutra bar Toviah said: How do we know that one
should recite a blessing upon smelling something good? It
is written: "Let every living soul praise the Lord" [Ps.
150:6]. What is it that the soul enjoys which the body does
not enjoy? Odors.[21]

No one should taste anything without first reciting a blessing over it, as it is said: "The earth is the Lord's, and its
fullness" [Ps. 24:1]. Whoever enjoys the goods of this world
without reciting a blessing has transgressed.[22]

How do we know that one must say grace after meals? It
is written, "You shall eat and be satisfied and bless the Lord
your God . . . " [Deut. 8:10]. This teaches that one is required to recite a blessing after a meal. What about before
the meal? Rabbi Ishmael used to say that this can be determined by using the *kal v'homer* method of reasoning: If
one is required to recite a blessing after he has eaten and
is satisfied, he surely should do so when he is hungry and
desires to eat. . . . How do we know that one must recite a
blessing before and after the reading of the Torah [at serv-
ices]? Rabbi Ishmael used to say that this can be determined
by using the *kal v'homer* method of reasoning: A meal,
which is merely for the purposes of this ephemeral life, must
be preceded and followed by a blessing. It is surely logical,
then, to infer that this is truer still of the reading from the
Torah, which is for purposes of life eternal.[23]

Rabbi Hiyya bar Ashi, citing Rav, said: A person whose
mind is not at ease must not pray.[24]

Rabbi Eliezer said: "The prayer of one who makes his prayer a fixed task is not supplication" (Mishnah *Berakhot* 4:4). How do you define prayer which is a "fixed task"? Rabbi Yaakov bar Iddi said in the name of Rabbi Oshaiya: The prayer of one who prays merely to fulfil a ritual obligation. The sages said: The prayer of one who does not use the language of supplication. Rabba and Rav Joseph said: The prayer of one who adheres to the set form, never uttering anything new. Abba bar Avin and Rabbi Hanina Bar Avin said: The prayer of anyone who does not pray at dawn and at sunset.[25]

This summary of laws of prayer is excerpted from the authoritative legal code, the *Shulkhan Arukh.*

One who prays must be conscious of the meaning of the words he utters, as it is written, "You will strengthen their heart; You will incline Your ear" [Ps. 10:17]. Many prayer books with explanations in other languages have been publisehd, and every man can learn the meaning of the words he utters in prayer. If one is not conscious of the meaning of the words, he must at least, while he prays, reflect upon matters which influence the heart and which direct the heart to our Father in heaven. Should an alien thought come to him in the midst of prayer, he must be still and wait until it is no more.

One should place his feet close together, as though they were one, to be likened to the angels, as it is written, "Their legs were a straight leg" [Ezek. 1:7], that is to say: their feet appeared to be one foot. One should lower his head slightly, and close his eyes so that he will not look at anything. If one prays from a prayer book, he should not take his eyes off it. One should place his hands over his heart, his right hand over his left, and pray whole-heartedly, in reverence and awe and submission, like a poor beggar standing at a door.

One should utter the words consciously and carefully. Every person should pray according to his own tradition, whether it be Ashkenazic or Sephardic or other; they share a sacred basis. But one should not mix the words of two traditions, for the words of each tradition are counted and numbered according to major principles and one should neither increase nor decrease their number.

One must be careful to pray in a whisper, so that he alone will hear his words, but one standing near him should not be able to hear his voice, as it is written of Hannah, "Hannah was speaking in her heart; only her lips moved, and her voice was not heard" [I Sam. 1:13].

One should not lean against any object for even the slightest support. One who is even slightly ill may pray while seated or even while lying down, provided that he is able to direct his thoughts cogently. If it is impossible for one to pray with the words of his mouth, he should at least contemplate with his heart. . . .

When one who is outside of the Land rises to pray, he must face in the direction of the Land of Israel, as it is written, ". . . and they pray to You toward their land . . . " [I Kings 8:48], and in his heart he should be directed toward Jerusalem and the Temple site and the Holy of Holies as well. Therefore those who dwell to the West of the Land of Israel must face the East (but not precisely East, for there are idolaters who pray in the direction of sunrise and their intention is to worship the sun), those who dwell to the East should face West and those who dwell to the South should face North (and those who dwell to the Northwest of the Land of Israel should face Southeast, etc.).

One who prays in the Land of Israel should face Jerusalem, as it is written, ". . . they pray to the Lord toward the city which You have chosen . . . " [I Kings 8:44], and his thoughts should be focused toward the Temple and the Holy of Holies as well. One who prays in Jerusalem should face the Temple site, as it is written ". . . when they come and pray toward this House . . . " [II Chron. 6:32], and his thoughts should be focused toward the Holy of Holies as well.

Thus the entire people of Israel in their prayer will be facing one place, namely, Jerusalem and the Holy of Holies, the Heavenly Gate through which all prayer ascends. . . .

If one is praying in a place where he cannot discern directions, so that he is unable to know if he is facing in the proper direction, he should direct his heart to his Father in heaven, as it is written, ". . . and they pray to the Lord . . ." [I Kings 8:44]. . . .

One must bow four times during the *Amidah*: At the beginning and at the end of the first benediction and at the beginning and at the end of the *Modim* prayer. When one says "Praised" he should bend the knee, and when he says "are You" he should bend over until the joints of his spinal column stand out, and also bow his head. Then, before one pronounces the name of the Lord, he should begin slowly to stand erect, according to the verse, "The Lord lifts up those who are bowed down" [Ps. 146:8]. . . .

It is forbidden to bow at any other place in the *Amidah*.

After the recitation of the *Amidah*, and before the worshipper recites "May He who ordains the order of the universe bring peace to us and to all Israel," he should bow and take three short steps backward, like a servant taking leave of his master.[26]

THE SYNAGOGUE

Even before the destruction of the Temple, perhaps even in early Biblical days, there were already rudimentary synagogues in ancient Israel. It clearly became the central institution for the cultivation of the faith during the Babylonian captivity. The restoration under Nehemiah and Ezra left a large Jewish Diaspora outside the Holy Land, and that Diaspora increased in succeeding ages. Its central institution was the synagogue. Here the Jews gathered to pray together, but that was not its most important function. The commandment to pray is incumbent upon every individual Jew, three times a day—morning, afternoon, and evening—and there is relatively little difference in the prescribed order of prayer between the service as said in public in the synagogue and the version of it that is prescribed for the individual.

The central function of the synagogue was to cultivate a value perhaps more important than prayer to Jewish faith, study of the Torah. On Sabbath and festivals, people gathered in the synagogue to hear a reading of a passage from the Torah and to be led in the understanding of its interpretation. This is enshrined in the central act of public worship in Judaism on every major occasion, to this day. The Scroll of the Torah, which is written in prescribed ancient form by hand on parchment, is taken from the Ark and an appropriate section is read. On the Sabbath, the cycle of readings from the Torah comprises a consecutive reading of the Five Books of Moses in the course of the Sabbaths of the year. At all other times the selection read is something from the Five Books of Moses appropriate to the occasion. A complementary section from Prophets, known as the Haphtarah, is also read on the Sabbaths and Festivals.

It should be added that much of rabbinic literature, including especially the moralistic sections, really represents ancient homilies given in the synagogue to explain and apply the teaching of the Torah reading.

They told Rabbi Johanan that there were elderly men in Babylonia. He was surprised, and said, "It is written 'that your days and the days of your children may be multiplied *on the land*' [i.e. in Palestine]. But outside of the land this is not so." However, when they told him that these Babylonians came early to the synagogue and stayed late, he said, "That is what helps them." This corresponds to what Rabbi Joshua ben Levi said to his sons: "Rise early and stay up late and go to the synagogue, that you may prolong your life." Rav Aha, son of Rabbi Hanina asked, "What verse [in Scripture] supports this statement?" He answered, " 'Happy is the man who listens to Me, watching daily at My gates, waiting beside My doors' [Prov. 8:34], and in the next verse it is written, 'Whoever finds Me finds life.' "[27]

This account of the synagogue in Safed around 1600 reflects a community at the apex of spiritual devotion. Here are the classic and lasting values of the synagogue put into practice at highest intensity.

In all the houses of prayer the whole community [of Safed] assembles immediately after the evening and morning prayer, in five or six groups in each house of prayer. Each group studies before leaving the house of prayer: one of them studies Maimonides seriatim, another Ein Jacob [a skillful arrangement of narratives from the Talmud], the third a section of *Berakhot* [the first tractate of the Talmud], a fourth one section of the Mishnah with commentary, a fifth a *halakhah* [legal statement] with Rashi and *Tosafot* [commentaries to the Talmud] and the others study the *Zohar* or the Bible only. In this way nobody can be found in the community who begins his daily occupation in the morning without having learned something of our teaching. And the same is done by the whole of Israel in the evening after the evening prayer.

On the Sabbath the whole people goes into the houses of prayer to listen to the sermons of the rabbis. And on each Thursday the whole community gathers in the big house of learning after the morning prayer and prays there for the good of Israel all over the world, for the banished *Shekhinah* and the destroyed Temple. Special blessings are said for those who sent money for the support of the poor in the Land of Israel, that the Lord may prolong their years, that their affairs may be successful and they themselves saved from every need and affliction. This prayer is recited by the whole community with great weeping and broken hearts. Before they begin to pray, the great and pious Moses Galanti ascends the pulpit and speaks in humble words and awakens Israel to the fear of the Lord, and brings them nearer to the love of their Creator with the sweetness of his language, the greatness of his wisdom and knowledge and the abundance of his holiness. After him two heads of the Yeshivot [Talmudic academies], great scholars and saints, ascend the pulpit. One of them is Rabbi Massod Sagi Nahor, who is my teacher and master, known in the whole of Israel through his great holiness and the extent of his knowledge; the other is Rabbi Solomon Maarabi, famous among the whole of Israel through his wisdom and exceptional humility and wonderful piety, and they begin to pray with anxiety and trembling and great reverence, and their eyes overflow with tears like twenty-two water brooks. Who would be able in the face of these prayers and loud cries uttered by Israel over the dispersion and destruction, and of the confession of sins, not to repent, not to confess his sins, and not to become zealous threefold?[28]

Here is the beginning of the Torah service.

There is none like You among the mighty, O Lord, and there are no deeds like Yours. Your kingdom is an everlasting kingdom and Your dominion endures forever. The Lord is King, the Lord was King, the Lord shall be King for ever and ever. May the Lord give strength to His people; may the Lord bless His people with peace.

Father of compassion, may it be Your will to favor Zion with Your goodness and to rebuild the walls of Jerusalem. In You alone we trust, O King, high and exalted God, Lord of the universe.

The Ark is opened:

When the ark was carried onward, Moses exclaimed: Arise, O Lord, that Your enemies be scattered and those who would deny You be put to flight. For out of Zion shall go forth the Torah, and the word of the Lord out of Jerusalem.

Praised is He who in His holiness gave the Torah to His people Israel.

The Torah is taken from the Ark:

Hear, O Israel: The Lord our God, the Lord is One. One is our God, great is our Lord, Holy is He.

The Torah is carried in procession:

Proclaim the greatness of the Lord; together let us exalt His glory.

Yours, O Lord, is the greatness and the power and the glory. Yours is triumph and majesty over all heaven and earth. Yours, O Lord is supreme sovereignty.

Exalt the Lord our God, and worship Him for He is holy. Exalt and worship Him at His holy mountain. The Lord our God is holy.[29]

It is the custom for men to be honored by being called to stand at the reading desk while part of the prescribed Torah reading is chanted. What follows are the blessings recited by the individual before and after the recitation of the section to which he has been called.

Blessing before the Reading:

Praise the Lord, Source of all blessing.

Praised is the Lord, eternal Source of all blessing.

Praised are You, O Lord our God, King of the universe, who chose us from among all peoples by giving us His Torah. Praised are You, O Lord, Giver of the Torah.

Blessing after the Reading:

Praised are You, O Lord our God, King of the universe, who gave us a Torah of truth, endowing us with everlasting life. Praised are You, O Lord, Giver of the Torah.[29]

The Torah is raised:

This is the Torah that Moses set before Israel.
This is the Torah given by God, through Moses.

On returning the Torah to the Ark:

Praise the glory of the Lord: His glory is supreme.

His glory is high over heaven and earth. He exalts His people and extols His faithful, the children of Israel who are close to Him. Halleluyah.

On replacing the Torah in the Ark:

When the ark was at rest, Moses said: Return,
O Lord, to the myriads of the families of Israel.
Return, O Lord, to Your sanctuary,
You and the ark of Your glory.

Let Your priests be robed in righteousness;
Let Your faithful sing with joy.
Do it for the sake of David, Your servant,
And do not reject Your anointed one.

Precious instruction do I give You:
Never forsake My Torah.

It is a tree of life to those who hold fast to it.
All who uphold the Torah are blessed.
Its ways are delight; its paths are peace.

Lead us back to You, and we shall return;
Renew our glory as in days of old.[29]

STATUTORY PRAYER

The first paragraph below is the beginning passage of the Shema. The long section which follows is the *Amidah*, here given in its weekday morning version. This prayer is recited silently by the individual who stands as he does so.

Hear, O Israel: The Lord our God, the Lord is One. Praised be His glorious sovereignty for ever and ever.

You shall love the Lord your God with all your heart, with all your soul, and with all your might. These words which I command you this day shall be in your heart. You shall teach them diligently to your children. You shall talk about them at home and abroad, night and day. You shall bind them as a sign upon your hand; they shall be as frontlets between your eyes, and you shall inscribe them on the doorposts of your homes and upon your gates.[30]

Open my mouth, O Lord, and I will declare Your praise.

Praised are You, O Lord our God and God of our fathers,
God of Abraham, God of Isaac, God of Jacob,
Great, mighty, revered God, supreme over all.

You bestow lovingkindness with gracious generosity.
You are mindful of the pious deeds of our fathers,
And will send a redeemer for their children's children
Because of Your love and for the sake of Your glory.

You are the King who helps, and saves and shields.
Praised are You, O Lord, Shield of Abraham.

Your might, O Lord, is eternal;
Your saving power brings the dead to life again.

You sustain the living with lovingkindness;
With great mercy You bring the dead to life again.
You support the fallen, heal the sick, free the captives;

You keep faith with those who sleep in the dust.
Who can compare with Your might, O Lord and King?
You are Master over life, and death and salvation.

Faithful are You in bringing the dead to life again.
Praised are You, O Lord, Who give life to the dead

Holy are You and hallowed is Your name.
Holy are they who daily praise You.
Praised are You, O Lord and holy God.

You graciously endow man with intelligence;
You teach him knowledge and understanding.
Grant us knowledge, discernment and wisdom.
Praised are You, O Lord, for the gift of knowledge.

Our Father, bring us back to Your Torah;
Our King, draw us near to Your service;
Lead us back, truly repentant before You.
Praised are You, O Lord, who welcomes repent-
    ance.

Our Father, forgive us, for we have sinned;
Our King, pardon us, for we have transgressed;
You forgive sin and pardon transgression.
Praised are You, gracious and forgiving Lord.

Behold our affliction and deliver us;
Bestow us with a speedy redemption,
For You are the mighty Redeemer.
Praised are You, O Lord, Redeemer of Israel.

Heal us, O Lord, and we shall be healed;
Help us and save us, for in You is our glory.
Grant perfect healing for all our afflictions,
O faithful and merciful God of healing.
Praised are You, O Lord, Healer of His people.

O Lord our God, make this a blessed year;
May its varied produce bring us happiness.
Bless the year with Your abounding goodness.
Praised are You, O Lord, who blesses our years.

Sound the great shofar to herald our freedom;
Raise high the banner to gather our exiles;
Gather our dispersed from the corners of the earth.
Praised are You, O Lord, who gathers the exiles of
    His people Israel.

Restore our judges as in days of old;
Restore our counsellors as in former times;

Remove from us sorrow and anguish.
Reign over us alone with lovingkindness;
With justice and mercy sustain our cause.
Praised are You, O Lord, King who loves justice.

Frustrate the hopes of those who malign us;
Let all evil very soon disappear;
Let all Your enemies be speedily destroyed.
May You quickly uproot and crush the arrogant;
May You subdue and humble them in our time.
Praised are You, O Lord, who humbles the arro-
gant.

Let Your tender mercies, O Lord God, be stirred
For the righteous, the pious, and the leaders of
Israel,
Toward devoted scholars and faithful proselytes.
Be merciful to us of the house of Israel;
Reward all who trust in You;
Cast our lot with those who are faithful to You.
May we never come to despair, for our trust is in
You.
Praised are You, O Lord, who sustains the right-
eous.

Have mercy, O Lord, and return to Jerusalem,
Your city;
May Your Presence dwell there as You promised.
Rebuild it now, in our days and for all time;
Re-establish there the majesty of David, Your
servant.
Praised are You, O Lord, who restores Jerusalem.

Bring to flower the shoot of Your servant David,
Hasten the advent of the Messianic redemption;
Each and every day we hope for Your deliverance.
Praised are You, O Lord, who assures our deliver-
ance.

O Lord, our God, hear our cry!
Have compassion upon us and pity us;
Accept our prayer with loving favor.
You, O God, listen to entreaty and prayer.

O King, do not turn us away unanswered,
For You mercifully heed Your people's supplication.
Praised are You, O Lord, who is attentive to
prayer.

O Lord, our God, favor Your people Israel and
their prayers.
Restore the service to Your Temple.
Accept with love Israel's offerings and prayers.
May our worship be ever acceptable to You.

May our eyes witness Your return in mercy to Zion.
Praised are You, O Lord, whose Presence returns
to Zion.

We thank You, O Lord our God and God of our
fathers,
Defender of our lives, Shield of our safety.
Through all generations we thank You and praise
You.
Our lives are in Your hands, our souls in Your
charge.

We thank You for the miracles which daily attend
us,
For Your wonders and favors, morning, noon, and
night.
You are beneficent with boundless mercy and love.
From of old we have always placed our hope in
You.

For all these blessings, O our King,
We shall ever praise and exalt You.

Every living creature thanks You, and praises You
in truth.
O God, You are our deliverance and our help.
Praised are You, O Lord, for Your goodness and
Your glory.

Grant peace and well-being to the whole house of
Israel
Give us of Your grace, Your love, Your mercy.

Bless us all, O our Father, with the light of Your
   Presence.
It is Your light that revealed to us Your life-giving
   Torah,
And taught us love and tenderness, justice, mercy
and peace.

May it please You to bless Your people in every
   season,
To bless them at all times with Your gift of peace.
Praised are You, O Lord, who blesses Israel with
   peace.[31]

This very personal prayer is by custom said at the end
of the *Amidah*. The prescribed *Amidah* itself speaks in
the normal plural, the "we" of Jewish prayer (compare
the introductory comment to the Confession, from the
Yom Kippur liturgy, to be found in Chapter IV).

My God, keep my tongue from evil, my lips from
   guile.
Help me ignore those who would slander me;
Let my soul be truly humble before all,
With my heart open to Your Torah,
And pursuing Your commandments.

Frustrate the designs of those who plot evil against
   me.
Speedily make naught of their schemes, for Your
   sake.
Do so for Your power, Your holiness, and Your
   Torah.

Answer me for the sake of Your beloved people.
May the words of my mouth and the meditations of
   my heart
Find favor before You, my Defender and My Redeemer.

He who ordains the order of the universe
Will bring peace to us and to all Israel.
Let us say: Amen.[32]

This is the first paragraph of the grace that is said after every meal at which bread is eaten.

Praised are You, O Lord our God, King of the universe. With goodness, with compassion, and with kindness You graciously nourish the whole world, providing food for every creature with everlasting mercy. Your great goodness has never failed us; Your great glory assures us nourishment. All life is Your creation, and You are good to all, providing every creature with food and sustenance. Praised are You, O Lord, who sustains all life.[33]

Before eating bread:

Praised are You, O Lord our God, King of the universe, who brings forth bread from the earth.

Before drinking wine:

Praised are You, O Lord our God, King of the universe, Creator of the fruit of the vine.

Upon viewing the beauty of nature:

Praised are You, O Lord our God, King of the universe, who has fashioned such beauty in His world.

On seeing a sage learned in Torah:

Praised are You, O Lord our God, King of the universe, who has given of His wisdom to those who revere Him.

Upon seeing a distinguished leader:

Praised are You, O Lord our God, King of the universe, who has given of His glory to mortal man.[34]

PRIVATE PRAYER

Jewish practice insists on the saying of the prescribed
service. It does not, however, rule out—indeed, it encour-
ages—private devotion. Here are a few examples of personal prayer chosen from literally thousands that might
be quoted.

The first is by a second-century rabbi, and appears in
the Talmud. The second is the prayer of a shepherd, from
twelfth-century Germany; the third is by Rabbi Elimelekh
of Lizhensk, in eighteenth-century Poland; and the last is
an undated prayer composed in Yiddish and used as a
meditation by women in the synagogue.

Rabbi Nehunya ben Hakaneh used to utter a brief prayer
whenever he entered the house of study and whenever he left
it. When they asked him, "What is the nature of this prayer?"
he told them: "When I enter I pray that I should not be the
cause of any offence, and when I leave I give thanks for my
lot."[35]

Lord of the universe!
It is apparent and known unto You,
that if You had cattle and gave them to me to tend,
though I take wages for tending from all others,
from You I would take nothing,
because I love You.[36]

Guard us
from vicious leanings and from haughty ways,
from anger and from temper,
from melancholy, talebearing,
and from all the other evil qualities.

Nor let envy of any man rise in my heart,
nor envy of us in the heart of others.

On the contrary:
put it in our hearts that we may see our
comrades' virtue,
and not their failing.[37]

God, it is true, before You there is no night, and the light is with You, and You make the whole world shine with Your light.

The mornings tell of Your mercy, and the nights tell of Your truth, and all creatures tell of Your great mercy and of great miracles.

Each day You renew Your help, O God! Who can recount Your miracles? You sit in the sky and count the days of the devout, and set the time for all Your creatures. Your single day is a thousand years and Your years and days are unbounded.

All that is in the world must live its life to an end, but You are there, You will always be there, and outlive all Your creatures.

You, God, are pure, and pure are Your holy servants who three times every day cry, "Holy," and sanctify You in heaven and on earth:

You, God, are sanctified and praised. The whole world is filled with Your glory for ever and ever.[38]

References

References

References

I PEOPLE

1. Gen. 17:1–8.
2. Ex. 6:2–8.
3. Ex. 19:5–6.
4. Lev. 20:22–27.
5. Num. 35:34.
6. Deut. 4:32–40.
7. Deut. 5:1–3.
8. Deut. 29:9–14.
9. Hosea 2:21.
10. *Pesahim* 87a–b.
11. *Song of Songs Rabbah* 1:15.
12. From a letter of Maimonides to the Jews of Yemen, in F. Kobler, ed., *A Treasury of Jewish Letters* (Philadelphia: Jewish Publication Society, 1954), Vol. I, pp. 184–86.
13. Deut. 4:5–8.
14. Deut. 7:6–13.
15. Deut. 9:5.
16. Mishnah *Avot* 3:14.
17. *Berakhot* 6a.
18. *Hullin* 89a.
19. *Megillah* 16a.
20. *Shekalim* 2b.
21. *Leviticus Rabbah* 30:12.
22. Judah Halevi, *Kuzari,* Part II.
23. Amos 3:1–2.
24. Amos 9:7–10.
25. *Song of Songs Rabbah* 1.
26. Gen. 9:8–15.
27. *Genesis Rabbah* 34:8.
28. *Seder Eliahu Rabbah,* Chap. 9.
29. *Exodus Rabbah* 19:4.
30. *Sifra, Aharei Mot* 86a (Weiss edition).
31. From a letter of Maimonides to Hasdai Halevi, in F. Kobler, *op. cit.,* Vol. I, pp. 197–98.
32. *Sifre,* Num. 71.
33. *Tanhuma* (Buber), *Lekh Lekha,* 6.
34. *Yebamot* 47a–b.
35. *Tanhuma, Lekh Lekha.*
36. From a letter of Maimonides to Obadiah the Proselyte, in F. Kobler, *op. cit.,* Vol. I, pp. 194–95.
37. Kaufmann Kohler, *Jewish Theology* (New York: The Macmillan Company, 1928), pp. 326–27.
38. Mordecai M. Kaplan, *The Future of the American Jew* (New York: The Macmillan Company, 1948), pp. 219–20.
39. Martin Buber, *At the Turning* (New York: Farrar, Straus and Young, 1952), pp. 36–37.
40. Edmond Fleg, "Why I am a Jew," in Arthur Hertzberg, *The Zionist Idea* (Garden City, N. Y.: Doubleday, 1959), pp. 481–85.
41. Samson Raphael Hirsch, *The Nineteen Letters of Ben Uziel* (New York: Bloch, 1942), Seventh Letter.
42. *Ibid.,* Fifteenth Letter.
43. Abraham Isaac Kook, "The Rebirth of Israel," in Arthur Hertzberg, *op. cit.,* pp. 424–25.
44. Trans. from the *Weekday Prayer Book,* Rabbinical Assembly of America, 1961.

II GOD

1. Gen. 1:1.
2. Isa. 40:12–25.
3. Trans. from the *Weekday Prayer Book,* Rabbinical Assembly of America, 1961.
4. Ps. 23.

5. Ps. 113; trans. from the *Weekday Prayer Book, op. cit.*

6. Trans. from the *Weekday Prayer Book, op. cit.*

7. Jer. 23:23–24.

8. *Numbers Rabbah* 13.

9. *Berakhot* 10a.

10. *Hullin* 60a.

11. *Genesis Rabbah* 19:7.

12. *The Zohar,* Gen. 103a–b; trans. by Sperling and Simon (London: Soncino Press, n.d.).

13. Saadia Gaon, *The Book of Beliefs and Opinions,* trans. by Samuel Rosenblatt (New Haven, Conn.: Yale University Press, 1948), Treatise II, Chap. 12.

14. Maimonides, *Guide of the Perplexed,* trans. by M. Friedlander (New York: Hebrew Publishing Co., 1881), Part I, Chap. 57–58.

15. *Genesis Rabbah* 1:10.

16. *Hagigah* 14b.

17. Hayyim ibn Musa, in N. Glatzer, ed., *In Time and Eternity* (New York: Schocken, 1946), pp. 74–75.

18. *Berakhot* 7a.

19. *Avodah Zarah* 3b.

20. *Exodus Rabbah* 43:6.

21. Israel Baal-Shem, in N. Glatzer, *op. cit.,* p. 87.

22. Deut. 6:4.

23. Ex. 20:2–7.

24. Ps. 115; trans. from *Weekday Prayer Book, op. cit.*

25. *Mekhilta, Pisha* 5.

26. *Shabbat* 55a.

27. Trans. from *Weekday Prayer Book, op. cit.*

28. Ex. 34:6–7.

29. Deut. 8:5.

30. Isa. 1:12–20.

31. *Sifre* Deut. 307.

32. *Megillah* 31a.

33. *Exodus Rabbah* 3:6.

34. *Leviticus Rabbah* 24:2.

35. *Tanhuma, Bereshit* 9.

36. *Genesis Rabbah* 12:15.

37. Franz Rosenzweig and Nahum Glatzer, *Franz Rosenzweig, His Life and Thought* (Philadelphia: Jewish Publication Society, 1953), pp. 304-5.

38. Deut. 6:5.

39. Deut. 10:12-22.

40. Ps. 117; trans. from *Weekday Prayer Book, op. cit.*

41. *Berakhot* 61b.

42. From the Testament of Shabtai Hurwitz. See Hebrew text in Israel Abrahams, *Hebrew Ethical Wills* (Philadelphia: Jewish Publication Society, 1948), pp. 255-56.

43. Moses Luzatto, *Mesillat Yesharim,* Chap. 11.

44. *Ibid.,* Chap. 19.

45. *Ibid.,* Chap. 19.

46. From the Testament of Israel Baal-Shem.

III TORAH—TEACHING AND COMMANDMENT

1. Deut. 6:20–25.

2. Deut. 30:11–14.

3. *Makkot* 23b.

4. *Makkot* 24a.

5. *Lamentations Rabbah,* Proem II.

6. *Numbers Rabbah* 17:6.

7. Louis Finkelstein, *The Jews: Their History, Culture, and Religion* (New York: Harper and Brothers, 1949), Vol. II, pp. 1739, 1792–93.

8. *Sifre* Deut. 45.

9. *Yoma* 72b.

10. Mishnah *Avot* 6.

11. *Tanhuma* (Buber), *Yitro* 7.
12. *Lamentations Rabbah,* Proem II.
13. *Sifre* Deut. 48.
14. *The Zohar,* Gen. 190a–b.
15. *Genesis Rabbah* 1:1.
16. *Mekhilta, Bahodesh* 1.
17. Trans. from *Weekday Prayer Book,* Rabbinical Assembly of America, 1961.
18. *Sifra* 86b (Weiss edition; Vienna, 1862).
19. *Sanhedrin* 74a.
20. Saadia Gaon, *The Book of Beliefs and Opinions,* Treatise III, Chap. 10.
21. *Ibid.,* Treatise III, Exordium.
22. Samson Raphael Hirsch, *The Nineteen Letters of Ben Uziel,* Fifteenth Letter.
23. Solomon Schechter, *Studies in Judaism,* First Series (Philadelphia: Jewish Publication Society, 1896), pp. 248–50.
24. Kaufmann Kohler, *Jewish Theology* (New York: The Macmillan Co., 1928), pp. 352–53.
25. Hayyim Nahman Bialik, "Address at the Inauguration of the Hebrew University in Jerusalem, 1925," in Arthur Hertzberg, *The Zionist Idea,* pp. 282–83.
26. Gen. 17:9–14.
27. Mishnah *Shabbat* 19:5.
28. Mishnah *Nedarim* 3:11.
29. *Yalkut Shimoni, Lekh Lekha* 71.
30. *Yalkut Shimoni, Beshalah* 268.
31. Gen. 2:18.
32. Gen. 2:24.
33. Deut. 24:5.
34. Prov. 31:10–12, 26–31.
35. Mishnah *Ketubot* 5:5.
36. Mishnah *Ketubot* 5:6.
37. Mishnah *Yebamot* 6:6.
38. *Yebamot* 63b.
39. *Yebamot* 64a.
40. *Yebamot* 62b–63a.
41. *Yebamot* 63b.
42. *Sotah* 17a.
43. *Tanhuma* (Buber), *Naso* 13.
44. Rabbi Nahman of Bratslav.
45. *Sh'elot Uteshuvot Mimaamakim* (New York, 1959), pp. 111–14.
46. *Ibid.,* pp. 151–56.
47. From the Marriage Service.
48. Ex. 20:12.
49. Deut. 27:16.
50. *Kiddushin* 30b–31a.
51. *Kiddushin* 31a.
52. *Jerusalem Peah* 1:1.
53. *Pesikta* 23.
54. *Kiddushin* 30b.
55. *Yebamot* 5b.
56. Mishnah *Keritot* 6:9.
57. *Kiddushin* 29a.
58. *Shabbat* 10b.
59. *Jerusalem Shabbat* 1:2.
60. *Kiddushin* 30a.
61. *Sifre Ekev.*
62. Gen. 32:33.
63. Ex. 22:30.
64. Ex. 23:19.
65. Lev. 11:2–8.
66. Lev. 11:9–11.
67. Lev. 17:10–14.
68. Deut. 14:21.
69. Mishnah *Hullin* 3:1.
70. Mishnah *Hullin* 8:1–3.
71. *Tanhuma* (Buber), *Shemini* 12.
72. Maimonides, *Guide of the Perplexed,* Part III, Chap. 48.
73. Ex. 23:10–11.
74. Lev. 19:9–10.
75. Deut. 14:28–29.
76. Deut. 15:7–11.
77. Job 29:12–16.
78. From letter of the Jews of Alexandria to Ephraim ben

Shamarya and the elders of the Palestinian community of Fostat, in F. Kobler, ed., *A Treasury of Jewish Letters*, Vol. I, p. 240.

79. Maimonides, *Mishneh Torah, Hilkhot Matanot Aniyim*, Chap. 10.
80. *Shulkhan Arukh, Yoreh Deah* 252.
81. *Shabbat* 31a.
82. Samuel Laniado, *Kli Hemda*, in N. Glatzer, ed., *In Time and Eternity*, p. 146.
83. Moses Luzatto, *Mesillat Yesharim*, Chap. 19.
84. Rabbi Israel Baal-Shem Tov.
85. Rabbi Nahman of Bratslav.
86. Rabbi Mendel of Kotzk.
87. Rabbi Isaac of Worka.

IV THE CYCLE OF THE YEAR

1. Gen. 2:1–3.
2. Ex. 20:8–11.
3. Ex. 31:12–17.
4. Deut. 5:12–15.
5. Isa. 56:1–7.
6. Isa. 58:13–14.
7. Jer. 17:24–25, 27.
8. Neh. 13:15–18.
9. Mishnah *Hagigah* 1:8.
10. Mishnah *Shabbat* 7:2.
11. *Shabbat* 49b.
12. Mishnah *Yoma* 8:6.
13. *Yoma* 84b.
14. *Shabbat* 118b.
15. *Genesis Rabbah* 11.
16. *Shabbat* 119a.
17. *Exodus Rabbah* 25:12.
18. Judah Halevi, *Kuzari*, Part II.
19. *Sefer Hasidim*, ed. Reuben Margaliot (Jerusalem: Mosad Harav Kook, 1959), Nos. 110, 149.
20. A. J. Heschel, *The Sabbath* (New York: Farrar, Straus and Young, 1951), pp. 6–10.
21. From the Prayer Book.
22. From the Prayer Book.
23. Trans. from the *Weekday Prayer Book*, Rabbinical Assembly of America, 1961.
24. Deut. 16:14.
25. Deut. 16:16–17.
26. Mishnah *Hagigah* 1:1.
27. *Pesahim* 68b.
28. *Pesahim* 109a.
29. *Tanhuma, Pinhas* 17.
30. Ex. 12:14–20.
31. Mishnah *Pesahim* 1:1.
32. Mishnah *Pesahim* 1:4.
33. Mishnah *Pesahim* 2:1.
34. Mishnah *Pesahim* 3:7.
35. Mishnah *Pesahim* 4:1.
36. Mishnah *Pesahim* 10:5
37. *Yalkut Shimoni, Emor* 23.
38. Mishnah *Pesahim* 10:4.
39. From the Passover Haggadah.
40. Deut. 16:9–12.
41. Ex. 20:1–14.
42. Comment of Rashi to Song of Songs 4:5.
43. Lev. 23:34–36.
44. Lev. 23:39–43.
45. Mishnah *Sukkah* 1:1.
46. *Sukkah* 28b.
47. Mishnah *Sukkah* 3:1.
48. *Sukkah* 55b.
49. *Sefer Hahinukh*.
50. J. Eibschutz, *Yaarot Dvash*.
51. From an unpublished sermon of my father, Rabbi Zvi Elimelech Hertzberg.
52. Lev. 23:26.
53. *Sukkah* 55b.
54. Lev. 23:24–25.
55. Neh. 8:9–12.
56. *Rosh Hashanah* 16a.
57. *Rosh Hashanah* 16b.
58. *Midrah Tehillim* 81 (order rearranged).
59. Maimonides, *Mishneh Torah, Hilkhot Teshuvah* 7:4.

60. S. Y. Agnon, *Yamin Noraim* (New York: Schocken, 1946), p. 177.
61. High Holy Day Prayer Book.
62. *Ibid.*
63. *Ibid.*
64. Lev. 23:27–32.
65. Mishnah *Yoma* 1:1.
66. Mishnah *Yoma* 3:8.
67. Mishnah *Yoma,* 8:1.
68. Mishnah *Yoma* 8:4.
69. Mishnah *Yoma* 8:5.
70. *Midrash Tehillim* 27:4.
71. Mishnah *Yoma* 8:9.
72. Mishnah *Ta'anit* 4:8.
73. Cited in S. Y. Agnon, *op. cit.,* p. 230.
74. *Belz,* M. J. Gutman (Tel Aviv, 1952), p. 75.
75. S. Y. Agnon, *op. cit.,* p. 243.
76. High Holy Day Prayer Book.
77. *Ibid.*

V LAND

1. Comment of Rashi to Gen. 1:1.
2. Gen. 17:8.
3. Gen. 47:29–30.
4. Deut. 30:1–5.
5. I. Kings 8:27–30.
6. *Tanhuma, Kedoshim*
7. Mishnah *Ketubot* 13:11.
8. *Ketubot* 110b–111a.
9. *Sifre, R'eh.*
10. *Leviticus Rabbah,* 34.
11. *Kiddushin* 49b.
12. Mishnah *Kelim* 1:6.
13. *Baba Batra* 158b.
14. *Jerusalem Nedarim* 6:8.
15. *Baba Kama* 80b.
16. *Genesis Rabbah* 59.
17. *Kiddushin* 49.
18. Isaiah Hurwitz, excerpt from a letter written in Jerusalem to his children in Prague (1621), in F. Kobler, ed., *A Treasury of Jewish Letters,* Vol. II, pp. 483–84.
19. Quoted in *T'kumat Yisrael* (Tel Aviv: Karni Publishers, 1958), p. 37.
20. Jer. 9:11–16.
21. Ps. 137:1–6.
22. *Tanhuma* (Buber), *Devarim* 7. The text is unhistorical for the emperor who conquered Jerusalem was Vespasian, and the commanding general was his son Titus.
23. *Mekhilta, Pisha* 14.
24. Judah Halevi, *Poetry of Judah Halevi,* trans. by Nina Salaman (Philadelphia: Jewish Publication Society, 1928), p. 2.
25. From a letter of Hasdai ibn Shaprut to Joseph, King of the Khazars, in F. Kobler, *op. cit.,* Vol. I, pp. 98–106.
26. From a letter of Joseph, King of the Khazars, to Hasdai ibn Shaprut, in F. Kobler, *op. cit.,* Vol. I, p. 113.
27. From a letter written by Obadiah of Bartinoro in Jerusalem to his father, in F. Kobler, *op. cit.,* Vol. I, p. 304. It is a ritual commandment that as a mark of mourning, garments are rent, whether it be for personal or national grief.
28. From a letter of the community of Salonica to the communities on the route to Palestine, in F. Kobler, *op. cit.,* Vol. I, p. 143.
29. From a letter of the Provençal Jews in Salonica to the Jews in Provence, in F. Kobler, *op. cit.,* Vol. II, pp. 344–47.
30. The Kaddish of Rabbi Levi Isaac of Berditchev, in N. Glatzer, ed., *In Time and Eternity,* pp. 94–95.

31. Solomon ibn Verga, *Shevet Yehudah* (Jerusalem: Mosad Bialik, 1947), pp. 163–64.
32. Jacob Emden, *Shaarei Shamayim.*
33. J. Eibschutz, *Yaarot Dvash.*
34. *Jer.* 29:4–14.
35. *Ketubot* 11a.
36. *Genesis Rabbah* 96.
37. *Tosafot* to *Ketubot* 110b.
38. Mordecai Kaplan, *The Future of the American Jew,* pp. 128–30.
39. *Jer.* 31:15–16.
40. *Tanhuma, Noah.*
41. Saadia Gaon, *The Book of Doctrines and Beliefs,* trans. by Samuel Rosenblatt (New Haven: Yale University Press, 1948), Treatise VII, Chap. 1.
42. Jacob Emden, from the introduction to his prayer book, in N. Glatzer, *op. cit.,* pp. 216–17.
43. Rabbi Nahman of Bratslav, quoted in N. Glatzer, *op. cit.,* pp. 206–7.
44. Leo Pinsker, *Road to Freedom,* ed. by B. Netanyahu (New York: Scopus, 1944), pp. 105–6.
45. Theodor Herzl, First entry in his diary (1895) in Arthur Hertzberg, *The Zionist Idea,* p. 204.
46. Solomon Schechter, *Seminary Addresses and Other Papers* (New York: Ark Publishing, 1915), pp. 91–104.
47. Abraham Isaac Kook, "Orot," in Arthur Hertzberg, *op. cit.,* pp. 419–22.

VI DOCTRINE

1. *Sefer Raziel.*
2. *Gen.* 1:27.
3. *Jer.* 9:22–23.
4. *Ps.* 8:4–7.
5. *Syriac Baruch* 14:17.
6. Mishnah *Sanhedrin* 4:5.
7. Mishnah *Avot* 3:14.
8. *Avot of Rabbi Nathan,* Version b, Chap. 30.
9. *Sanhedrin* 38a.
10. *Ecclesiastes Rabbah* 7:13.
11. *Genesis Rabbah* 8:5.
12. *Ta'anit* 22a.
13. *Tanhuma Buber, B'hukotai* 6.
14. Judah Halevi, *Kuzari,* Part III.
15. Rabbi Nahman of Bratslav.
16. *Ibid.*
17. *Deut.* 30:19.
18. *Deut.* 11:26–28.
19. *Prov.* 6:16–19.
20. Mishnah *Avot* 4:2.
21. Mishnah *Avot* 3:15.
22. *Megillah* 25a.
23. *Kiddushin* 40b.
24. *Leviticus Rabbah* 4:6.
25. *Erubin* 13b.
26. *Berakhot* 28b.
27. *Avodah Zarah* 4a.
28. *Baba Metziah* 83a.
29. *Sotah* 14a.
30. *Berakhot* 17a.
31. *Pesahim* 113a.
32. *Pesahim* 113b.
33. *Jerusalem Kiddushin* 66d.
34. *Nedarim* 10a.
35. Mishnah *Eduyot* 5:6.
36. Rabbi Eliezer the Great, *Paths of Life.* See Hebrew text in Israel Abrahams, *Hebrew Ethical Wills,* pp. 40–41.
37. From a letter of Judah ibn Tibbon to his son Samuel, in F. Kobler, *A Treasury of Jewish Letters,* Vol. I, pp. 156–64.
38. From a letter of Nahmanides to his son, in Abrahams, *op. cit.,* pp. 95–98.

39. Rabbenu Asher, in Abrahams, *op. cit.*, pp. 119–25.
40. Moses Luzatto, *Mesillat Yesharim*, Chap. 11.
41. *Ibid.*
42. *Ibid.*, Chap. I.
43. Rabbi Israel Baal-Shem Tov.
44. *Idem.*
45. Rabbi Nahman of Bratslav.
46. *Idem.*
47. Eccles. 7:20.
48. Ezek. 18:30–32.
49. *Tanhuma* (Buber), *Hukkat* 39.
50. *Yoma* 9b.
51. *Shabbat* 55a–55b.
52. *Nedarim* 32b.
53. *Jerusalem Berakhot* 7d.
54. *Song of Songs Rabbah* to 5:2.
55. *Seder Eliahu Zuta*, Chap. 4.
56. *Midrash Tehillim* 90:16.
57. *Pesikta Rabbati*, Chap. 44.
58. *Leviticus Rabbah* 7:2.
59. *Avot of Rabbi Nathan*, Version a, Chap. 39.
60. Moses Luzatto, *op. cit.*, Chap. 5.
61. *Berakhot* 5a.
62. *Baba Metzia* 85a.
63. *Menahot* 29b.
64. *Makkot* 24b.
65. Saadia Gaon, *The Book of Beliefs and Opinions*, Treatise V, Chap. 1.
66. Rabbi Israel Baal-Shem Tov.
67. Rabbi Nahman of Bratslav.
68. Rabbi Mendel of Kotzk.
69. Martin Buber, *At the Turning*, pp. 55–56.
70. André Schwarz-Bart, *The Last of the Just* (New York: Atheneum, 1960), pp. 372–74.
71. Job 14:7–12.
72. Ps. 6:6.
73. Dan. 12:1–2.
74. Mishnah *Sanhedrin* 10:1.

75. *Sanhedrin* 90b.
76. *Tosefta Sanhedrin* 13:2.
77. *Berakhot* 28b.
78. *Midrash Mishle* 17:1.
79. *Tanhuma* (Buber), *Vayigash* 9.
80. *Berakhot* 17a.
81. *Berakhot* 34b.
82. *Sifra* 85d.
83. Saadia Gaon, *op. cit.*, Treatise VII, Chap. 1.
84. Maimonides, *Mishneh Torah, Hilkhot Teshuvah* 8.
85. Moses Luzatto, *op. cit.*, Chap. 4.
86. From the Daily Prayer Book.
87. Trans. from the *Weekday Prayer Book*, Rabbinical Assembly of America, 1961.
88. Isa. 2:2–4.
89. Jer. 23:5–6.
90. Mal. 3:23.
91. *Sanhedrin* 98a.
92. *Avot of Rabbi Nathan*, Version b, Chap. 31.
93. Saadia Gaon, *op. cit.*, Treatise VIII, Chap. 5.
94. Maimonides, *Mishneh Torah, Hilkhot Melakhim*, Chap. 11–12, in N. Glatzer, ed., *In Time and Eternity*.
95. Zvi Hirsch Kalischer, *Derishat Tsiyyon*, in Arthur Hertzberg, *The Zionist Idea*, pp. 111–13.
96. From the commentary of Maimonides to Mishnah *Sanhedrin* 10:1.

VII PRAYER

1. *Yebamot* 64a.
2. *Berakhot* 32b.
3. *Ta'anit* 2a.
4. Num. 14:17–20.
5. From the Testament of Jonah ben Landsofer.
6. Rabbi Israel Baal-Shem Tov.

7. Rabbi Nahman of Bratslav.
8. Deut. 10:20.
9. Deut. 8:10.
10. Mishnah *Berakhot* 2:1.
11. Mishnah *Berakhot* 2:4.
12. Mishnah *Berakhot* 2:5.
13. Mishnah *Berakhot* 3:1.
14. Mishnah *Berakhot* 4:1.
15. *Tanhuma* (Buber), *Miketz* 11.
16. Mishnah *Berakhot* 4:5.
17. Mishnah *Berakhot* 4:6.
18. Mishnah *Berakhot* 9:1.
19. Mishnah *Berakhot* 9:2.
20. Mishnah *Berakhot* 9:3.
21. *Berakhot* 43b.
22. *Tosefta Berakhot* 3.
23. *Mekhilta, Pisha* 16.
24. *Erubin* 65a.
25. *Berakhot* 29b.
26. *Kitzur Shulkhan Arukh*, Section 18, *Hilkhot T'filat Shmoneh Esreh.*
27. *Berakhot* 8a.
28. From the letter of a Moravian Jew, Shlomoh Shlomiel, son of Hayyim, written from Safed in 1607, in F. Kobler, ed., *A Treasury of Jewish Letters*, Vol. II, pp. 395–96.
29. Trans. from the *Weekday Prayer Book*, Rabbinical Assembly of America, 1961.
30. Deut. 6:4–9; trans. from the *Weekday Prayer Book, op. cit.*
31. Trans. from the *Weekday Prayer Book, op. cit.*
32. *Ibid.*
33. From the Daily Prayer Book.
34. *Ibid.*
35. Mishnah *Berakhot* 4:2.
36. *Sefer Hassidim*, trans. in N. Glatzer, ed., *Language of Faith* (New York: Schocken, 1947), p. 78.
37. *Ibid.*, p. 74.
38. *Ibid.*, p. 14.